MW00946026

AWS

Advanced Networking
Exam Guide

ANS-C01

1st EDITION

AWS Advanced Networking Exam Guide, ANS-C01, FIRST EDITION

Copyright © 2022 KAM AGAHIAN

All rights reserved. No portion of the book may be reproduced or utilized in any form or by any means, electronic or mechanical, including photocopying, recording, or by any other information storage and retrieval system, without permission in writing from the author.

Warning and Disclaimer

Unless otherwise indicated, all the names, characters, businesses, places, events and incidents in this book and its scenarios are either the product of the author's imagination or used in a fictitious manner. Any resemblance to actual networks and businesses is purely coincidental.

This book is designed to provide information about networking in Amazon Web Services (AWS). Every effort has been made to make this book as complete and as accurate as possible, but still no warranty or fitness is implied. The information is provided on an "as-is" basis. The author and his team shall have neither liability nor responsibility to any person or entity with respect to any loss or damage arising from any information contained in this book. Every production network is different and each case needs to be looked into by an expert individually. The nature of the public cloud space could make the topics covered in this book obsolete quicky. The readers are strongly encouraged to cross-check the technical details with the official documentation by AWS for the latest updates.

At the end of the pain is success.

This book is dedicated to Shapur I, the second Sassanian King of Kings, whose life story taught me how to be the person I am today.

About the author, reviewers and contributors

Kam Agahian (CCIE No.25341) is a seasoned network and cloud engineering leader and a part-time fitness coach and avid participant in events and competitions such as the Murph Challenge. He has more than 20 years of experience in designing and implementing complex network architectures and solutions for companies including Amazon, Cisco Systems and DIRECTV as well as teaching various networking courses as a Certified Cisco Systems Instructor (CCSI No.33326). Kam possesses expert level and versatile knowledge in IP/MPLS backbones, cloud architecture optimization and systems engineering. Over the past two decades, Kam has interviewed hundreds of network engineers, architects and leaders in North America, Europe and Asia Pacific and developed content and presentations for technical and behavioral interview best practices, balance and fairness. He also holds two CCIEs (emeritus) in Service Provider and Routing and Switching and a master's degree in telecommunications engineering from the University of Melbourne, Australia. Kam lives in sunny Orange County, CA with his wife and two boys, and his loyal German Shepherd, Gunner. You can follow him on Twitter @kagahian.

Khaled Abuelenain (CCIE No. 27401) is Consulting Director at Acuative Corp. Khaled holds two CCIEs and is an expert in service provider networks, SD-WAN, network automation, and cloud networking. Khaled is also a contributing author on "Routing TCP/IP Volume II, 2nd Edition" by Jeff Doyle and is the author of the Cisco Press book "Network Programmability and Automation Fundamentals, First Edition". You can follow him on Twitter @kabuelenain.

John Breth is Founder/Managing Principal of J.B.C (jbcsec.com) and is an experienced architect and author with 18 years' experience helping the nation's federal agencies, defense and intelligence agencies, and critical infrastructure companies identify, implement, and protect against cyber threats. John has designed and implemented mission critical systems to support a Tier 1 ISP's cyber protections for the federal government, numerous DoD joint networks, and Air Force One's secure network. John has earned multiple high-level certifications from (ISC)², Cisco, AWS, Juniper, and CompTIA (and others), as well as having earned a Master of Science (MS) with a focus on Information Technology from Johns Hopkins University. He also enjoys creating tech content for new folks in the industry with a specific focus on networking, cybersecurity, and cloud technologies on his YouTube channel, CyberInsight. You can follow him on Twitter @jbizzle703.

Daniel Dib (CCIE #37149, CCDE #20160011) is a Senior Network Architect at Conscia. He works with designing scalable, modular, and highly available networks that meet business needs. Daniel has a background in implementation and operations and achieved his CCIE certification in 2012. In May 2016 he became the second person in Sweden to achieve the Cisco Certified Design Expert certification. The last couple of years Daniel has been working mainly with SD-WAN and networking in public clouds such as AWS and Azure. He is an active part of the networking community and writes a blog at https://lostintransit.se. You can follow him on Twitter @danieldibswe.

Shervin S. Joor Shervin with a PhD in Aerospace Engineering and is a lifelong learner of engineering simulation and computer science. When he is not absorbed in the latest Cloud computing technology, Shervin loves to spend time with his family.

Eric Leung Wan Chung (CCIE #19489, JNCIP-SEC) is a network specialist with over 10 years of experience on datacentre networking. He works as the networking team leads in multiple multinational financial companies. He is interested with multicloud networking in recent years and actively contributing in the cloud networking community. You can follow him on Twitter @ericlwc.

Alvaro Solano is a cloud and network architect at DXC Technology. He is an experienced technical trainer in cloud computing, architecture and infrastructure (AWS technologies). You can follow him on Twitter @alvarosolanom

A special thanks go to a team;

Technically, this work is based on the "AWS Advanced Networking" kickstart book that Kam published in 2020-21. However, the recent updates to cover the ANS-C01 were made by a group of authors and reviewed extensively by a team of seasoned contributors and experts mentioned above.

CONTENTS

PART 2: ANS-C01 MOCK EXAM

Introduction (a must-read)

Welcome to the Second Edition!

The challenge of preparing for and passing IT certifications is an interesting one. Since 1997 when I started as an engineer and began working on my early certifications, I have been asked many times: why would anyone in IT want to be certified? Is it worth the time? I got asked the same question about MCSE or RHCE, later about CCIE, and nowadays very often about the public cloud certifications. After 25 years, my answer remains the same.

It can very much be worth the time and resources you spend on it *if* you do spend such time and resources. While this might sound a bit confusing, I believe it best describes the world of certifications.

That is exactly where this book comes into play.

My journey to this book, and a similar title on OCI, began with a couple of innocent questions that a friend of mine asked me: I want to switch to cloud networking; do you happen to have any real-world scenarios about all the tools and features? Also, how do I practice for the AWS Advanced Networking exam beyond the official sample questions and still fully respect the NDA? How about learning other public cloud providers, including Oracle OCI and Microsoft Azure? Looking back, my initial reaction was half-baked. I went to great lengths to explain how the official documentation would help and why one should read every single page. I also emphasized the importance of checking back in case the documents had changed. His next question punched holes in my suggestion; is there a shortcut for someone with a network or systems engineering background? What if the same engineer isn't so patient and has little time? Let's say just a weekend right before the interview or the actual ANS-C01 exam. These questions would keep me awake for days to come.

There was no shortcut.

Then I hit the biggest challenge; the public cloud is an ever-changing space. No feature remains exactly the same for more than a few months, and new features or updates keep coming out.

By this time, I was confident I had answers to two main questions. Firstly, I could see why no one else had taken on this challenge before. Secondly, I understood why when I was working on the first edition, five out of the six people I contacted to join us as technical reviewers had declined the offer!

How is the book structured?

Simple. The book comprises three main parts and assumes you have passed the AWS associate and professional exams and possess some network engineering knowledge. The book includes: the course recap, reference architectures, and mock exams, along with their answers. You will find everything in a well-structured, mostly bullet-point format in the lessons recap sections. Most sections introduce well-known reference architectures that are used in real life. Absolutely to the point and not too verbose. The lessons are followed by three sets of mock multiple-choice mock exams and comprehensive answers to the questions. We attempted to make sure the mock exams would give the candidate a very similar experience as the real ANS-C01 test while adhering to the NDA and the exam integrity. We also made a conscious choice to avoid long paragraphs and replace them with bullet points - as much as possible.

Can I just take the tests and skip the course recap?

Don't. The ANS-C01 exam blueprint is extremely broad, and my team tried to cover the entire blueprint in a concise and still attractive way. While the exams cover many key topics we discussed in the book, they do not necessarily cover every single line of lessons. A well-prepared candidate must study both. Never skip a section, ever.

I am going to skip some of the not-so-important sections

Don't. The field of cloud engineering, in general, is unique in several amazing ways. One of them is the breadth of topics required for an engineer or architect to be successful. The ANS-C01 exam follows the exact same pattern. You are expected to know BGP and the other traditional network engineering topics, but at the same time, you need to be well-versed when it comes to DNS, DHCP, and other services, as well as the basics of security. You also need to be familiar with what many engineers usually deem as "boring," and that's the topic of monitoring, logging, and log digestion through tools such as CloudWatch Logs/Events, EventBridge, and Athena. Last but not least, you will find quite a few tiny details, including numbers, in the book. This could be the maximum number of sessions a service can take or a community string that BGP can send. They are all important, and any architect or engineer worth their salt must know them by heart.

What about the containers and all the Kubernetes stuff?

First off, if you are one of those network engineers who have developed *Kube-phobia*, I have some good news for you. Even outside the context of public cloud certifications, mastering the topic of containers for a senior-level engineer should not take more than 60 hours. This is more like several weekends if you are into self-studying. So, I would absolutely fix that. It is doable, well-documented, and a real money-maker. Do that today.

Secondly, the subject of container networking is not a huge part of the ANS-C01 exam blueprint. In fact, given the blueprint, I would not expect that to be a game changer when you are taking the actual test. Yet, I put together a fairly comprehensive section in the book. It's so detailed that the exam, hopefully, will be a subset of that. The containers section of this book offers an overview of container networking and both ECS and EKS services as far as they are related to a network engineer.

What if I have been preparing for the ANS-C00 exam?

You can still use at least 70% of your knowledge here. Some key topics have changed or been updated. For example, in the previous exam, the Virtual Gateways (VGWs) were the main routing constructs, but in the new exam, everything is about Transit Gateways (TGWs). When we took the previous test, many services did not exist, such as DNS Firewalls, Network Firewalls, Gateway Load Balancers, Private NAT, DNS Inbound/Outbound endpoint, MACsec for Direct Connect, and DNSSEC. Now they do, and the book has extensively covered them. The huge mistake you can make is skipping the course recap, jumping to the exams, scoring 80% there, and concluding that you are prepared *even* for the new exam. Once again, never skip a section.

I studied one section but feel I need more details on it

The official documentation always has the most comprehensive version of the details. Do not underestimate that, if you want to go beyond the context discussed here – which I am confident is sufficient to help you master the topics and be successful on the exam.

What about the topics that are not covered in the book?

The book is structured around the ANS-C01 exam and its blueprint. The beta version of the exam went live in early 2022, and the final version of it became available in July 2022. Some topics were never covered in the blueprint, and I skipped those. The Cloud WAN is one of those examples. I am reasonably confident they have fallen outside the scope of the ANS-C01 exam, but to maintain the highest quality of contents in the book, if the blueprint changes, I will go and add those in the future editions. For now, the book is based on what you need to know based on the official exam blueprint. Please keep in mind, this book is not designed to redo the entire AWS documentation as they're updated. The commitment here is to ensure you will succeed on one particular exam, which is the ANS-C01!

Do I need any hands-on experience?

Absolutely. Fortunately, most public cloud providers offer free or very low-cost tiers that are just good enough to get some real-world experience. Do not underestimate it. In most cases, all you need to do is create an account and log into the AWS management console.

Always keep an eye on the billing section of the AWS console; many students end up with unexpected bills after they leave their EC2 instances up and running, their DNS zones active, or transit gateways in service unnecessarily, and there are many other examples. A quick clean-up after you are done with your lab can sometimes save you quite a bit.

My favorite part of the book?

The answers to mock exams. I could have chosen to provide simple answer sheets but decided to get into the details and turn each answer into an opportunity to either teach something new or recap a key piece of information. This is essential. Because, first, each comprehensive answer is a reminder of what the student has learned in the book's lessons. Then, each answer is a window to teach less experienced architects and engineers how to approach various technical issues in a structured manner. This is what we usually refer to as the thought process. Finally, the answers may include technical points that have not been directly covered in the lessons sections.

How much time do I need to fully study the book?

Although this might sound like a very subjective question, it is not. Despite differences between one brain and another, as with any technical topic loaded with details, if you turn this into a never-ending project of several months, you will have to go back and redo the earlier sections. Ideally, a seasoned network or system engineer should be able to finish the book in about four to five weeks. But what if you don't? It won't be the end of the world as the book is designed with that possibility in mind. It is concise enough to be reviewed quickly if your busy schedule warrants a recap of the key concepts. I strongly recommend taking notes or highlighting the text as you progress. Never ignore the numbers or little details here and there.

I passed the exam or my job interview; now what?

Congratulations! Big milestone. Celebrate and take a break. Don't forget to the news with me on Twitter (@kagahian). Also, I would love to hear your suggestions and topics for future updates to this book, blog posts, or YouTube videos.

From here, there are two paths before you. You can move to other public cloud providers with solid and structured learning tracks and content, such as Oracle Cloud Infrastructure (OCI), or you can start looking into other emerging and (to some extent) related areas, such as security or containers in the cloud. Many students also pursue automation and development tracks, which are equally great and interesting. I know of others who explore completely different areas, such as Big Data and High-Performance Computing (HPC) in the cloud.

My blog posts, conference talks, and other stuff...

Here are a few of my recent blog posts on Packet Pushers that you might find relevant and useful. I am sure you can look them up:

- How to Break into a Cloud Engineering Career? (Great resource for the absolute beginner)
- The Future of Network Engineering; some possibilities through 2040 and beyond
- SD-WAN: Reasons to Think Twice. A Curious Case of Inaction; Operators and Vendors
- Failed the CCIE lab. Now what? (Although here I talked about CCIE, you can essentially apply the same principles to any IT certification)

Every now and then, I give talks at different events, including the NANOG conferences. You might want the following videos on YouTube interesting:

- Some boring network engineering interview questions and how to replace them with smarter ones
- The Anatomy of the Most Challenging Network Engineering Interview Question

Last but not least, as a fitness coach and sometimes career coach, I share my experiences in blog posts like this one:

- Six Coaching Principles That Took Me Years to Learn (I am sure many can benefit from these lessons to further enhance their career in IT).

Final thoughts...

I am committed to keeping all the other contents we create including the Udemy training videos of the highest possible quality. This book is no exception and is supposed to set an example for quality exam preparation material while respecting the integrity of the test. Usually, several times a year, we release a new revision with minor updates, and once or twice a year (depending on the feedback), we publish a new edition. Twitter (kagahian@) is usually where Kam makes the announcements. Furthermore, we are always looking for smart individuals to assist us with content development for different public cloud providers or other technical topics. If you are interested, please feel free to reach out.

PART 1

AWS Advanced Networking Course Recap

CHAPTER 1

Virtual Private Clouds (VPCs)

Let's Zoom Out

The AWS network comprises a group of separate geographical areas called regions such as the us-west-1, us-east-1, and ap-east-1. In each region of the AWS network, there are a number of Availability Zones (AZ) that are essentially groups of data centers. For instance, the Availability Zones of us-east-1a, us-east-1b, and us-east-1c are located in the us-east-1 region.

- That's a vast pool of resources such as servers and storage, but each customer needs their very own piece or pieces of it.

- Virtual Private Cloud (VPC) is the main construct in the modern-day AWS (generally after 2013) to provide a private network for the customers within the region. By default, each customer can currently have up to 5 VPCs per region.

- Historically and before VPC, we only had a flat environment called EC2-Classic.

  - EC2-Classic was a single flat network that customers shared with each other.

  - It still is available, but only to its original customers. All new users now get a VPC.

  - These days, many EC2-classic customers are assigning their best engineers and architects to plan migrations off of EC2-classic to VPCs.

- Each VPC consists of a number of subnets with dedicated CIDR blocks. That is where you can launch various resources such as your EC2 instances and their network interfaces (NICs) and start grabbing IP addresses.

- After the most recent changes in 2021 and 2022 currently AWS supports three subnet types

  - IPv4-only subnets

  - IPv6-only subnets

- The most recent addition with strong demand especially from the federal government. Instances in these subnets will not receive an IPv4 address – which is obvious. Right?
  - Dual-stack subnets
    - Where communications can happen over both IPv4 and IPv6.
- Each VPC can have up to 200 subnets.
  - IPv4 main VPC CIDR size must be between /16 and /28 and each IPv4 subnet when you create and use must be between /16 and /28
  - IPv6 main VPC CIDR block size must be fixed at /56 and each IPv6 subnet when you create and use must be fixed at /64
- Subnets can be public or private; with or without access to the Internet.
- AWS VPCs can spread across multiple Availability Zones (data centers in the same region). However, AWS subnets are limited to one Availability Zone.
  - The only exception here is the concept of Local Zones, which we will investigate later in the book.
- Although now the concept of IPv6-only "subnets" exists, still when you are creating a VPC, you must also specify the IPv4 CIDR block for the VPC itself.
  - Later on, if you specify an IPv6 CIDR block for the VPC, when you are creating its subnets, you can check a box to identify the subnet as IPv6-only.
  - I understand it might sound a bit intimidating to run IPv6 only environments, but many AWS services and the Internet provide a much wider range of options to what we had 5 years ago in terms of IPv6 destinations.
    - If you are not familiar with the concept of IPv6 Internet routing table, not for the ANS-C01 exam but in general, I strongly suggest you start learning the topic.
- Each EC2 instance in a VPC gets a private IPv4 address by default.
  - You can add a public IPv4 address to your instances. If the public IP address is assigned through an Elastic NIC, it will be preserved until released by the user. It is a virtual network interface and a great choice if keeping the same public address is important.
    - There is a small fee associated with unused Elastic interfaces. Do not park them unused.
- For the subnets that you create and have IPv4 or IPv6 ranges, although by default the auto-assign option is not enabled for public IPv4 and IPv6 addresses, you can manually enable the feature for both address spaces.
  - Enabling this option for IPv6 will result in assignment of an IPv6 address only and not both.

Propagating DHCP options

Similar to traditional networks, AWS supports the propagation of various network settings via the DHCP options called "DHCP options sets" that are applied to the customer's VPCs.

The DHCP options sets:

- Are configured at the VPC level

    - Cannot be modified after creation. So that, to make a change, delete and create a new one. This can be disruptive in production networks.

- Can be used to distribute several key pieces of information, such as:

    - IPv4 or IPv6 DNS server addresses while the keyword "AmazonProvidedDNS" is also an acceptable value[1]

    - IPv4 or IPv6 NTP server addresses

    - NetBIOS name server addresses

        - Be proud of yourself if you operated such networks in the 90s!

    - Domain name: That is used by hosts to form a complete FQDN. Without them, the default AWS domain names are used. For example, ec2.internal (US East naming convention) and region.compute.internal (All the other regions)

- Be mindful of a major limitation in the current implementation of IPv6 on AWS. If your subnets are dual-stack (and not IPv6-only), the IPv6 hosts will only receive their IP address from the DHCP server and not any of the other network settings such as the DNS server addresses. Another reason to start embracing the concept of IPv6-only subnets.

- Once a set is created it takes time for the settings to apply to the host.

    - The IP settings of the hosts can be refreshed from within the operating system for immediate effect.

- Finally, the most annoying characteristic of the DHCP options sets; once created, they cannot be edited. You would need to create a new one from scratch and attach it to your VPC.

    - As a VPC-level configuration, this could lead to outages and service disruptions. Make sure you plan ahead of time.

    - Food for thought: Can you think of some major design challenges if you have different NTP or DNS servers for different parts of the VPC?

---

1. We will extensively cover the concept of Amazon DNS later in the book.

AWS Outposts and Local Zones

For a variety of reasons, including ultra-low-latency or strict compliance requirements, some customers cannot afford to allow their workload to leave their data centers even though the closest AWS Availability Zone might be only 5ms away. In such cases, AWS offers a service called AWS Outposts that brings a limited number of services such as EC2, S3, EMR, EKS, RDS, and EBS to the customer's environment.

- Fully configured and managed by AWS

- Runs on the same hardware as AWS data centers

- The customer provides space, power, and cooling (obviously, as the racks will be placed in their data center)

The third option between the two offerings of Availability Zones and Outposts is called Local Zones. It offers a limited number of services but outside the customer on-premises environment and still outside any full-blown Availability Zone. This could be a major metropolitan area where AWS does not have an AZ, but major customers have a large concentration of end users.

- Generally speaking, the end users can hit the Local Zone with single-digit latency

- AWS provides connectivity directly into the AWS backbone, and the Local Zone will be treated as a stripped-down AZ, managed by AWS.

§*Exam Tip: While the details of AWS Outposts and Local Zones, including how they are set up and billed is outside the scope of the ANS-C01 exam, you need to be familiar with both concepts and use cases of each.*

We learned AWS is made of tens of geographical regions where in each region they have set up multiple data centers called Availability Zones. These data centers host a large number of servers and network devices. Each customer is allocated their own isolated part of a massive pool, and it's called a VPC, where they can create their IPv4 or IPv6 subnets. The subnets are confined within one Availability Zone. AWS has recently started supporting IPv6-only subnets. One way or another, you could use DHCP Options Sets to assign to your EC2 instances not just their IPv4 or IPv6 addresses but also some other network configurations such as the DNS and NTP IP addresses.

In case you're curious, in hyper-scale network implementations, companies tend to (or even maybe have to) use Software Defined Networking (SDN), White-boxes (network devices based on some merchant silicon), and proprietary Operating Systems (OS). This is different from a large enterprise network for many reasons, including hardware and software costs at scale, proprietary architectures, and logistics.

Final point, the DNS name resolution and communication processes for IPv6-only subnets using DNS64 and NAT64 are covered in the Route 53 section of the book. It requires some foundation that we will build and then discuss the topic.

Reference Architecture(s)

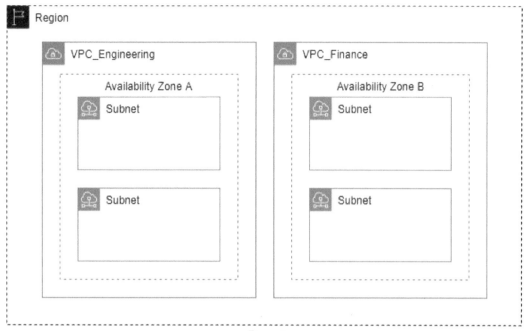

Figure 1

Basic architecture showing multiple subnets per AZ. As shown here, each VPC can spread across multiple AZs but the subnets must reside in one AZ.

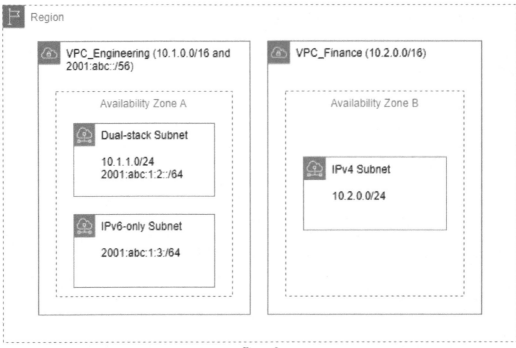

Figure 2

This figure reaveals more details and possilities about IP addressing. VPC_Engineering is a dual-stack VPC featuring the recently announced IPv6-only subnets. VPC_Finance has a traditional IPv4 design. Later in the book when we cover Route 53, I will explain how the different types of IPv6-enabled subnets can communicate with each other and the outside world. In the most recent updates to the AWS products, a Resource-based Name (RBN) is created for IPv6 resources in DNS and (by default) the settings are enabled to create AAAA records for them such resources.

We will also look into the possibity of having overlapping IP ranges (which is awful but sometimes inevitable – like a merger or acquisition case) and how to navigate around them.

CHAPTER 2

Routing and Networking Beyond VPC

Basics of routing in AWS architectures

- Routing within and outside VPC is governed by Route Tables (routing tables)
  - Each AWS VPC has one main (default) route table that comes with your VPC after its creation.
    - It cannot be deleted, but you can add multiple custom route tables and, if needed, replace the main route table.
  - Each route table contains an essential route that facilities routing within the VPC. It's called the local route.
  - By default, AWS subnets cannot communicate with resources beyond what the local route takes them to. In other words, by default, communication is limited to and from resources within the VPC.
    - However, those resources can be reached by using other AWS constructs such as Internet Gateways or VPC endpoints.
  - Each subnet must be associated with only one route table.
    - Upon creation, subnets are implicitly associated with the main route table, but as you create custom route tables, you have the option to associate a subnet with another route table.
    - Unlike the traditional route tables, each route cannot have an IP address as its target or next hop, it has to point to an endpoint, network interface, or local; to "something" and not "some IP."

Internet Gateways (IGWs)

AWS Internet Gateway (IGW) is a cloud construct that is attached to a VPC and used to provide inbound and outbound IPv4 and IPv6 connectivity between VPCs public subnets and the public Internet.

- First things first, is your security team comfortable connecting a VPC potentially directly (or even indirectly) to the Internet over both IPv4 and IPv6?

- Think strategically; how do you scale later? How do you secure it?

- Your subnet would need a default route pointing to the IGW as the target (next hop) to use it. This route needs to be manually added. Once again, keep in mind in the world of AWS, your next hop, instead of an IP, is the construct itself.

- EC2 instances need public IP addresses to directly leverage the IGW, or you would need another construct called NAT Gateway. You can use the Elastic virtual network interfaces or even bring your own public IP address to AWS.

- It is technically possible to have a VPC with no communications with the public Internet, although most operating systems and tools need to be updated regularly.

Public and Private NAT Gateways

In conjunction with IGW, AWS public NAT Gateway is used to provide connectivity between the VPC's subnets and the public Internet.

- Both in production environments and on the ANS-C01 exam, NAT Gateways are considered an expensive cloud construct, as you will see later in the billing section

- Only supports Source NAT, which basically is a simple form of Port Address Translation (PAT)

- Is created in a public subnet and requires an Elastic IP address; which, of course, is public

  - Once assigned to the NAT Gateway, the Elastic IP cannot be modified. You would need to recreate the Gateway; a traffic-disrupting operation

  - Unlike some other cloud providers, the NAT gateway can have only ONE public IP assigned to it

- Similar to any PAT/NAT gateway, it permits outbound traffic and denies inbound traffic initiated on the outside

- The subnet would require a route pointing to the NAT Gateway. Similar to traditional routing, each route table can only have one NAT or Internet Gateway.

  - This is covered in the reference architectures

- Like many other cloud constructs, NAT Gateway's scalability is managed by AWS but only one is created in each Availability Zone.

- If you need multi-AZ redundancy, you can have multiple NAT Gateways for different subnets in different Availability Zones. In some existing architectures, it might need costly and significant updates to the architecture to split resources between different AZs to use different NAT Gateways for different subnets.

- Provides some degree of security by limiting connections to those established from the inside to the public Internet.
  - I have been to many architecture review sessions where a junior designer was trying hard to sell a NAT Gateway as a security tool. It is not. Simple NAT Gateways cannot prevent a wide range of attacks, including data exfiltration.
- The NAT Gateways have certain limitations that need to be taken into account by the architect:
  - Only support TCP, UDP, and ICMP
  - Do not support IP fragmentation for TCP and ICMP
  - Do support IP Fragmentation for UDP
  - Currently can scale up to 45Gbps, 4 million packets per second, and 55000 concurrent connections. The latter is per unique destination and not the total. Also, they can currently accommodate a climbing rate of 900 connections per second. If you have a single NAT Gateway and an aggressive multi-threaded application on multiple servers behind it, you might need to consider using multiple subnets and gateways.
  - Any violation of the limits can result in port allocation errors as the gateway would fail to translate and assign ports. This condition can be closely monitored from CloudWatch. Read on for further details on this.

If needed, the architect can run their own NAT gateway on an EC2 instance.

- The scale will depend on the NAT software and the EC2 instance type.
- The customer will be responsible for any licensing fees, software updates, and the EC2 hourly rates.
- This architecture supports some of the key designs not supported by AWS NAT Gateways, including 1:1 NAT. Keep in mind, the cloud construct is barely a PAT VM in your VPC.

In 2021, AWS removed the traditional dependency of its NAT Gateways on IGWs to enable customers to deploy private NAT Gateways between private subnets. Private NAT Gateways can use private IP addresses to reach on-premises or other VPCs using VGWs or TGWs. Before that, NAT Gateways would have to be connected to IGWs and would only serve the purpose of connecting the AWS footprint to the public Internet.

- Private NAT Gateways are ideal in many scenarios, including the following:
  - *IP group masking:* Where you want your log server sees only one IP address for a large fleet of visiting hosts in your subnets
  - *IP whitelisting:* Where instead of configuring many policies on your firewall, you only configure one permit policy allowing the IP address of the private NAT Gateway and place every visiting host behind it

- *IP overlapping:* Where you are connecting two subnets in two VPCs with overlapping IP addresses. This is a common issue in merger and acquisition scenarios

- Private NAT Gateways only have private IP addresses (obviously) and do not need an Elastic IP address (public). This private IP address comes from the subnet inside which you have created the NAT Gateway

- Similar to public NAT Gateways, you cannot change the IP address of a private NAT Gateway, and if you had to update the "translate-to" IP address, you would need to delete and create a new NAT Gateway

  - This is not an unlikely scenario in production networks; hence it demands careful maintenance window planning as it would disrupt the traffic. For example, you might be using a private NAT Gateway to mask 100 IP addresses behind it and only whitelist the IP address of the NAT Gateway on your firewall. Any change to the IP address seen by the firewall and permitted by its policies would not be an easy operation. There are several interesting mini-scenarios on this in the book as well as a reference architecture on one of the use cases of Private NAT (aechiecting around overlapping CIDR blocks) in the Tarnsit Gateway section.

Finally, monitoring, accounting, and logging are critical for an expensive construct like a NAT Gateway.

  - CloudWatch is the main resource for connectivity troubleshooting for NAT Gateways. It offers several key *metrics* that, in many DevOps scenarios, you would want to monitor, such as the total number of active connections, attempts, bytes, and packets in and out and port allocation errors for when you have exhausted the available ports to translate to.

  - VPC Flow Logs is the main resource for connection investigation initiatives, including identifying the top talkers. The Flow Logs can be captured off the Elastic Network Interface (ENI) of the NAT Gateway (or the VPC itself) and sent to either an S3 bucket or CloudWatch *Logs*. I personally prefer the bucket, especially if it is a quick check or investigation.

    - If you direct the logs to CloudWatch Logs, you can create a simple filter query and sort based on bytesTransferred

    - If you have opted for the quick and dirty option of using S3, you can use another AWS service called Athena, turn the logs into a table and run the good old SQL queries against it using the SELECT and WHERE keywords. Then sort using the ORDER keyword. That is another reason for me to prefer Athena, as most people I know are way more familiar with the standard SQL query structure than the proprietary query model of CloudWatch.

§Exam Tip: *Due to their billing model, the AWS NAT Gateways are always considered expensive choices. This could affect many architecture decisions throughout the book as we prefer other solutions to avoid excessive costs.*

- IPv6 routing and addressing the security concerns

All AWS-assigned IPv6 addresses are publicly routable and reachable from the IPv6 internet as soon as the IGW is up. If this behavior is undesirable, you can use the AWS Egress-only Gateway construct to limit the IPv6 communications with the IPv6 Internet to those initiated from within the VPC.

- You need to add an IPv6 default route (::/128) to the route table for the Egress-only gateway to work.

Beyond the basics of routing: VPC Ingress Routing

In 2019, AWS simplified the process of adding security appliances to their cloud architectures. In traditional networks, we had several ways to redirect traffic to appliances and servers that were not necessarily deployed in-path (or inline). In such environments, we had a wide range of options, including Policy-Based Routing (PBR), Web Cache Communication Protocol (WCCP), and all sorts of routing tricks and tunnels.

Today, with VPC Ingress routing, you can define specific routes for your IGW (traffic to/from the Internet) and VGW (traffic to/from VPN) to pick out traffic to certain destinations and route it to an Elastic Network Interface (ENI) on an EC2 instance – that you have designated as your security appliance, such as a firewall or an IPS.

For instance, if you need to inspect the incoming traffic for the protected subnet of 192.168.100.0/26 in one of your VPCs, all you need to do is to create a route in a dedicated route table for the IGW called the gateway route table. This route will direct anything for the destination of 192.168.100.0/24 to eni0, which would be the interface of your virtual firewall. All the other traffic will take the path via the local route (e.g.,192.168.100.0/24).

Once the traffic is received by the security appliance, it will be processed and then, if permitted, forwarded to its ultimate destination. All the security appliances available on the Marketplace, such as firewalls by major vendors, can handle this operation.

However, if you are using a Linux server as your appliance, similar to most on-premises Linux-based firewalls, you would need to manually allow IP traffic forwarding using the sysctl command. Furthermore, you would need to disable the source/destination checking process using the AWS CLI command of *aws ec2 modify-instance-attribute* with the parameter of *--no-source-dest-check*.

This architecture had scalability issues. For instance, it was not straightforward to increase the number of security appliances if the designs needed more horsepower or better redundancy. As you will see, the Gateway Load Balancers that came out later improved the scalability of the customers' designs, but the VPC Ingress routing remained a key part of security-oriented architectures. We will take the 3rd step when we introduce AWS Network Firewall. Stay tuned.

Reference Architecture(s)

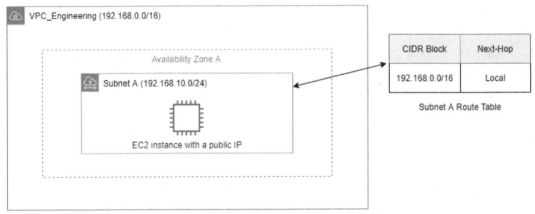

Figure 3

The most basic form of routing within a single VPC with no communications to the outside world. The routing process here, for this subnet and all the other subnets, can be controlled by the local route.

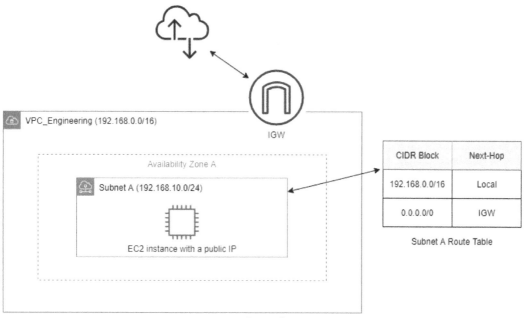

Figure 4

The quickest and one of the least secure methods to connect VPCs to the Internet. Please pay close attention to the route table; the traffic within the same subnet is handled locally by the internal router of the VPC (operated implicitly by AWS), and anything Internet-bound is routed to the IGW. IGW is scaled by AWS and supports either hosts with public IP addresses or without public addresses. The ones without public IPs will need a NAT gateway before the traffic hits the IGW. Very few architects notice that even if the hosts have public IP addresses assigned to them, the communication between the IGW and them is based on their private addresses, and the IGW performs implicit NAT to keep the intra-VPC communication private only. As you will see, this architecture is widely despised by CISOs!

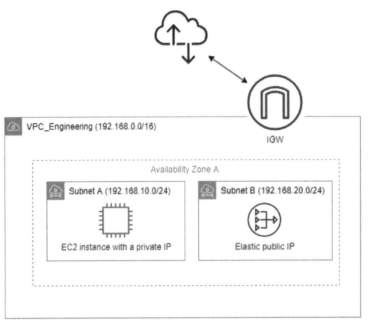

Figure 5

Basic NAT architecture in one AZ to support a single subnet. The NAT construct is, in fact, a PAT virtual device in your tenancy. It scales automatically by AWS and supports both private to public and private to private address source translation. Pay close attention to the separate subnet needed by the NAT gateway. It cannot share the subnet with the hosts that it is translating. Here, we showed a public NAT construct. In 2021, AWS added support for private NAT gateways (to translate private IP addresses to private IP addresses), but the construct, essentially, remained a PAT device. For anything beyond PAT, such as 1:1 address translation, the architect would need to deploy EC2-based NAT instances such as those on Linux with IPtables.

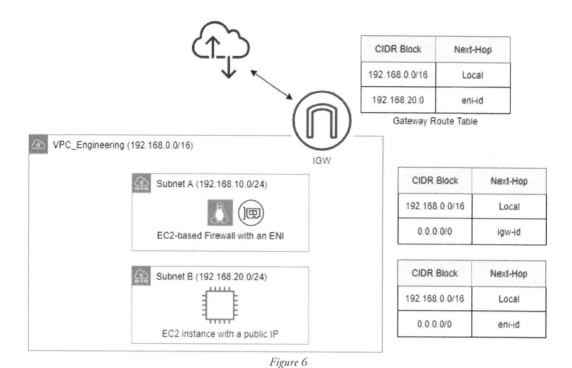

Figure 6

Simple reference architecture to deploy a Linux-based security appliance with a single ENI. The IGW has a gateway route table using the VPC Ingress feature. Pay close attention to the flow of the packets from the IGW all the way to the EC2 instance. The IGW feeds the packets bound for the EC2 instance to the ENI of the appliance, and the appliance sends them down to the EC2. The return traffic takes the opposite path. Notably, the appliance's subnet has a default route pointing to the IGW to route the EC2 traffic out to the Internet. Follow the traffic flow a few times to make sure you fully understand it. Many more complex scenarios are built on top of this.

CHAPTER 3

VPN Connectivity Between AWS and Customers

Most customers need connectivity between their on-premises and AWS footprint. There are two primary connectivity solutions: site-to-site IPSec VPN or Direct Connect (DX):

- IPSec VPN provides a quick, secure but not-so-reliable/high throughput/scalable solution.

- AWS Direct Connect takes more time to establish but provides better reliability and potentially higher bandwidth. AWS Direct Connect, over time, tends to be a more affordable solution. However, this may vary from one location to another and from one-use case and deal to another. The topic of AWS Direct Connect will be examined extensively in a dedicated section, and here we will remain focused on site-to-site IPSec VPN.

Regardless of the choice of VPN or DX by the architect, there are two primary constructs for connecting AWS to customers' on-premises network:

- Virtual Gateway (VGW)

- Transit Gateway (TGW): To be covered in a dedicated section.

The customer would also need a customer gateway on their side. In most cases, this is a router or a firewall.

§*Exam Tip:* *Although both VGW and TGW topics are covered in the book, one of the main transition points in ANS-C01 compared to ANS-C00 is exactly that. The older exam was solely based on VGWs, while the new exam is primarily based on TGWs. This does not mean you can skip VGWs. They are still part of the test and many customer architectures out there.*

A closer look at site-to-site IPSec VPN

Site-to-site VPN is an IPSec encrypted channel over the public Internet that connects the customer's network to AWS:

- Can be established to both VGW and TGW on the AWS side

- Has two underlying IPSec tunnels

- Supports both static and dynamic routing using BGP

- Supports both 2 and 4-Byte Autonomous System Numbers (ASN)

- You can send up to 100 routes to the VGW and receive up to 1000 routes. If you attempt to send more than 100 routes, the connection will reset. Also, if you have more than 1000 routes, only 1000 routes will eventually be sent down to the on-premises network.

- When creating an IPSec VPN connection, depending on your on-premises router or firewall vendor, you might be able to download the configuration details specific to your customer gateway from the AWS website. If needed, you can always customize the configuration file prepared by AWS for your on-premises router or firewall.

- AWS VPN tunnels have Dead Peer Detection (DPD) timeout configured

  - No response to 3 consecutive DPD messages is considered a dead peer

- Each IPSec VPN connection, in theory, can handle up to 1.25Gbps.

- As you will see later in the book, if you use TGWs instead of VGWs, you can have multiple tunnels and perform Equal Cost Multipath (ECMP).

- Currently, IPv6 over site-to-site VPN is only supported if the AWS end is a TGW.

- Over time AWS has added a wide range of encryption and hashing algorithms. For example, AES-128/256, 128-bit-GCM-16, or 256-GCM-16 and SHA-1 or SHA-2 with different key sizes and a wide range of Diffie-Hellman groups are supported. Recently you also have the option of using certificates in addition to pre-shared keys for peer authentication.

§*Exam Tip: As you will see later in the book, choosing the more expensive construct of TGW over VGW has many architectural benefits. One of the less obvious ones is the ability to run ECMP across multiple VPN tunnels, which is impossible with the older VGW.*

The customer can always build their own VPN headend on an EC2 instance if their desired encryption, hashing, or authentication functions are not supported by AWS. This approach applies to several other key AWS constructs, including gateways and databases. In such cases, the customer will be responsible for scalability, security, licensing, labor, and the EC2 hourly rates.

Keep in mind, doing the math and weighing all the options are parts of the architect's responsibility. Do not outsource those.

§Exam Tip: *VPN is one of the broad concepts in IT. What is covered here is site-to-site VPN to provide connectivity between on-premises and cloud. AWS also supports client VPN based on OpenVPN to support secure single-user access to AWS. Do not confuse the two terms.*

Simple VGW Hub-and-Spoke using CloudHub

An interesting use case of Virtual Gateways is called CloudHub, which can be used by enterprise customers with multiple remote sites. This is the poor man's hub and spoke WAN architecture and always reminds me of the frame relay networks from early 2000.

- The VGW in AWS acts as the hub.

- The VGW may or may not be attached to a particular VPC. If it is attached, the remote sites may also have connectivity to the VPC.

- All the remote sites and facilities act as the spokes.

- The spokes can have different or the same AS numbers in BGP designs.

- The spokes cannot have overlapping CIDR blocks.

- The inside IP addresses of the tunnels need to be unique too.

Over time, the CloudHub concept has lost much of its momentum. As you will see later in the book, now there are better alternatives, including SD-WAN.

§ Exam Tip: *Once, the AWS CloudHub was an important architecture for job interviews and the older ANS-C00 exam. Although it is still supported, AWS now has other service offerings that have overshadowed this "trick."*

Reference Architecture(s)

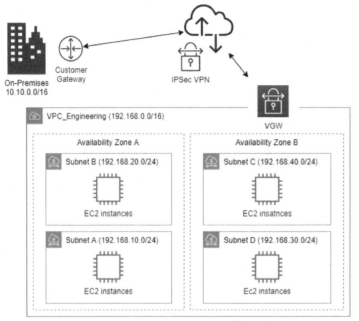

CIDR Block	Next-Hop
192.168.0.0/16	Local
10.10.0.0/16	vgw-id

CIDR Block	Next-Hop
192.168.0.0/16	Local
10.10.0.0/16	vgw-id

CIDR Block	Next-Hop
192.168.0.0/16	Local
10.10.0.0/16	vgw-id

CIDR Block	Next-Hop
192.168.0.0/16	Local
10.10.0.0/16	vgw-id

Figure 7

The most common reference architecture to access AWS footprint via site-to-site IPSec tunnels from on-premises. An alternative to this design is to use transit gateways. One of the notable differences between the two architectures is the lack of multi-tunnel support in this design, where the architect cannot have more than one IPSec VPN to ECMP. The customer gateway can be a router, firewall, or basically any device or server that supports IPSec VPN tunnels within the settings that AWS supports. What if you need an encryption type not supported by AWS? Use your own VPN servers on both ends (EC2 to on-premises).

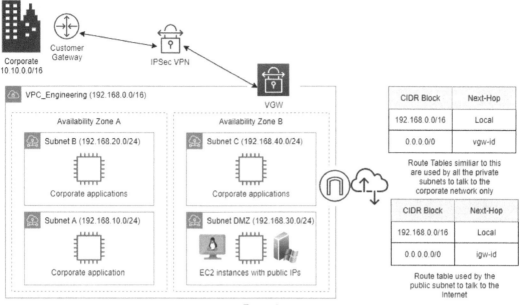

Figure 8

Multiple subnets with two different external destinations. In this case, some subnets want to communicate with the Internet while the rest of them need to reach the on-premises network (either one and not both). In this case, the architect has designed two types of route tables; one with a default gateway to the IGW and another with a route table to the VGW. They could have a mix of the two if they had a subnet with both requirements, although the route table for that subnet could not have two default gateways. In such architectures, the route pointing to the on-premises network needs to be more specific than 0.0.0.0/0 (perhaps only the on-premises subnets).

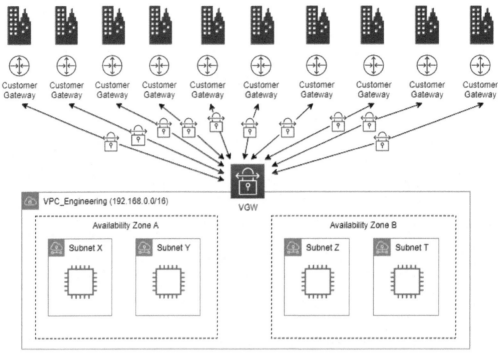

Figure 9

One of the most basic architectures to support hub and spoke designs with VGWs where the customer has a large number of remote offices. In traditional networks, the architect would have to deploy 1 or 2 mighty routers in a central data center and connect the offices to the hub using IPSec tunnels. That model can be replaced by this architecture. Please note, as you will see, the newer SD-WAN designs are gradually replacing this model. Finally, in this architecture, the remote sites could also have access to the VPCs on AWS. In this book, we cover a number of scenarios on how to design the autonomous numbering and routing strategy for this scenario. Remember what you just read about the AS numbers of this architecture in the lessons sections.

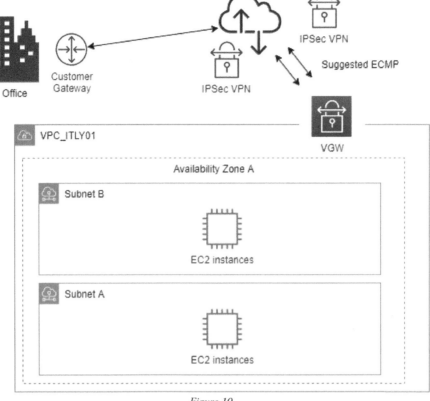

Figure 10

This is an INVALID architecture.

You cannot do ECMP between on-premises and VGWs. This would need a transit gateway and dynamic routing.

CHAPTER 4

Direct Connect[2]

§Exam Tip: You are about to start one of the most important exam topics and it has always been so!

The most basic form of connectivity between on-premises and AWS is still site-to-site IPSec VPN. While VPN provides the customers with a quick and entry-level solution, many customers have different needs, including greater reliability which cannot be achieved via the public Internet. Direct Connect is for those customers with strict performance and throughput requirements to access private and public resources on AWS. Today many companies extensively use both; Direct Connect as the primary channel to AWS and IPSec VPN as the backup path.

- AWS, at the time of this writing, has over 100 Direct Connect locations worldwide.
    - In contrast to the physical address of the actual AWS data centers, the location of the Direct Connect "POPs" is not confidential and can be obtained from the AWS Web site.
- Similar to any data center, there are AWS cages and racks with their routers to accept cross-connect fiber links from the customers' or partners' routers. The customers may or may not have equipment in the target Direct Connect location.

    There are two possible scenarios:
    - If the customer has a footprint in the same Direct Connect location, they can simply create the connection through the console and work with the data center owners (such as Equinix or CoreSite) to run a cross-connect fiber between their router and the AWS Direct Connect router.
        - AWS has strict layer 1 requirements for the cross-connect links:
            - Single mode fiber. This makes perfect sense given the distance between cages in large data centers
            - 1000BASE-LX (1310 nm) optics for 1Gbps links

---

2. Please note the transit gateway and Direct Connect use cases will be examined in the Transit Gateway section.

- 10GBASE-LR (1310 nm) optics for 10Gbps links
- 100GBASE-LR4 for 100Gbps links. The 100Gbps service was added in 2021.
- Port Speed and Duplex (full) must be hardcoded.
    - Helps avoid any confusion or bugs that might affect the negotiation process
- AWS also has detailed requirements for higher layers:
    - Only BGP is supported (no static routing) with both IPv4 and IPv6.
    - BGP must be protected by MD5 passwords.
    - VLAN tagging through 802.1Q must be supported. AWS maps the VLAN tags to your VPCs so you can use a single link to have access to up to 50 VPCs (or AWS public services such as S3) on a single dedicated Direct Connect connection.
    - It is recommended to have asynchronous Bidirectional Forwarding Detection (BFD). This feature helps you detect a dead peer without having to wait for the BGP timer to expire.
- If the customer has no presence in the target Direct Connect location, there are multiple ways to have IP connectivity between their facility and the Direct Connect location.
    - Many service providers (also known as carriers) offer a wide range of connectivity options, including various flavors of MPLS circuits such as VPLS (Layer 2) and L3 VPN to connect the customer's data center to the Direct Connect location.

§Exam Tip: *Although you might think nuances such as the physical layer details and how the BGP connections are set up are not to be memorized, that is not the case. All ANS-C01 candidates are expected to know the details of the physical layer, as well as how BGP is set up.*

Services available via Direct Connect and how to reach them?

Generally speaking, AWS Direct Connect is used by customers to access two types of public and private services:

- Private services within VPCs
    - Also reachable via traditional VPN connections with less reliability
    - Accessible through Private Virtual Interfaces (Private VIF)
- Public services such as Amazon S3 and DynamoDB
    - Also reachable via the public Internet with less reliability and potentially lower throughput

- Accessible through Public Virtual Interfaces (Public VIF)
- To set up, you need to either own a public AS number or use a private AS number (ASN 64512-65535).
    - If you choose to use a private AS, it comes with the caveat that you will not be able to leverage the AS_PATH attribute in BGP to influence the path selection process.

Both types of services can be accessed over one Direct Connect link between AWS and the customer device at the same time. You will use different VLAN numbers (tags) for each virtual interface (mapped to the physical sub-interfaces).

The basics of BGP over Direct Connect

When the BGP session on your Direct Connect is up, depending on the type of Virtual Interface (VIF), different sets of routes are advertised to you:

- If you have a public VIF to access AWS public services
    - AWS advertises thousands of routes with the NO_EXPORT BGP community for all the public services in all the regions to you. This enables you to reach any AWS public services in any region from any region and helps you prevent them from leaking out of your network and Autonomous System. This is the default behavior unless you override it using BGP policies. For example, you can reach an S3 bucket in APAC from US East if you have a Direct Connect with a public VIF in the us-east-1 region.
    - Also, it might be undesirable to receive such a large number of routes especially in the case of low-end routers on the customer's side.
        - AWS attaches the BGP communities of 7224:8100, 7224:8200 and no tag to mark prefixes belonging to the same region, same continent, and global, respectively.
        - You can configure your BGP policies to match the communities on your router to accept just enough routes depending on which destinations you want to reach.
        - A complete and updated list of Amazon's public prefixes is regularly published in JSON format at: ip-ranges.amazonaws.com/ip-ranges.json. The list shows a fairly comprehensive breakdown of IP addresses assigned to services in each region.
    - Similarly, over Direct Connect, you can advertise to AWS the public IP ranges that your business owns. You can also leverage the BGP communities to tell AWS how far on their backbone you want your prefixes to travel.

- AWS recognizes and honors the BGP communities of 7224:9100, 7224:9200, and 7224:9300 when attached to the routes received from the customer. AWS has BGP inbound policies to map the BGP communities to keep-in-the-local-region, keep-in-the-continent, and propagate-globally, respectively, where the global advertisement is the default.

- You can advertise up to 1000 routes using a public VIF to AWS.

- If you have a private VIF to access your VPCs

  - You can advertise up to 100 routes to AWS.

  - For each VPC, you will have a unique VLAN tag to accommodate 50 VIFs on a single link.

  - Private VIFs can have the MTU value of 1500 Bytes or 9001 Bytes.

    - The larger value, when supported by everything along the path, can improve your overall throughput.

    - Changing the value can be service disruptive and has to be done during a planned maintenance window.

§Exam Tip: Congratulations, you just finished one of the most important parts of this book. The past two pages are extensively required at work and are absolutely fair game in any job interview. The ANS-C01exam's blueprint cares a lot about them as well. If I were you, I would go back and review this section before moving on to the next.

Take your architecture beyond one region using Direct Connect Gateway

By default, after setting up Direct Connect into an AWS region, you will only have access to the VPCs in that particular region. You can use the AWS Direct Connect Gateway (DXGW) construct, a global resource, to address this issue and more.

- Works with both Virtual Gateways and Transit Gateways.

- Allows you to have Direct Connect in one location in a specific region and have access to your VPCs in other regions.

- Simplifies the BGP configuration by sitting between VPCs and your Direct Connect setup.

  - On one side, it has a number of VGW associations to each VPC, and on the other end, there is a Private Virtual Interface to the Direct Connect location

- The member VPCs can belong to different AWS accounts.

Hosted or Dedicated connection? Go directly or via a partner?

Depending on their architecture, customers have two options for the type of connection when ordering a new Direct Connect link: Hosted Connections and Dedicated Connections.

- Hosted connections

  - You work with an AWS partner (member of the AWS partners network), and they create the connection for you. Most of the technical work, especially the field part, is handled by the partner.

  - Traditionally was only used for sub-1G connections as low as 50Mbps but recently has had its limits removed and can be used for various bandwidth options, especially when the customer prefers to delegate most of the technical work to a third party or have specific port speed requirements beyond the three choices of 1G, 10G and 100G offered by Dedicated connections. For example, with the Hosted connections, you can have port speeds of 300Mbps, 500Mbps, 2Gbps, 5Gbps, and more.

  - The biggest limitation of Hosted connections and the main reason many customers end up with Dedicated connections is the limit of 1 VIF of any type you can have on them. For example, you can connect to 1 VPC using 1 Private VIF but create 1 Public VIF and consume all AWS public services globally.

  - Loosely speaking, the partner works directly with AWS and purchases the capacity at a wholesale rate. Then they sub-lease the capacity to smaller consumers.

  - This is not to be confused with the Hosted VIF, which is a VIF owned by a different AWS account from the account that owns the Direct Connect port.

- Dedicated connections

  - The customer works directly with AWS and the data center owner to create the connection and run the cross-connect.

  - The customer currently has three port speed choices of 1Gbps, 10Gpbs, and 100Gbps. The 100G option was added in 2021.

  - To create a dedicated connection, the customer needs to:

    - Use the console, CLI, or API to create a new connection.

    - Wait until the Letter of Authorization Customer Facility Access (LOA-CFA) becomes available through the console. The letter specifies how AWS will participate in this connection, including the cage, rack, patch panel, port, optics, and connector types information. With this authorization from AWS and the details specified, a data center technician can implement the physical changes.

    - Download the form and share it with the data center operators within 90 days.

    - Wait until the cross-connect fiber is in place and confirm the completion of the deployment with the owner of the data center and through the console.

Direct Connect and the challenges of resiliency and availability

You can improve your Direct Connect resiliency by provisioning more than one connection. This architecture can be further improved by diversifying your AWS Direct Connect locations and even having more than one Direct Connect at each location. Needless to say, this increases your AWS and data center costs but reduces the chance of losing connectivity in the case of losing a router, link, or an entire AWS Direct Connect location.

To achieve greater redundancy and availability, AWS Direct Connect customers with multiple Dedicated connections of the same speed and bandwidth can place up to 4 Dedicated Direct Connect links in one bundle called Link Aggregation Group (LAG) for 1Gbps and 10Gbps links and up to 2 connections for 100Gbps links.

- The behavior is similar to the traditional concept of port channels with a hashing algorithm and its all-active links.
- The dedicated connections must be made to the same AWS endpoint in the same location.
- You can define the minimum number of surviving links in a bundle to keep it operational.
  - This helps in certain architectures such as active-passive designs with BGP, for example, where you have 4 dedicated Direct Connect connections in one location and 4 in another. You would like to stop using a Direct Connect location and switch over to the next if 2 Direct Connect links. When the minimum number of members is reached, the bundle is taken down, which triggers a BGP routing switch over.
- AWS Direct Connect Resiliency Toolkit was released in 2021. This new addition to the console helps customers use a GUI to decide how to achieve their desirable Service Level Agreements (SLA) goals. This tool also allows customers to design, order, and test Direct Connect links.

Direct Connect and the long-standing question of security

Although a Direct Connect connection is a private fiber link between AWS and the customer, many companies still need to encrypt traffic on AWS Direct Connect. This could be due to regulatory mandates or general policies for traditional networks that now have become applicable to the cloud space.

- Currently, there are three main approaches to providing encryption on AWS Direct Connect:
  - Encryption at Layer 2 using MACsec (IEEE 802.1AE)
    - Added in 2021
    - Point-to-point encryption
    - Only available to 10G and 100G links

- Higher throughput compared to IPSec

  - On the exam, this could be your best guide to the right choice

- Provides confidentiality, origin authenticity, data integrity, and protection against replay attacks

- Being a point-to-point encryption mechanism has the obvious disadvantage that the solution will not easily work if any routing (a Layer 3 process) is involved. For example, it will not function if Layer 3 MPLS VPN is used. Cross-connect fiber and leased lines are perfect candidates for MACsec encryption

- Encryption at the application level, such as the use of HTTPS instead of HTTP

  - May not work for some customers, especially those with legacy applications.

- Site-to-site IPSec VPN over Direct Connect with 3 main architectures

  - IPSec VPN tunnel over Public VIF to VGW

    - Establish the tunnel between the customer gateway and the public IP address of the VGW.

  - IPSec VPN tunnel over Public VIF to an EC2 instance

    - Establish the tunnel between the customer gateway and the public IP address of the elastic interface on an EC2 instance within the VPC.

  - IPSec VPN tunnel over Private VIF to an EC2 instance

    - Establish the tunnel between the customer gateway and the private IP address of an EC2 instance.

Routing over Direct Connect

BGP routing with AWS Direct Connect with or without the backup VPN channel leads to very interesting architecture cases. Keep in mind, AWS Direct Connect is always preferred over VPN if it's up and the prefix lengths are the same. You must run BGP over the Direct Connect connection, and the traditional BGP decision process applies in the same order. The list partially includes: Weight – Local Preference – Locally originated over learned – AS_PATH – Origin – MED.

At a high level, with Direct Connect, there are two main routing architectures, and each has its own branches:

Routing over public and private Virtual Interfaces (VIFs)

- Routing over Public Virtual Interfaces (Public VIF) when multiple Direct Connect connections are present:

  - Active-Active architectures

- Public AS number used: Keep the BGP attributes and prefix lengths the same. BGP starts using all the available Direct Connect links.

- Private AS number used: Keep the BGP attributes and prefix lengths the same. BGP starts using all the available Direct Connect links.

- Active-Passive architectures

  - Different prefix lengths

    - If you advertise more specific routes via one Direct Connect connection, AWS will always prefer that link to reach your network.

  - The same prefix lengths

    - Public AS numbers used when creating the connection

      - Inbound into your network from AWS: Use the BGP AS_PATH prepending technique to advertise longer AS_PATH out of the less preferred link. AWS will avoid that as long as the more preferred Direct Connect path is up

      - Outbound out of your network to AWS: Use the BGP Local Preference attribute to assign a higher value to the routes received from AWS through the preferred link. Your BGP routers will prefer the path to reach the AWS prefixes.

    - Private AS numbers used when creating the connection

      - Inbound into your network from AWS: You are limited to manipulating the prefix lengths to make AWS prefer one link over the other. This is a caveat of using private AS numbers with AWS Direct Connect.

      - Outbound out of your network to AWS: Use the BGP Local Preference attribute to assign a higher value to the routes received from AWS through the preferred link. As a result, your BGP routers will prefer the path to reach the AWS prefixes.

- Routing over Private Virtual Interfaces (Private VIF) when multiple Direct Connect connections are present:

  - Active-Active architectures

    - Keep the BGP attributes and prefix lengths the same. BGP starts using all the available Direct Connect links.

  - Active-Passive architectures

    - Inbound into your network from AWS (in the order of priority):

- Here, in addition to the AS_PATH, we have the ability to change the Local Preference on the AWS side by leveraging the following BGP communities to signal AWS the preference of the paths into your network.
  - 7224:7100 - Low
  - 7224:7200 - Medium
  - 7224:7300 – High
- For example, if AWS learns a prefix through a connection with the community of 7224:7300 when sending traffic using that route to you, it would prefer that Direct Connect reach your network.
- Use the BGP AS_PATH prepending technique to advertise longer AS_PATH out of the less preferred link
- Use the BGP MED attribute to influence the path selection process. The prefixes you advertise to AWS with a lower MED value indicate the path you want AWS to use when sending traffic to those destinations
- Outbound from your network to AWS:
  - Use the BGP Local Preference attribute to assign a higher value to the routes received from AWS through the preferred link. Your BGP routers will prefer the path to reach the AWS prefixes.

§*Exam Tip:* *Although you might not like it, as an ANS-C01 candidate, you must memorize all the BGP communities mentioned in the book. And it is not just about the exam; they're easily found in any production network too.*

Direct Connect convergence in case of failures

Similar to traditional networks, on AWS you can deploy BFD to detect issues with your Direct Connect links. The timers set for the BGP and BFD process used on the AWS side of the Direct Connect can negotiate with the customer end. This flexibility helps reduce the number of trouble tickets to the support teams.

- The BGP timers will set to the lowest value of the two for the quickest convergence
  - Default values on the AWS side: 30 seconds Keepalive – 90 seconds Hold timer
  - In case you're curious, these are the default values for Juniper routers
- The BFD timers will set according to the longest interval to accommodate the less capable hardware
  - Default values: 300 milliseconds and 3 attempts to declare a dead end. This results in detecting a dead peer in 900ms.

Monitoring Direct Connect links

AWS Direct Connect can be closely monitored by Amazon CloudWatch.

- The comprehensive metric data points, by default, are presented every 5 minutes.
- Some key metrics to monitor:
  - ConnectionState: 1 and 0 for Up or Down states
  - ConnectionBpsEgress: Outbound from AWS. Keep in mind, Direct Connect charges you for the egress traffic only.
  - ConnectionErrorCount: Vital error counters, including the CRC errors, which is a good indicator if your optics need to be cleaned up or replaced.

Direct Connect Troubleshooting

The troubleshooting process for the AWS Direct Connect is very similar to the same process for any circuit to your carrier with a BGP session on top of that. Here is a quick list of items to check off when you are in a Direct Connect troubleshooting scenario:

- Make sure the link build-out is complete. This could be a cross connect to be run by your data center operator or any other types of WAN connectivity by your carrier of choice. This would eliminate any doubts around circuit readiness. This could save you hours.

- In case of cross connects, make sure the light level and all the other physical aspects involving the optics (send/receive) are at an acceptable level. This would eliminate any doubts around the physical layer. I would also make sure the port is not inadvertently shut down; yes, I know!

- Make sure the VLAN settings and IP address on the virtual interfaces are accurate. Check the ARP tables to ensure the MAC is present. Issues at this stage could also keep the virtual interface (VIF) down. If everything is rosy, the virtual interface is up, and you are able to ping the AWS peer router, hence you can move on to BGP troubleshooting.

- The BGP troubleshooting is very classic and similar to any other network. You need to make sure if you have any firewalls in between TCP 179 is permitted through. Also ensure that the peer IP address, AS number, and the MD5 password (mandatory) are correct. Then you need to check if you are exceeding the maximum number of routes that you can advertise to AWS. As usual, on your router you can run all sorts of tools to diagnose routing issues, such as the traceoptions for BGP in Juniper or debugging and logging in Cisco.

§*Exam Tip:* *DX troubleshooting is an interesting topic. Although, for the most part, it is not different from regular BGP troubleshooting, since the layer 1 and 2 designs are (sort of unique) to public cloud environments, you are expected to fully understand each step, symptoms, solutions, and recommendations. The exam won't quiz you on Cisco or Juniper capabilities, but you need to know the overall troubleshooting workflow described above.*

§*Exam Tip:* *The topic of DX connectivity won't end here. We will revisit and expand this when we get to the Transit Gateway section of the book.*

Reference Architecture(s)

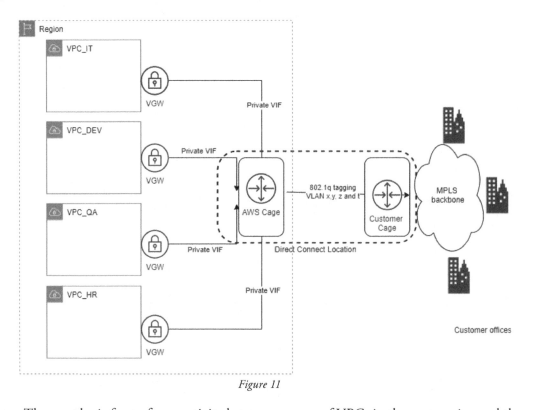

Figure 11

The most basic form of connectivity between a group of VPCs in the same region and the on-premises network is via Direct Connect. Notably, the customer is using VGWs instead of transit gateways. They only have a presence in one region (hence no need for DX gateway). As always, AWS uses VLAN tagging (802.1q) sub-interfaces on the routers to distinguish between the traffic of each VPC. It's not shown here, but if the Direct Connect link is point-to-point 10Gbps or 100Gbps, you might also be able to encrypt it using MACsec. At the time of this writing, there is no native way to use IPSec for non-P2P circuits, although it might come out at some point, and as you will see, there are custom architectures that we will discuss extensively. One way or the other, the million-dollar question remains; do we need encryption on a private dedicated fiber between your device and AWS? Some security experts and auditors would require that. That is a battle rarely won by the cloud and network architects.

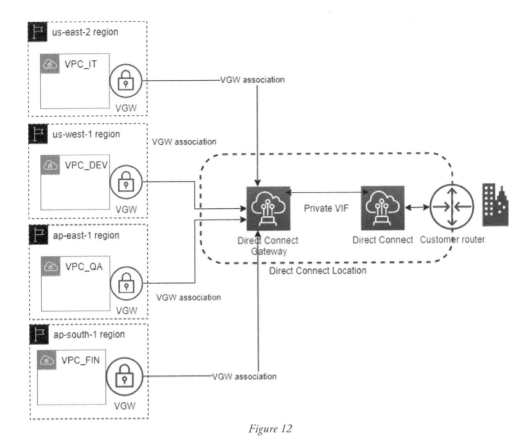

Figure 12

Simple multi-region reference architecture for Direct Connect. Here, although the architect could have used the DX link to reach VPCs in one region, she is using another construct called DX gateway to provide global reach to multiple regions. This design is based on VGWs, but as you will see in the following sections, this model is also extensively used when we have transit gateways (TGWs).

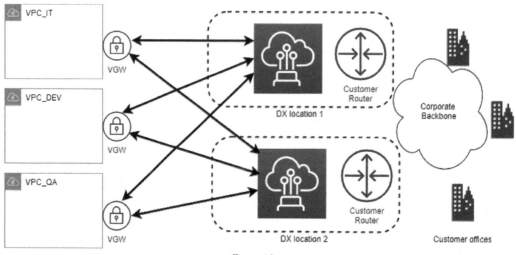

Figure 13

Further enhancements to the previous models by going to multiple Direct Connect locations and using dedicated routers on the customer side. Predictably, the cost would be higher but better numbers in terms of availability can be achieved. The main cost components would be those related to the hourly fees of each one of the four Direct Connect links, the cost of customer equipment, and if any redundancy is needed on the network between the office and those locations, the cost of introducing that also need to be taken into account. Customers with strict availability requirements might require diverse paths from different carriers to get to the AWS locations (if not co-located) and diverse paths within their own backbone (if co-located but have offices in other places).

Detailed cost analysis and budget justification are always among the architect's responsibilities; without them, anyone could design the most available networks in the world with many "9s".

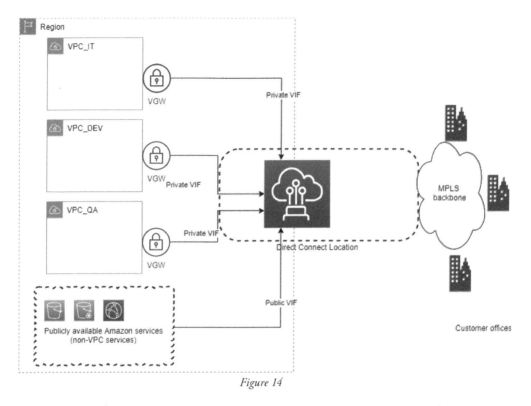

Figure 14

A common reference architecture used by Direct Connect customers with requirements to connect to both a group of VPCs and AWS public services. Notably, the VLAN tagging process would allow you to carve out a dedicated channel for the public VIF and treat it similar to another VPC. The architect needs to keep in mind that a public VIF could potentially give them access to public resources in more than one region, while the private VIFs would be dedicated to one region if no DX gateway is used. At this point, you need to ask yourself; what would happen to (1) access to the VPCs (2) access to S3/Glacier if we were to lose the DX location? With or without the backup VPN, their fate would not necessarily be the same.

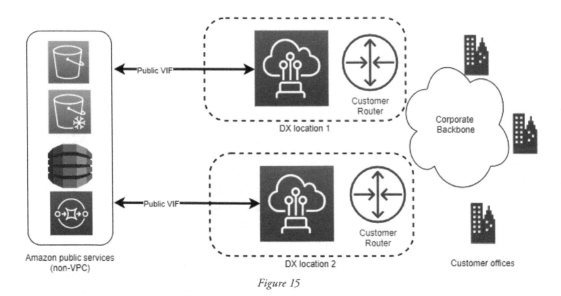

This figure shows a simple architecture used by a customer with the only requirement of accessing the AWS public services via Direct Connect. As you see, there is no trace of VPCs, and the architect has chosen to use more than one AWS DX location to improve the service availability in case they were to lose one of the AWS DX locations altogether. This architecture can be used by customers who need low latency and reliable access to services such as S3, DynamoDB, and Glacier.

A quick flashback: Although not shown here, since those services are available via the public Internet, some architects might have the option to better engineer their Internet traffic to/from AWS. For instance, a public peering agreement with the public cloud provider or a tier-1 carrier might give you a similar low-hop low-latency experience. That said, the dedication and private nature of a DX link cannot be beaten, especially in terms of security for customers such as those in the healthcare and financial sectors.

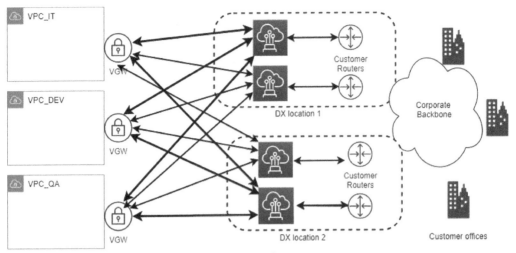

Figure 16

Similar architecture to the previous model but with enhanced availability for VPC access. In this mode, the architect has gone to two different AWS Direct Connect locations, and the design should be able to tolerate a complete failure of one location. Although, if such a catastrophic outage were to happen, the convergence time would also depend on a range of variables, including the BGP configuration, its timers and/or BFD settings, and the network between the DX location and offices. Needless to say, the cost of implementing such architecture would be significantly higher than the cost of a single-threaded design involving only one AWS Direct Connect location.

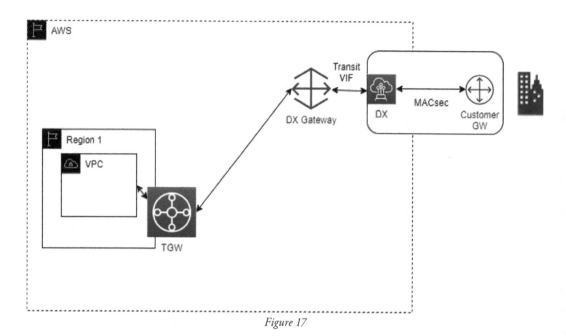

Figure 17

Although we will cover Transit Gateways later in the book but this is a simple reference architecture for MACsec deployment.

Although your point-to-point circuit might satisfy the basic requirements of MACsec, you need to keep in mind, AWS only provides MACsec on 10G and 100G links. This limitation is related to the type of switches/routers on the AWS side and cannot be changed by the architect.

CHAPTER 5

Taking the First Steps to Secure Your VPC

Up to this point, you have learned about VPCs and how the routing process in AWS works. But, how about securing an environment that is already outside your traditional perimeters? Remember, it took years for many IT professionals to get along with this idea.

EC2 instances in VPCs can have multiple layers of protection, including Security Groups (SG) and Network Access Lists (NACLs).

- Security Groups
  - Work in a similar way as any stateful host-based firewall.
  - Outbound traffic is permitted by default.
  - The return traffic for what's left is automatically permitted in.
  - Sessions initiated on the outside need to be explicitly permitted into the instance.
  - They are easy to configure but without automation, can be hard to manage and audit at very large scales.
- Network Access Lists (NACL)
  - They are similar to stateless firewalls for the VPC at the subnet level.
  - By default, they permit all inbound and outbound traffic.
  - Can be associated with multiple subnets, but each subnet can have only one NACL associated with it.
  - Similar to traditional ACLs the NACLs follow an ordered model from low to high (up to 32766).
  - Being stateless, they are less convenient (and less preferred) than the Security groups.
    - The return traffic needs to be accounted for and permitted in (e.g., ICMP ECHO REPLY)

- For the return traffic, pay close attention to the ephemeral ports (above 1024). They are used by resources outside the VPC to respond to your requests and are denied by default and vary from one operating system (and sometimes version) to another.
- If allowed by the security policies, make sure your main troubleshooting and optimization tools and their return traffic are permitted too.
  - Ping/Pathping
  - Traceroute
  - Path MTU discovery
- Combining the Security Groups and NACLs without proper accounting and automation can lead to confusing troubleshooting scenarios. If configured, it would be one of your key connectivity troubleshooting steps.
  - AWS Traffic Mirroring, as you will see, or 3rd party tools such as Wireshark or TCPdump can be helpful in such cases.

§*Exam Tip: Although the list of differences between NACLs and SGs is long, my favorite is how they handle the return traffic, also known as stateless vs. stateful. If you are not familiar with the topic at all, I recommend you have a look at some basic security books, but the key point here is that NACLs can easily turn into a real operations nightmare as they are stateless.*

Inspecting flows using VPC Flow Logs

VPC Flow Logs is a tool to monitor the flow data of each VPC.

- It is not a packet capturing tool and cannot replace AWS Traffic Mirroring, TCPdump or Wireshark.
- Offers insights into each flow at a high level and their fate; ACCEPTED or DENIED
- The logs can be sent to an S3 bucket or shared with CloudWatch.
  - In CloudWatch, you would have the option to analyze the logs and trigger actions via alarms if certain patterns are found within defined periods of time. For example, you can investigate too many Telnet login failures.
- The tool captures the following key pieces of information about the flows:
  - Interface-id, source and destination IP address, source and destination port number, protocol, and the action taken; ACCEPTED or DENIED
  - In 2021, AWS added flow direction, service name, and traffic path to the list of fields that you can capture and study
- The tool does not capture certain flows:
  - Instance metadata at 169.254.169.254. Do not worry if you are not familiar with EC2 metadata. There are some interesting examples of this in the mini-scenarios.

- Amazon Time Sync Service (NTP) at 169.254.169.123

- All the communications with the Amazon DNS server (the Resolver) at 169.254.169.253 or CIDR+2; which means the base of the subnet plus 2. This topic, too, will be extensively discussed later in this book

- DHCP traffic

- Amazon Microsoft Windows license activation

§ *Exam Tip:* *The Flow Logs have certain advantages and use cases. The most important takeaway that I want to make sure every reader has gained at this point is what they are and what they are not. The flow logs are data about flows and not the actual flows or packets. They are logs showing what sessions were established and between what points of the environment (e.g., source/destination IP/port). If your goal is to see the inside of each packet, then Wireshark or AWS Traffic Mirroring would be the right answer.*

CHAPTER 5

The Endpoints to Venture
Out of the VPC

§*Exam Tip: Remember the exam tip right at the top of the Direct Connect section? This is the second section of the book that I need to give everyone a wake-up call before we dive in. The Endpoints are an integral part of any production environment, and the exam's blueprint has a great emphasis on them. Make sure you fully grasp the concepts.*

Thus far, you have learned how to route traffic inside a VPC and how an architect can add virtual constructs such as the IGWs and NAT Gateways to go outside a VPC to access the public Internet. From a traditional enterprise networking perspective, this would cover most of our requirements. But all public cloud providers, including AWS, offer numerous other services that customers would want to consume. In the case of Oracle OCI, this could be the high-throughput Autonomous Database (ADB) system, and in the case of Microsoft Azure, this would be one of the storages or Cosmos DB.

AWS is no exception. Many services are owned and hosted by AWS, such as S3 bucket storage and DynamoDB, in addition to thousands of other services offered on AWS by 3rd party SaaS providers.

But how do we access those from within the VPC?

Some of these services, such as S3 and DynamoDB, can easily be accessed from the public Internet. Hence, from your on-premises network, you could hit the public side of those services; likewise, from within the VPC, you could take the path via a NAT Gateway to an IGW and again hit the public IP address of those services. In fact, for a number of years, that was the only way to have access to specifically S3.

Building such architecture had two obvious challenges:

Security: Many CISOs and other security decision-makers, regardless of any Layer 7 encryption such as those offered by SSL/TLS, simply do not like traversing the public Internet; I tend to agree with them, although I am used to hearing long-winded lectures on HTTPS security for *commercial* use-cases by my young engineers and architects. Well...

Cost: I hope this far in the book, as an architect, you have developed enough consciousness around all the costs associated with the AWS NAT Gateways. Pushing your S3 storage traffic through a NAT Gateway most likely won't sit well with your CFO or whoever pays your AWS bills!

§Exam Tip: Ironically, you will see this architecture in many production networks, and if cost and strict security requirements are not the main concerns, it could also be considered a valid option in the exam too.

The answer to both challenges is here. AWS VPC endpoints are special cloud constructs that are used to leverage the AWS private network and still communicate with services that traditionally were only reachable via the public Internet, such as S3. This provides better security and usually lower costs by keeping the traffic on the AWS backbone and away from the Internet.

- Currently, AWS supports 2 types of VPC endpoints[3]:
  - Interface VPC endpoints (Powered by PrivateLink)
  - Gateway VPC endpoints

Interface VPC endpoint (Powered by PrivateLink)

- Is an elastic network interface with a private IP address of the IP range allocated with the subnet that sits in your subnet and provides a link back to the target service
- Is used to reach 3 main types of services without leaving the AWS network (and taking security risks or incurring extra costs):
  - Many AWS-owned services (including support for S3 that was added in 2021).
  - 3rd party services offered by SaaS providers such as the ones available on the Marketplace
  - Shared services created by the same company for their departments or users
- Can support 10Gbps per Availability Zone which can burst to 40Gbps
- Supports only IPv4 and TCP traffic
- Can be accessed using the endpoint-specific hostnames generated by AWS. They are long and made of random characters as well as the name of the region and Availability Zone.
- Interface VPC endpoints can be used to reach SaaS offerings across AWS. For your popular SaaS offerings as a provider, you can create a name using your domain name. You can prove the ownership of a public domain name.
- AWS would require you to create a special TXT record under your public domain name for ownership verification.

---

3. AWS also supports other types of endpoints including Network Firewall endpoints and Gateway Load Balancer endpoints that will be examined in great details later in the book.

- For AWS-owned services and those on AWS Marketplace, to be accessed by an interface endpoint, if the private DNS option is enabled, the default DNS name for the service is available, and when the endpoint becomes active, it responds with a private IP address from your subnet pointing to the service such as ec2.us-west-2.amazonaws.com which could respond with 192.168.50.222 instead of 54.240.251.132.

- Keep in mind private DNS option is enabled for AWS-owned services and those available on the Marketplace.

- To use private DNS, both VPC attributes of enableDnsHostnames and enableDnsSupport need to be enabled.

Gateway VPC endpoint

- In early generations of AWS architectures without the endpoints, when we wanted to provide access to S3 and DynamoDB from within VPCs, the connection had to be made through the public Internet

  - As you might have guessed, the combination of EC2 instances accessing S3 buckets and NAT Gateways would skyrocket the monthly AWS bills!

- With Gateway VPC endpoints, you can access (ONLY) S3 and DynamoDB directly and privately from within the VPC. This obviates the need to traverse the public Internet and incur costs associated with the NAT Gateways and egress traffic

- It becomes reachable through injecting a route into the route table of the subnet. The route includes a prefix list defined as pl-xyz, indicating the IP range of the destination service and an endpoint such as vpce-xyz as the target (i.e., the next hop to get there)

- Predictably, it is a less expensive service in terms of data transfer rates compared to Interface endpoints (currently $0.0035 vs. $0.01 per GB data processed)

The endpoints and the challenge of transitive routing from on-premises

One of the critical topics not just for the ANS-C01 exam, but also in real-world public cloud environments with any vendor is to create a strategy to access service "indirectly." But what does that mean when an architect needs to access a service such as S3 indirectly?

Imagine a simple architecture where you only have one VPC with a Gateway VPC endpoint. In your VPC, all the EC2 instances happily access the S3 buckets through the endpoint with no issues. At the same time, users located in your headquarters access the same S3 buckets over the Internet. After setting up a 10Gbps Direct Connect, your CISO is excited and wants the S3 users to switch from the public Internet to the Direct Connect link and through the Gateway VPC endpoint.

There are two rules to follow to answer such questions on the exam:

- Gateway VPC endpoints (S3 and DynamoDB only) CANNOT be accessed from on-premises via both site-to-site VPN and Direct Connect links. To many customers, this is a key disadvantage. In many architectures, on-premises applications need to talk to

S3 buckets without traversing the public Internet. With Gateway VPC endpoints, this goal is only achieved if the consumer applications are located in a VPC. That's one of the main reasons AWS added S3 to the list of services supported by PrivateLink in 2021.

- Hence S3 can be accessed through VPC endpoints not just from within the VPC but also from on-premises, but much higher data transfer rates are applied

- Interface VPC endpoints CAN be accessed from on-premises via both site-to-site IPSec VPN and Direct Connect links. This is a huge advantage when compared to Gateway VPC endpoints

§Exam Tip: Since this topic has evolved over the years, it is empirical for the ANS-C01 candidates to fully understand the concept of transitive routing using the endpoints, how it behaves in different types of endpoints and how it changes over time. Again, not every customer has the latest and greatest architecture, nor is everyone able to afford it. Take a hypothetical customer and architect their environment using different types of endpoints; add, remove, replace, upgrade and along the way, explain to your customer the pros and cons of each.

In the old days, well before 2021, when the architects wanted to provide transitive (indirect) access to S3 from on-premises, they had to get creative. One of the ways to build such architectures was to deploy proxy servers inside the VPC as a jump box to hop on to get to S3 via the endpoint. It actually still works, although maintaining high availability for the proxy servers and incurring charges for their instances would be a separate challenge.

§Exam Tip: At this point, I need you to pick up a pen and paper, and draw your own table of comparison between the two types of endpoints. Don't forget a great part of any architect's job is service comparison. X vs. Y and why we choose X over Y. What if neither X nor Y is possible? Apply the concept to everything you've learned so far in this section of the book. Once again, remember, now there are multiple different ways to access S3 and similar services such as SQS; make sure you are fully aware of each and their pros and cons.

The endpoints and the challenge of tightening access to destination resources

Although both types of endpoints provide a convenient way to privately venture outside our VPCs and access other services such as S3, they also open doors that need to be properly secured.

How do we decide which AWS accounts IAM users/roles can access the destination services through the endpoints? And then, what sort of access is granted?

AWS allows you to create endpoint policies in the same familiar JSON IAM format and attach them to both types of Gateway and Interface endpoints.

As a quick reminder from the Solutions Architecture course, the IAM policies had a few components, as shown below. Keep in mind you can only attach one policy to each endpoint.

Statement: Beginning of the body of your policy.

Effect: What would the policy do; allow or deny? (i.e., the keywords "allow" or "deny")

Principal: Who is allowed or denied access to a resource? (e.g., an AWS account ID)

Action: What actions are you applying the policy to? (e.g., S3:* means all S3-related operations such as listing, S3:GetObject to download, S3:PutObject to upload, etc.)

Resource: What are you protecting? (e.g., arn:aws:s3:::MyExampleBucket01 or just "*" for everything related to that service via this endpoint).

Below is a sample policy that can be attached to an endpoint to tighten access via the endpoint. In this case, the policy is attached to the endpoint; everyone (indicated by *) can only access the S3 bucket of test-bucket and can only perform the operation of GetObject against the bucket.

```
{
    "Version": "2022-11-11",
    "Id": "Policy1234",
    "Statement": [
        { "Sid": "Limit-all-to-download-test-bucket",
          "Principal": "*",
          "Action": ["s3:GetObject"],
          "Effect": "Allow",
          "Resource": ["arn:aws:s3:::test-bucket",
                       "arn:aws:s3:::test-bucket/*"]
        }
    ]
}
```

Needless to say, this is an example related to S3, and all the other services available via both types of endpoints will have their own set of "actions." For example, if you are creating a policy to protect an endpoint that is used to access AWS Kendra (an ML-based search service), "Query" becomes a valid "action" to call.

Building a SaaS business on AWS

To build and become a 3rd party SaaS provider in AWS, use the following blueprint:

- Use the endpoint services option from the AWS console. This option allows you to host a service that can be reached by endpoints that could be used by your customers.

- Create a Network Load Balancer on the provider side. Your servers will be sitting as targets behind the NLB.

- Your customers need to create interface VPC endpoints pointing to your NLB as the service and request access. You will have the option to accept or reject.

- Traffic between the consumers and your servers will not leave the AWS network.

- You can protect your service by defining IAM rules/users or even AWS accounts.

- The consumer and SaaS VPCs can be in different AWS accounts to represent true SaaS provider and SaaS customer.

§Exam Tip: I have reference architectures on this point. Make sure you fully understand the concept. Go get a pen and paper and design your own SaaS on AWS by following the guidelines provided above. I would do that a few times until you are comfortable with the overall architecture.

Finally, keep in mind some endpoints can have their own access policies attached to them. Additionally, certain services such as S3 also have their own set of access policies. The two sets work independently.

- With no VPC endpoint policy attached to an endpoint, AWS will grant full access to the endpoint to reach the resource where the resource policies decide.
  - This is critical point in any production environment.

Reference Architecture(s)

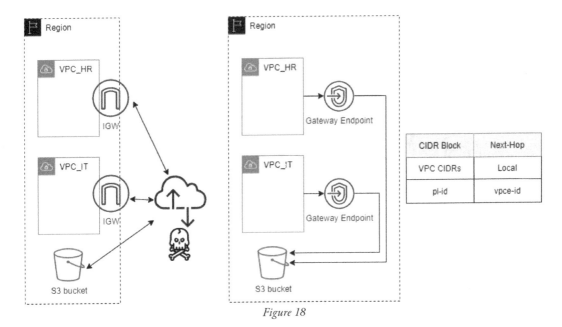

Figure 18

This architecture shows how S3 (or DynamoDB – And just these two services) can be accessed privately from within VPCs using Gateway endpoints without traversing the Internet. This is critical to healthcare and financial sector customers. Although this type of endpoint is quite handy and low-cost, it cannot be extended over to on-premises.

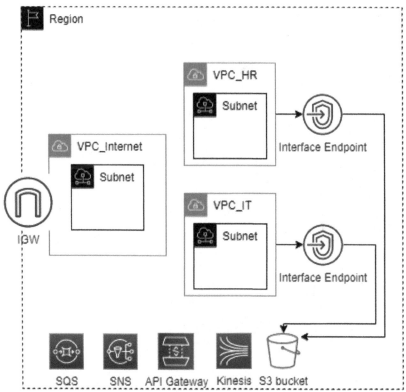

Figure 19

Here the architect is using interface endpoints to access a wide range of services outside the VPCs. The only point that stands out here is the fact that in 2021, AWS updated the service to be able to access S3, which traditionally was only accessible via gateway endpoints, as shown in the previous architecture. The interface endpoints can be accessed from on-premises, have higher data transfer charges compared to gateway endpoints, and can reach a wide range of services.

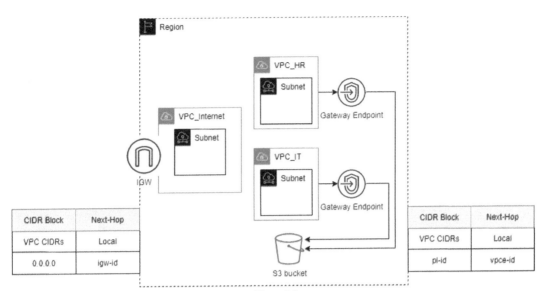

Figure 20

Avoiding the Internet by deploying gateway endpoints. In contrast to interface endpoints that cover a wide range of AWS services such as Kinesis, SNS, and SQS, the gateway endpoints only support S3 and DynamoDB. In this design, the architect still maintains the IGW but uses it for other purposes, such as providing Internet connectivity to VPC_Internet. Needless to say, it's never a good idea to attach an IGW without enough inspection and protection. Pay close attention to the route tables.

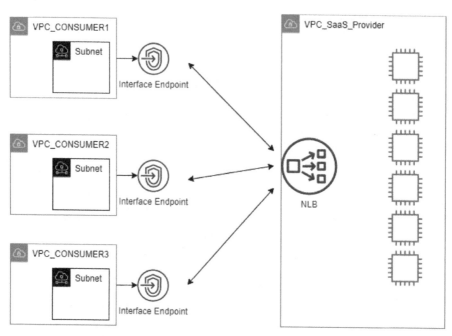

In reality, ENIs using AWS PrivateLink to the NLB
in a different AWS account

Figure 21

The reference architecture for implementing a simple SaaS provider on AWS. Using the endpoint services option of the AWS console, you can offer this service to your internal or external customers. On the provider side, at a minimum, you have a group of servers behind a high-throughput NLB, and each client VPC uses an interface endpoint (and not gateway endpoint) to reach your service. This architecture is easy to scale and, as you will see later, can be hardened by introducing firewalls to the SaaS VPC. Another use case of this architecture is to work around overlapping CIDR blocks if they exist in the source and destination VPC. In this book, we evaluate a few different solutions to that problem, including the private NAT architectures and using the Endpoint services option (depicted here).

The name resolution part of this architecture needs great attention and has been discussed multiple times in the book.

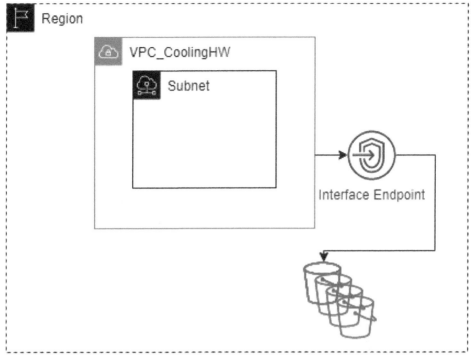

Figure 22

As shown above, an arhicteect has proposed a design in which they will use an *interface* endpoint in one of their VPCs to access several S3 buckets. This solution is valid, not just from within the VPC but also over Direct Connect from their office, should one become available in the future.

They must use the new interface endpoints for S3 and NOT the gateway endpoint to transit if they bring Direct Connect to the picture. The customer also needs to be careful as the rates for Interface endpoints are higher than those of their gateway endpoints.

CHAPTER 7

VPC Peering

VPC peering allows you to create 2-way all-port/protocol connections between two VPCs in the same or different regions under the same or different account without involving a virtual router or a Transit Gateway[4].

- Supports both IPv4 and IPv6

- Usually is established within the same company or where there is enough trust between two VPCs. When the right routes are in place, it enables communications between two VPCs, so enough caution must be exercised.

- The IPv4 and IPv6 CIDR blocks of the two peering VPCs must not have any overlap.

- Routing between the two VPCs must be manually configured. You can add routes to each route table of the participating VPCs and define the peering connection as the next hop (target) to the peer VPC. Similar to static routes, this change needs to be made on both sides; otherwise, the return traffic will fail.

- Inter-region VPC peering is supported

  - Works well in mass data replication scenarios from one region to another, although inter-region data transfer charges need to be carefully considered.

  - Helps businesses keep their data within AWS and encrypted.

  - The MTU value is capped at 1500 Bytes.

  - Can be costly.

- The creation of the VPC peering connections is a request-and-acceptance process.

- The security groups applied to the EC2 instances in the destination VPC remain effective.

  - It is a common troubleshooting case where the engineers forget to update the security groups with the source IP addresses of their peering VPCs.

---

4. As you will see in later sections of the book

- Even after creating the peering connections, the public hostnames within the peering VPCs are still resolved to the public IP addresses, which could cause issues.

  - AWS offers an option called DNS hostname resolution. If enabled, the same hostnames will resolve to the private IP addresses of the destination instances. In many architectures, this is a security requirement.

The common design challenges of extending VPC peering and transitive routing

- VPC peering does not support transitive routing. Hence, a VPC peering between A and B and then B and C won't create peering or routing between A and C.

- VPC peering relationships cannot be extended to on-premises over VPN or Direct Connect. Currently, without using a potentially complex overlay, you cannot use VPC peering to connect to one of your VPCs from the corporate office and then have access to all its peering VPCs.

- VPC peering relationships cannot be used to access a Gateway VPC endpoint (currently to S3 and DynamoDB) from a peering VPC. You cannot have a central VPC for S3 or DynamoDB access and use the peering to get to S3 or DynamoDB from other VPCs. Normally, each VPC would need its own Gateway VPC endpoint.

- VPC peering relationships cannot be used to share Internet access through an IGW or NAT Gateway with a peering VPC, also known as transitive routing. You cannot have a central VPC for Internet access and use the peering to browse the Internet from other VPCs.

- The idea of creating a hub VPC and using peering between that and a group of spoke VPCs is not always a bad idea. You can still deploy the architecture to access your own or third-party services located in a central VPC. A large business can have a vault VPC, hosting all their authentication services consumed by hundreds of peering VPCs. We will examine some of these architectures later in the book when we cover Transit Gateways.

§*Exam Tip: Before the advent of TGWs, the VPC peering architectures, for years, were one of the primary methods to provide end-to-end connectivity in multi-VPC environments. Today they still are (especially due to the lower overall cost compared to TGWs), although TGWs offer a lot more flexibility and manageability.*

Reference Architecture(s)

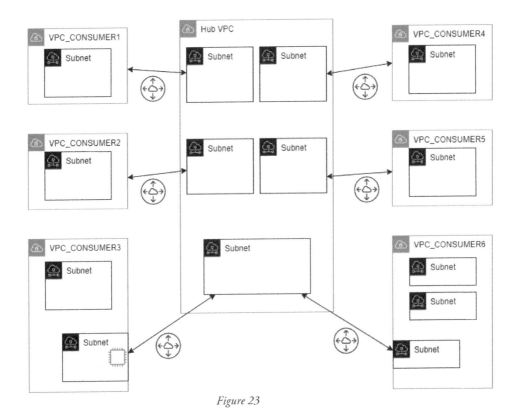

Figure 23

Before the advent of transit gateways, VPC peering was the most common method to connect multiple VPCs when there was enough trust between the two. The peering is done on a per-subnet basis and both sides would need routes to reach each other's subnets. Later, AWS started supporting inter-region VPC peering, while the data transfer cost has remained a major factor up to now. Although it might seem to be extreme, the architecture above still shows most of the possibilities with VPC peering. Here, we also show the fact that the peering relationship can be broad to cover every subnet of a VPC or as specific as peering to a single EC2 instance in a subnet of a VPC. This can be achieved by using the /32 address of a node in the route table, instead of the wider IP address range of the subnet.

CHAPTER 8

Transit Gateways and Going Beyond VGWs

§*Exam Tip: This marks the third wake-up call before we start a critical section of the book. Many modern AWS production networks operate TGWs, and the exam blueprint has a great focus on them.*

In 2018 after a long wait, AWS finally introduced the concept of Transit Gateways (TGW), a long stride in the direction of providing similar capabilities as what traditional routers would support in IP networks. Before that, for several years, AWS recommended the customers build their large-scale architectures based on third-party solutions such as Transit VPCs using Cisco Cloud Services Routers (CSR) or other routers or firewalls in a central VPC.

Finally, the AWS's own router called Transit Gateway became available in November 2018, with a Service Level Agreement (SLA) of 99.95% that increased to 99.99% in 2021, dramatically changing the network landscape architecture in AWS. In contrast to regular routers, TGW has built-in High-Availability (HA) capabilities, and the operator does not need to provision more than one to guarantee greater redundancy.

Currently, the TGW can replace the third-party routing solutions in traditional Transit VPC architectures as the hub. The TGW also, in many scenarios, can also replace the VPC peering architectures although the overall cost when considering all the fees related to a TGW would be higher than the costs of VPC peering.

It can also be deployed in several other key architectures, including:

- **Site-to-site IPSec VPN:** Replacing the functionality of VGW by connecting to the customer gateway. Now, if you use BGP, you can scale your VPN throughput beyond the classic 1.25Gbps per tunnel by using Equal Cost Multi-path (ECMP) and terminating multiple VPN tunnels on the TGW.

- **Direct Connect:** Effectively replacing the functionality of VGW by connecting to the Direct Connect Gateway construct via a new VIF type called Transit VIF.

- **VPC to VPC connectivity:** Facilitating connectivity between two VPCs or among a large number of VPCs. This solution tends to be more scalable than the traditional VPC peering.

- **Deployment of SD-WAN solutions:** By supporting a special type of attachment based on GRE tunnels and BGP, called Connect, a wide range of SD-WAN vendors can natively connect to your AWS footprint

You might have noticed the pattern: many functionalities shouldered by VGWs or 3rd party routers can now be fulfilled by Transit Gateways.

§*Exam Tip:* *Up to this point, let's agree on the fact that a TGW is a virtual router with a bunch of interfaces sitting in your AWS tenancy. You can bring all sorts of different connections to it and have routing between them. This includes routing between different VPCs and on-premises locations over VPN or DX.*

The architecture of AWS Transit Gateway

Each TGW comes with a default route table but can have up to 20 routing tables and 1000 routes. The functionality offered by the route tables in TGW is very similar to what Routing and Forwarding instances (VRF) offer in regular routers with separate route tables. In a traditional router, each interface (or attachment) can be placed in a separate VRF, and then it injects its routes into a route table. That route table is shared with other interfaces in the same VRF. A similar concept exists in the world of TGWs where the routes from an attachment are propagated to the TGW and populate the route table specified by the network operator.

If the attachment type is VPC, the propagation of routes from the VPC to the TGW takes place automatically using internal APIs. However, this process is one-way only, from the VPC to the TGW. Therefore, the network operator has to create a static route on the VPC side to send traffic upstream to the attached TGW. Similar to VPC peering scenarios, broadly speaking, you cannot attach VPCs with overlapping CIDR blocks to a TGW.

If the attachment type is VPN, in addition to static routing, BGP is used to propagate routes from the on-premises network to the TGW and vice versa. Similarly, if the attachment is Direct Connect, BGP becomes the only possible option to propagate the routes.

Here, I strongly suggest you go back to the previous paragraph and make sure you fully understand the difference between how routing takes place with each attachment type and how BGP can be a life and time saver.

Besides, with the VPN attachment type, if, as an architect, you need to perform ECMP across multiple tunnels to go beyond 1.25Gbps, you must use BGP. This cannot be done by static routes.

§ *Exam Tip:* *We talked about this before in the VPN section. Once again, going above 1.25G and leveraging multi-tunnel VPN architectures using ECMP currently is only possible with TGWs and not VGWs. You can make the same comment about IPv6 routing over VPN tunnels.*

Later in this book, we will cover the SD-WAN attachments and their details.

Network segmentation with Transit Gateways

You can use an AWS TGW to implement various segmentation strategies in your architectures:

- You can attach all your resources, such as VPCs, or VPN tunnels (or DX), to the same TGW and propagate their routes to the same route table (in simple English, put all the routes from all the attachments in the same route table). In that case, you will have full connectivity among the attachments with no restrictions at the TGW level.

  - This is ideal when you have no security concerns and do not mind having a flat network with end-to-end connectivity. I usually do.

- You can also connect all your resources, such as VPCs or VPN tunnels (or DX), to the same TGW but create different route tables for each group of attachments.

  - Each group, obviously, can have full connectivity among themselves. However, to achieve connectivity between two attachments (which again can be a VPC, VPN, DX, etc.) linked to two different route tables, you would need to propagate their routes not just to their respective route tables but also to the other route table to have two-way communication.

    - For example, finance VPC can talk to the HQ via DX, HR VPC can talk to HQ via the DX, but finance and HR cannot directly talk to each other.

Advanced architectures with Transit Gateways

To accommodate global Transit Gateway architectures, AWS supports Transit Gateway peering in inter-region scenarios.

- This architecture can be used by large enterprises with a presence in multiple regions.

- Now instead of creating Transit VPCs and supporting virtual routing instances running 3rd party codes, you can deploy TGWs in each region and peer them in any desired architecture, such as mesh. In such scenarios, route propagation between the two TGWs is not supported, and each TGW will get a static route to reach its peers.

Similar to traditional VPC peering, when attaching VPCs to a TGW, you have the option to enable "DNS support," which will allow your VPC to resolve public hostnames to private IP addresses when queried from EC2 instances in a peering VPC. An obvious benefit of this setting is to enhance your traffic security by keeping it local within AWS.

Attaching VPCs to the same Transit Gateway gives access to resources located in peering VPCs such as PrivateLinks, Load Balancer, and NAT Gateways. This is a major enabler when you are architecting central services VPCs. Here you might want to go back to the endpoints section of the book and once again review the design details.

Transit Gateways and Multicast traffic

After years of resistance against multicast, AWS is finally opening up its environment to multicast. Multicast is a huge topic by itself. If you are unfamiliar with it, I strongly recommend you build some knowledge base around it before trying to architect multicast-based solutions on any public cloud provider. But as a quick refresher for those who are familiar with it, here are some key points:

- Multicast streaming is one of the very first ways explored by IP engineers to preserve bandwidth and horsepower on the source

- Multicast streams flow from the source and can feed multiple receivers. The data-plane traffic (e.g., the video feed) is strictly one-way.

- Without multicast, each receiver would have to run its own unicast session from the source. This would lead to unnecessary use of bandwidth and resources on the source (CPU, memory, disc time, network, etc.)

- Multicast uses UDP/IP and works with both IPv4 and IPv6. In the context of the public cloud, for now, everything is IPv4.

- In traditional environments, multicast routing is done by Protocol Independent Multicast (PIM), and it's used by routers. PIM is not used in AWS networking yet.

- In traditional environments, multicast receivers (such as your laptop when your customer is watching a video over multicast) use the Internet Group Management Protocol (IGMP) to contact their upstream router to request the feed (i.e., join the multicast group; aka. Join the TV channel you are streaming). The receivers can also use IGMP to signal their intention to leave the group; which would allow the upstream device to stop participating in sending down or even receiving any further traffic for that "TV channel."

After a quick multicast premier, let's look at how it's done on AWS:

- Multicast can be enabled on a new AWS TGW where the AWS region supports it

- TGW is practically a virtual router, and with multicast support, it becomes similar to a multicast-enabled cloud router.

- Currently, TGW with multicast does not support even a fraction of what a PIM router would support in a traditional environment such as various routing scenarios. As you see more, you might suspect it is more like a multicast-enabled switch than a router! Although AWS would never use this term.

- Currently, as of 2022, a multicast-enabled TGW does not support multicast routing between anything but VPCs. So, we cannot architect solutions involving Direct Connects, VPN, or other extensions such as VPC peering to route multicast natively. Although you can still build a hard-to-manage overlay.

- As described above, a multicast-enabled TGW can support multicast routing from one VPC to another (i.e., between VPC attachments). So, you can have architectures involving one or more sources located in one subnet and a large number of receivers in other subnets/VPCs.

- Similia to traditional networks, on AWS too, you can have dynamic or static multicast receivers. The dynamic receivers use IGMPv2 to join or leave multicast groups, while the static members need to be manually added to the group by the engineers via the CLI or console.

- Multicast on AWS currently has very few knobs and ways to optimize and is extremely easy to set up. Multicast over VPC attachments to TGWs are controlled by two main knobs that cannot be enabled both at the same time:

  - *IGMPv2 Support:* Can be enabled or disabled.

  - *Static Sources Support*: Can be enabled or disabled.

- Depending on how the two knobs are set, the behavior of the multicast environment changes. If the IGMPv2 support is enabled, your receivers can dynamically join and leave the group with no static subscription required. If you turn this option off, the receivers need to be defined manually, for example, via the console. On the other hand, if the static source support option is enabled, you enforce strict control over who can be a source, and any new source must be manually registered using the (funny) CLI command of `register-transit-gateway-multicast-group-sources`. Currently, there is no console support to register multicast sources. Finally, if the static source support is disabled, any node can become a multicast source (sender).

- Finally, the behavior of a multicast-enabled TGW is similar to a traditional router in the sense that it uses IGMP QUERY messages every 120 seconds to find out if there is anyone else interested in receiving the multicast "feed" over that attachment.

§*Exam Tip:* *Although the details of multicast routing remain outside the scope of the ANS-C01 exam, since AWS is expanding the multicast capabilities of their environment through TGWs, I expect the topic to be at least lightly covered in the exam.*

Transit Gateway Network Manager

Via the AWS Console, the network operator can use the TGW Network Manager to centrally visualize, monitor, and (to some extent) manage their global network infrastructure. This includes how the TGWs are connected to the WAN and other on-premises locations. This reminds me of how the early versions of SolarWinds would monitor Wide Area Networks, although the current tool offers integration with CloudWatch Metrics and CloudWatch Events (or the newer generation of CloudWatch Events called EventBridge).

- To build the global view of the network, the majority of the work is about registering your Transit Gateways with Network Manager and adding the on-premises locations. The rest is visualized by the console for you.

- The tool uses CloudWatch to receive raw data and generate near real-time metrics for key data points such as bytes in/out, VPN connection status, and potential packets dropped.

- The Network Manager tool can also keep an eye on a wide range of network events and the number of their occurrence. Having such data on those events could save hours in troubleshooting. The list of events includes VPN attachment deletion, BGP for VPN down/reestablishment, new route installation/uninstallation on one or more TGW, and IPSec VPN down.

  - CloudWatch Events (now EventBridge) can also receive and process the events mentioned above.

  - In that case, you would have the ability to create rules, check the incoming event, and trigger appropriate actions such as sending them to a Lambda function. This would enable you to design a seamless chain from detection of an event to action. For example, a VPN connection goes down, or a route is added or missing. The event is received in CloudWatch Events (or later EventBridge), checked against the rules, and routed to the matching Lambda function, which would trigger a Python code to take further actions defined by the SRE team.

Transit Gateway Route Analyzer

In a typical TGW environment, when the source and destination cannot communicate, the network engineers usually follow a set of classic steps that we inherited from the days of traditional networking. We check the route tables for both static and propagated routes, then the attachments and all the other components that are somehow involved along the path. In May 2020, AWS introduced Route Analyzer a feature that takes the source and destination IP addresses and their TGWs as well as their attachments and investigates the entire path.

- At a very high level, the outcome of this feature is similar to Traceroute, although in this case, the result is applicable to the cloud architectures where the customer might have more than one TGW and presence in multiple regions.

- The output of the process can be used to take remedial actions such as adding any missing routes or fixing the attachments to establish end-to-end connectivity between the source and destination as the traffic goes through different TGWs.

- Similar to Traceroute, this feature is focused on the "routers" along the way, their routing tables, and attachments (in this case, the TGWs).

VPC Reachability Analyzer

In Late 2020, the VPC Reachability Analyzer tool was added to the list of observability and troubleshooting tools. The tool is used to conduct network diagnostic in troubleshooting reachability issues between two endpoints in one or more VPCs, such as two EC2 instances. The VPCs can be connected in any possible way. If you have complex Security Groups or Network Access Lists (NACLs) with various ingress and egress policies and are experiencing connectivity issues, this is probably the best tool for quick troubleshooting.

Reference Architecture(s)

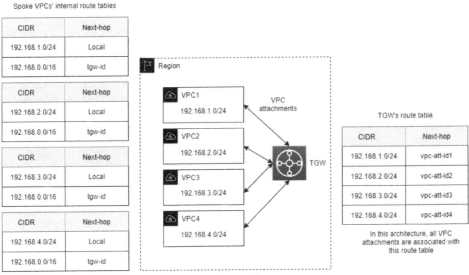

Spoke VPCs' internal route tables

CIDR	Next-hop
192.168.1.0/24	Local
192.168.0.0/16	tgw-id

CIDR	Next-hop
192.168.2.0/24	Local
192.168.0.0/16	tgw-id

CIDR	Next-hop
192.168.3.0/24	Local
192.168.0.0/16	tgw-id

CIDR	Next-hop
192.168.4.0/24	Local
192.168.0.0/16	tgw-id

Region

VPC1
192.168.1.0/24

VPC2
192.168.2.0/24

VPC3
192.168.3.0/24

VPC4
192.168.4.0/24

VPC attachments

TGW

TGW's route table

CIDR	Next-hop
192.168.1.0/24	vpc-att-id1
192.168.2.0/24	vpc-att-id2
192.168.3.0/24	vpc-att-id3
192.168.4.0/24	vpc-att-id4

In this architecture, all VPC attachments are associated with this route table

Figure 24

The most basic reference architecture to deploy a TGW on AWS. This figure shows a totally flat network where all the VPCs can use the "hub" to communicate with each other. Currently, there is only one route table on the TGW that each VPC is associated to. This route table is used to find the destination attachment (VPC) if the traffic does not match the local entry of each spoke route table.

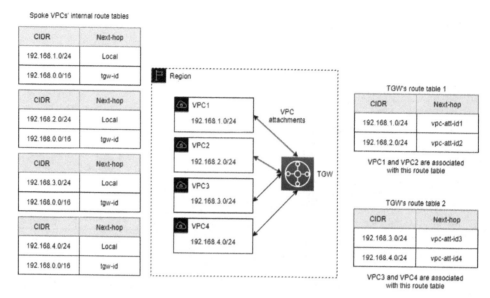

Figure 25

A common reference architecture for simple network segmentation on AWS using TGWs. Each group (also known as segment) of VPCs is attached to the same route table of the same TGW and routes whatever is not local (meaning in the same VPC) to its "hub router," known as the TGW. In this case, VPCs 1 and 2 are in the same group, and VPCs 3 and 4 are in another segment. Each segment uses the route in the corresponding route table of the TGW to find the other VPC members of the same group.

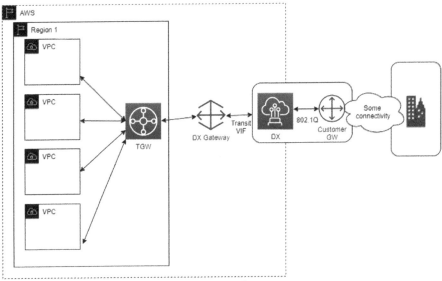

Figure 26

The architecture shows a simple single-region network with Direct Connect and TGW. In contrast to the traditional VGW-based architectures, here, we use the DX gateway between the DX and TGW. The VIF between the two is of a special type called transit VIF. As you will see in the following designs, this architecture can be easily expanded to multiple regions.

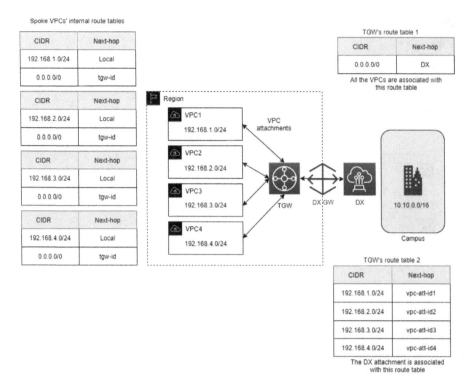

Figure 27

Reference architecture for strict VPC segmentation (grouping). In this architecture, no VPC can communicate with each other, but all of them have access to the Direct Connect link. Route table 1 is used by the VPCs to find the DX, and route table 2 is used by the traffic coming from the on-premises network to find its way to each of them spoke VPCs.

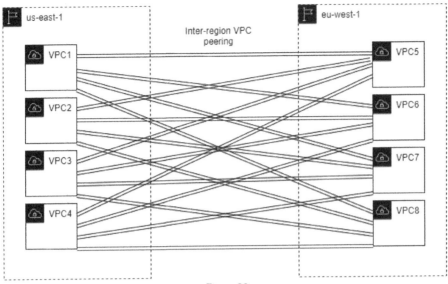

Figure 28

Probably the least efficient model to provide full-mesh connectivity among all the VPCs located in two regions using VPC peering. As you will see in the following architectures, this model and transit VPCs, with the advent of TGWs, can be easily replaced by more efficient designs.

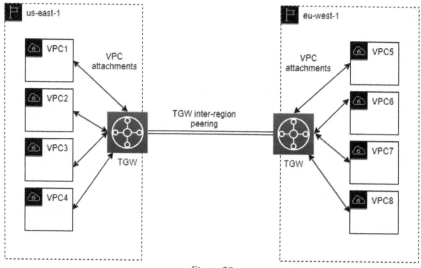

Figure 29

This architecture shows the peering attachment between two TGWs. This design at scale can replace the old transit gateway model where we had to designate a VPC with a third-party router as the hub. Furthermore, this model shows much better scalability compared to the VPC peering model, where the architect would have to create sessions between every pair of VPCs. In this model, the cost of inter-region data transfers must be considered carefully.

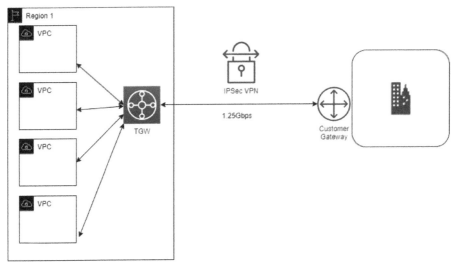

Figure 30

Single IPSec VPN session between a transit gateway and the on-premises network. Although this design simplifies the number of tunnels between the two environments compared to the traditional VGW design, with only one VPN session, it's still capped at 1.25Gbps. Keep in mind, in this case, as you will see, the architect has the option to introduce ECMP to their design. Having said that, check out the next architecture for a bad decision.

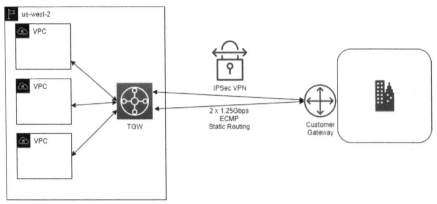

Figure 31

Currently, the customer has 1 VPN tunnel terminating on the TGW. They use static routing, and it has been very stable. This is a proposal to add a secondary tunnel to perform ECMP and increase the overall throughput to over 2 Gbps.

This is an INVALID architecture.

You cannot achieve ECMP with static routes. Deploying BGP would resolve their issue.

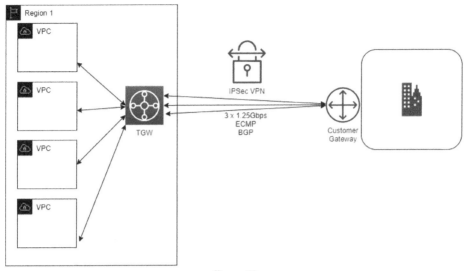

Figure 32

This simple architecture shows one of the key advantages of using TGW for site-to-site IPSec VPN over VGW. As shown here, the architect can create more than one VPN tunnel and utilize them simultaneously by using ECMP. It goes without saying that the customer gateway should support ECMP. Some firewalls running older codes or limited hardware might have restrictions. This architecture helps network designers go beyond the historical 1.25Gbps bandwidth available to VGWs for their VPN sessions. Here, the architect must use BGP because static routing is no longer an option. Keep in mind, you cannot have ECMP with static routing over VPN connections.

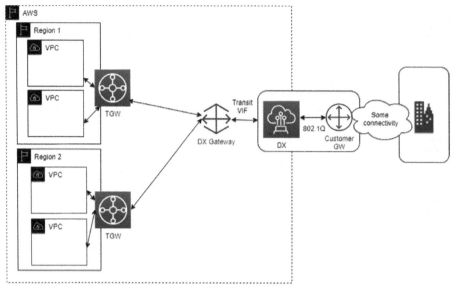

Figure 33

Simple and single-threaded DX architecture with TGWs. The company will lose connectivity to its cloud footprint when any outage happens along the path. This includes the last mile, service provider backbone, customer router, cross-connect, AWS devices, or even the entire AWS-owned DX location. The architect can improve the availability number by taking steps such as adding more DX locations or using IPSec VPN as a low-cost (but unreliable) backup channel.

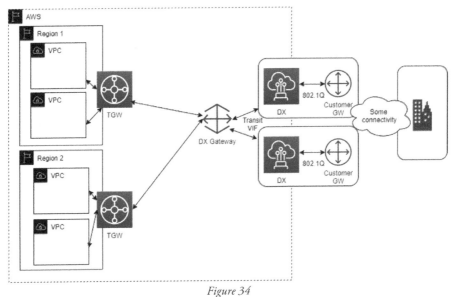

Figure 34

The only design aspect that stands out here is the DX redundancy that the architect has added to the design. At an extra cost, if one of the AWS DX locations were to go down, it would not cause an outage on the customer side. The rest of the architecture is similar to other simple TGW/DX integrations with DX gateway constructs. Here, the customer remains vulnerable to outages outside the DX locations.

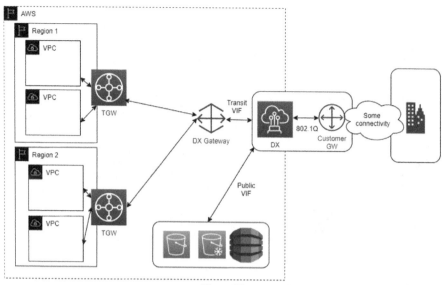

Figure 35

This figure shows how the architect provides access to public and private types of resources using one Direct Connect link. Here, the on-premises network has access to VPCs in two different regions. It also leverages a public VIF to access publicly available AWS services such as S3, Glacier, SQS, and SNS over DX. The latter can potentially enhance their end-user experience by reducing the number of hops and latency compared to the path via the Internet. Also, to some customers in the healthcare or financial sectors, the public VIF is a must, as they cannot afford routing, even their encrypted traffic easily over the Internet.

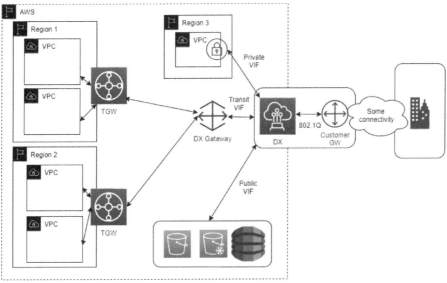

Figure 36

An expanded version of the previous architecture. The design here provides access not just to regions 1 and 2 via the TGW but also to region 3 via the traditional VGW. This reference architecture can be used in migration cases where not all the regions and VPCs have TGW connectivity yet, or in cases where financially, it does not make sense to migrate from VGW to TGW due to its data transfer fees and billing model.

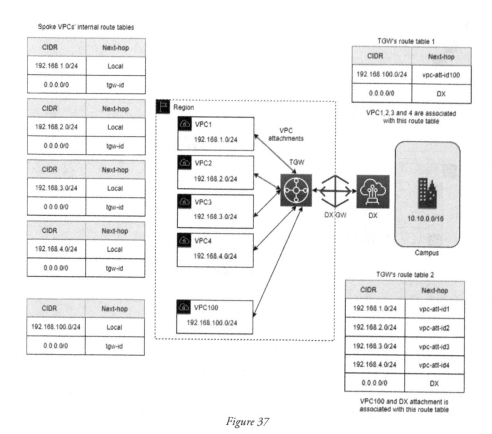

Figure 37

A single-region multi-segment reference architecture with a TGW. Here, VPC1,2,3 and 4 cannot communicate with each other but will have access to VPC100, which can be hosting services such as AAA. The architecture also allows them to communicate with the on-premises network via DX.

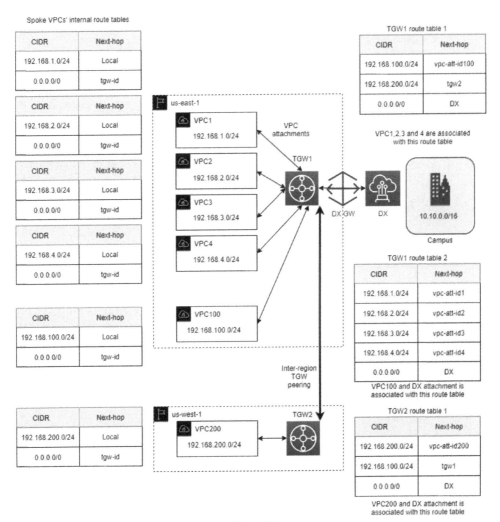

Figure 38

The diagram demonstrates an example of a multi-segment multi-region network with Direct Connect connectivity. Here, VPC100 is acting as a host for central shared services that are to be accessed by VPC1,2,3 and 4, a group of VPCs with no east-west access among them. The group can also communicate with the on-premises network via DX and with VPC200 in us-west-1 via the inter-region peering session between the two TGWs. Once again, the architect needs to take the inter-region data transfer fees into account carefully in such designs.

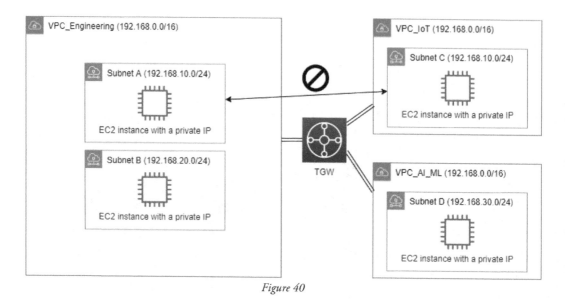

Figure 40

Simple reference architecture for a network with overlapping IP address ranges. I suppose all network designers are well aware that they must not have overlapping ranges but it still happens. For example, when your company acquires another company or when a merger takes place even within the same company. So that, it is not unlikely for an architect to run into a situation like the one depicted here. The next diagram shows one of the potential solutions using Private NATs that came out in 2021.

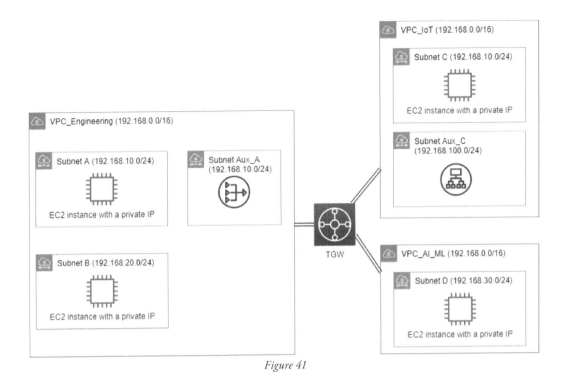

Figure 41

This reference architecture depecits one of the possible solution to the problem of having overlapping IP addresses. While deploying VPC Endpoints to implement a one-to-many SaaS-like architecture remains a solid solution (especially at scale), here the customer has decided to implement a different design using auxulary subnets and a private NAT Gateway. If you recall from the early chapters, NAT Gateways no longer need IGWs to operate and the concept of "private" NAT Gateways work perfectly fine.

Let's forget about the Subnet B and D and focus on the rest of the architecture. Subnet A and Subnet C cannot commucniate due their IP addressing. The architect creates an auxulary subnet, in this case Aux_A and places a private NAT construct in it. The NAT Gateway receives an IP address from the range of Subnet Aux_A. The architect, also, places an ELB, in this case an ALB in the auxulury subnet of the destination VPC, in this case Aux_C. The traffic from Subnet A to Subnet B will go through the private NAT Gateway and get translated to the non-overlapping IP address of the gateway. On the other side, that is what the ALB sees and routes the traffic to its registered targets, which are located in Subnet B, that would not have been routable due to the overlapping IP addresses. The concept of load balancing will be discussed shortly. Please bear with me.

CHAPTER 9

Resource Sharing with
Resource Access Manager (RAM)

It is very common with large customers to have and manage multiple AWS accounts. Traditionally, each account had to create its own set of resources and worry about managing and then securing them. This, obviously, was too much overhead. Starting in late 2018, AWS introduced Resource Access Manager or RAM that would enable resource owners to share those resources with other AWS accounts (principles).

- First and foremost, to share a resource with other AWS accounts, you need to be the owner of the resource.

  - Along the same lines, you cannot share resources that have been shared with you.

- Currently, there is a good integration between RAM and CloudTrail and RAM and CloudWatch to provide detailed visibility into the shared resources and what is happening to them.

- Not every AWS cloud construct can be shared, but the list is fairly comprehensive.

  - To cover the scope of the ANS-C01 exam, you primarily need to be familiar with the networking-related resources that can be shared.

- In addition to individual AWS accounts (the simplest form of sharing), you can share resources with accounts in AWS Organizations or even IAM roles and users.

  - The details of this topic are more part of the AWS security-focused exams. Again for this exam, you need to know several networking resources such as TGWs can be shared, and once they are shared, the receiving side can use them in their architecture.

§*Exam Tip:* *You might see various questions and scenarios in the book or on the exam involving cloud constructs shared with RAM. Do not let them distract you. Almost always, from a network engineering perspective, the goal of the question does not change, regardless of how the resource has become available and to whom. The fact that a TGW is shared with user A won't change how a TGW works.*

Sample networking scenarios to leverage AWS RAM

Prefix lists: You can create prefix lists centrally in one account and share them with other AWS accounts. This is a simple but very useful, sharable resource where you can remain consistent in terms of your Security Groups as you need to reference a PrefixList later in other places such as routing policies. This significantly reduces certain security risks, including choosing too narrow or too wide CIDR blocks by mistake or simply by random people's preference in one organization, which can later undermine your overall security posture. You create what is right and share it with other accounts.

Subnets: One of the most commonly used sharable resources where you create subnets centrally and allow other AWS accounts to have access to it to launch their resources such as EC2 instances, RDS databases, or Lambda functions. This could be one of the main building blocks of a central VPC where multiple AWS accounts are supposed to build their footprint without having to create their own individual subnets.

- The only catch here is that to share subnets in various scenarios, you need to make sure you have the following permissions: ec2:DescribeSubnets, ec2:DescribeVpcs, and ram:CreateResourceShare.

Transit Gateway: Very similar to traditional enterprise networks where the IT teams would set up a core switch/router and different departments would connect their networks to individual interfaces, the same need and concept also exist in multi-account AWS environments. In such places, different AWS accounts might want to connect their VPC to a centrally created and managed Transit Gateway (i.e., a virtual router) and route traffic between that and even engage their on-premises network. This architecture can be built by sharing Transit Gateways and allowing attachments from different accounts to it.

- Just like sharing subnets, you need to make sure you have the following permissions: ec2:DescribeTransitGateway and ram:CreateResourceShare.

Traffic Mirror Targets: Finally, in multi-account environments, it is possible to share traffic mirror targets. Hence, multiple AWS accounts, instead of setting up their own targets, could all send their mirrored traffic to one centrally managed destination (i.e., target). This would not need any special permissions such as the "describe" statements required when sharing subnets and Transit Gateways.

§Exam Tip: I handpicked a few key networking components to cover here. As the feature expands, I am sure you can find quite a few more examples in the official documentation. But before going after the extra, make sure you fully understand the key blocks I dissected here; the subnets, traffic mirroring, TGW, and prefix list.

CHAPTER 10

Foundations of Name Resolution with Route 53

Similar to private and public IP addresses, various types of nodes on computer networks can have DNS hostnames or Fully Qualified Domain Names (FQDN). For decades, we used on-premises DNS servers for local name resolution and used the external DNS hierarchy to resolve addresses with public domain names.

- An FQDN has several key components:
    - server01.payroll.castlenica.com.
        - Host: server01
        - Sub-domain: payroll
        - Second level domain: castlencia
        - Top level domain: .com
        - Root: .
- With the advent of the cloud, the model has expanded to cover more architectures:
    - In the cloud, we need full name resolution to reach on-premises, cloud-based, and Internet-based resources
    - From on-premises, we may need to perform name resolution for cloud-based resources
    - All the existing key DNS definitions, such as zones and records, are carried over to the cloud.
    - The traditional global DNS resolution hierarchy will remain unchanged.

When you create a VPC instance, your instance is assigned a private IP address. Also, optionally your instance might be assigned a public IP address. Both IP addresses are mapped to auto-assigned DNS hostnames such as xyz.ec2.internal (for the us-east-1 region only) or xyz.region.amazonaws.com (for other regions).

- The private DNS name is only resolved from within the VPC and returns the private IP address of the instance.

- The public DNS name can be resolved globally to the public IP address, but if called from within the VPC or a peering VPC, it is smart enough to resolve to the private IP address of the instance (Yes, the private address of it) and keep the conversation internal to AWS.

In the AWS ecosystem name resolution plays a critical role and is performed in two general ways:

- Full-scale name resolution using Amazon Route 53

  - Where you can have private and public zones with a rich set of traffic routing policies and health monitoring features.

- **Basic name resolution using Amazon Route 53 Resolver server** (called a bunch of other names, Amazon-provided DNS, VPC internal DNS, Amazon DNS)

  - Extremely simple DNS service available to each VPC

  - Located at 169.254.169.253 or the base of the IPv4 range + 2 (also known as CIDR+2)

    - This service and its IP address is not reachable from on-premises.

  - Performs name resolution for AWS auto-assigned names of the EC2 instances.

  - Is controlled by two DNS attribute knobs at the VPC level:

    - enableDnsSupport: If set to true, enables the Amazon Route 53 Resolver server for the VPC.

    - enableDnsHostnames: If set to true, creates public DNS hostnames (at amazonaws.com) only if the instance has a public IP address.

  - Can use a built-in firewall called Amazon resolver firewall to block queries made to untrusted or malicious domains. In high-security environments, you can also take the opposite approach by white-listing the domains that you trust. Either strategy will limit the domains, your VPC resources can query. This firewall was added in 2021.

§*Exam Tip:* *Make sure you fully grasp the concept of Route 53 resolver and where it sits (CIDR+2). We will be using this extensively in the rest of the book.*

Full-scale name resolution with Amazon Route 53

For anything beyond simple name resolution within your AWS ecosystem, you would need to configure the full-blown Route 53. Amazon Route 53 offers 3 main functionalities:

- Domain registration

- Similar to many public domain registration websites, you can look up, find the domain name you like, and for a fee, register the domain under your name for a number of years.

- DNS traffic routing

  - Sitting at the heart of Route 53, with this functionality, you can manage your DNS zones and records. You can also decide how to route traffic to your resources.

- Health check monitoring

  - By sending constant prob messages to backend resources, you can divert traffic from unhealthy servers.

DNS traffic routing using Route 53

Route 53, just like traditional DNS servers, uses the concept of zones that, in reality, are buckets designed to hold DNS records such as:

- A and AAAA records to map hosts to the corresponding IPv4 or IPv6 addresses and PTR records that perform the reverse functionality of A records.

- Canonical Name (CNAME) records to assign aliases to hostnames.

- Start of Authority (SOA) records to maintain some key information about the domain, such as the name of the DNS server and the TTL value for the records in the zone. Every zone must have an SOA record.

- MX records to define mail servers.

- NS records to indicate the name of primary (and perhaps secondary) DNS servers that are responsible for the zone. This is also used when you create delegation meaning another DNS server will be responsible for the parts of the domain you define. Later in the book I will introduce a similiar type of record; the DS records; bear with me.

- And finally, the Alias records that are technically Route 53 extensions to DNS and have special characteristics. While on the surface they look similar to CNAME records, Alias records can do more.

  - For instance, define alias names for AWS resources such as Elastic Load Balancers where the underlying IP address of the resource might change.

  - Also, you can define an alias record for the zone apex (root) of a DNS name, an operation that is not possible with CNAME records such as an alias, for example .com.

  - Alias records only exist for a subset of records supported by Route 53.

    - They are available for resources such as Network and Application Load Balancers, S3 Website endpoints, VPC endpoints, and CloudFront distributions.

Public and Private Hosted Zones in Route 53

- Public Hosted Zones

  - With publicly registered domain names are used to route the Internet traffic to your AWS or on-premises resources.

  - By default, these zones come with an NS record and an SOA record.

    - The NS records point to 4 randomly selected DNS servers from a pool of Amazon-owned DNS servers such as ns-410.awsdns-51.com or ns-576. awsdns-09.net that respond to the queries from the Internet for the public domain.

    - You can create delegations and let the other departments of your organization manage subdomains of a public-hosted zone on their own servers.

- Private Hosted Zones

  - To route traffic within AWS VPCs

  - This type of zone only responds to queries received from Amazon DNS (Route 53 resolver) and not directly from on-premises.

  - A Private Hosted Zone can be associated with one or more VPCs.

    - Queries from resources within VPCs are captured by Route 53 resolver. Then the Private Hosted Zone and its records are consulted. If a matching record is found, a response is sent to the querying node.

    - For this functionality to work properly, both enableDnsHostnames and enableDnsSupport options must be enabled.

    - You cannot define zone delegation with Private Hosted Zones.

Scalable traffic routing using Amazon Route 53

On traditional DNS servers, you have the option to create simple records such as DNS A records to point to the IP address of the servers. You could improve your architecture by introducing some basic forms of traffic distribution such as round robin or, even further, by adding load balancers to your local or global network architecture. For decades, these architectures allowed network designers to receive and process DNS queries at large scales. Additionally, with some level of certainty, the network operators could direct their users to resources close to them to achieve the best user experience.

With Amazon Route 53, when you create a record, you can also choose from a variety of traffic routing policies. Currently, the following routing policies are available:

- Simple

  - Suitable to point to a single resource such as one database or Web server

- Failover
  - Suitable in active-passive scenarios where you have two resources or pools of resources
- Latency-based
  - Suitable to direct users to the closest resource in AWS multi-region architectures
  - Although it's based on the average latency over time yet, due to the significant variations in the public Internet's condition, it might result in unpredictable routing patterns.
- Weighted
  - Suitable for cases where you give more weight to certain resources to have Route 53 attract more users to them, maybe because they are more powerful servers.
- Multi-value answer
  - Suitable when there are multiple resources available, and in the response, you want to provide a group of them to the querying users.
- Geolocation
  - Suitable in scenarios where your goal is to direct your users to resources based on their geographical locations - which may or may not result in the lowest latency
- Geoproximity
  - Suitable in scenarios where you want to direct your users based on their location and the location of the resources. Also, by adding a parameter called "bias," you can potentially attract more users to certain AWS or non-AWS resources, such as cases where you have more capacity provisioned in one AWS region compared to its neighboring region.
    - This mode can be configured through Route 53 Traffic Flow, which is currently a paid service.

Global name resolution enhancements with Amazon Route 53

Network operators have always been looking for ways to improve the accuracy of Traditional Global Server Load Balancing (GSLB) mechanisms. In other words, when a DNS query is received, and you have presence in multiple data centers around the world, which one should be used to serve the user? How to improve its accuracy?

- AWS supports Extension Mechanisms for DNS or specifically the ENDS Client Subnet or EDNS0 for short, as described in the RFC-7871.
- The premise is simple; when performing recursive name resolution, it would be nice for the DNS resolver to include some information about the network that originated the DNS query without violating the user's privacy:

- For instance, including the first 3 octets of the IPv4 would help the DNS infrastructure have more information about the location of the querying client based on where the IP address is registered.

- The Geoproximity, Geolocation, and Latency-based routing policies of Route 53 would greatly benefit from the feature.

- Although the DNS servers and possibly firewalls that will see larger UDP packets for DNS would need modifications, the clients would not require any changes, which is a huge benefit to implementing an idea like this on a global scale.

- If a DNS resolver does not support EDNS, Route 53 will use the source IP address of the resolver itself. Although this works in most scenarios, it could cause issues in cases such as large enterprises where the resolver and clients are not in the same geographical areas. For instance, when the corporate office in Vancouver, BC, uses the DNS resolver of the larger office in Seattle, WA, and it does not support ECS. In this case, Route 53 will decide based off of the source IP address of the resolver in Seattle, WA.

CHAPTER 11

Advanced Topics in Route 53

Name resolution in hybrid environments

§*Exam Tip: You are about to begin the most important part of this chapter, as almost any AWS customer would have questions about this. This topic is also called out by the exam blueprint. So be 100% prepared.*

Route 53 is a highly scalable DNS service with decent availability of Service Level Agreements (SLA). However, many customers are expected to maintain at least part of their on-premises DNS infrastructure for years to come. This, of course, will support many client computers and IoT devices. Historically, up until mid-2018, although you could have separate DNS infrastructures for on-premises and AWS, to implement name resolution between the two, you had to architect some intermediary service such as Microsoft Active Directory, Unix BIND, or AWS Directory Services as your DNS forwarders to forward the requests back and forth.

One of the biggest hurdles that the architects had to overcome was the fact that they could not send queries over Direct Connect or VPN directly to their Amazon DNS resolver at 169.254.169.253 (or the famous CIDR+2).

- In late 2018 AWS greatly simplified this model by introducing inbound and outbound endpoints for Route 53 Resolver.
  - Inbound endpoints (i.e., inbound from your data center into AWS):
    - You create them in your VPC, and they are contacted by the on-premises DNS infrastructure to forward DNS queries for what you are hosting in Route 53.
    - The inbound endpoints are assigned private IP addresses and are available via VPN or Direct Connect. Hence, this solution directly addresses the issue described above by contacting the Amazon DNS address from on-premises. Once configured, you need to go to your Microsoft or Unix DNS servers

in your data center and configure conditional forwarding for the zones in AWS. Going forward, such requests will be forwarded to your endpoints.

- To make your service more scalable, you can have multiple inbound endpoints in multiple Availability Zones.

- Outbound endpoints (i.e., outbound from your VPC to on-premises DNS):

  - You create them in your VPC, and they are contacted by the resources in the VPC, to forward name resolution queries from your VPCs to on-premises. Similar to the inbound endpoints, they are also assigned private IP addresses, and you can create multiple endpoints in multiple availability zones.

- A major difference between the inbound and outbound endpoints lies in a powerful feature called outbound rules.

- Similar to the conditional forwarding rules on traditional DNS servers, Route 53 allows you to create rules and define which domains you want to forward the requests to the on-premises DNS infrastructure. There are two types of rules:

  - Forwarding rules are used to forward queries for a specific domain to the on-premises DNS servers.

  - System rules are used to carve exceptions out of the broader forwarding rules. For instance, you can use system rules to exclude queries for one of the subdomains of a parent domain from being forwarded to the on-premises DNS server. In other words, this rule helps you keep them "local" in AWS, although the main domain is being forwarded.

Finally, if you have multiple private hosted zones with overlapping names, the more specific match is used. For instance, if you have a rule to forward castlencia.com and apps.castlencia.com, your traffic will be routed based on the more specific match. Also, keep in mind that rules can be applied to multiple VPCs.

§*Exam Tip*: *A big mistake you can make here is to ignore the older architecture where we had forwarders on each side and focus dedicatedly on the new architecture where we have the endpoints. Although in most cases, the endpoints are the recommended approach, you still might encounter very large customers running the older architecture. The same concept applies to the ANS-C01 exam. The endpoints are extremely important but will not abolish all the other possible architectures. My recommendation is the same as before, grab a pen and paper and design both architectures at least 10 times for a range of hypothetical customers. Take redundancy into account, follow the traffic pattern, and explain the pros and cons to your customer.*

Simulating Dynamic DNS (DDNS) on AWS

Those network engineers with a systems engineering background appreciate the value of Dynamic DNS. I personally started to value it in 1999-2000, when Microsoft integrated DNS and Active Directory, and I, as a network administrator, didn't have to manually "register" the hostnames (i.e., A or PTR records and sometimes both) for each device that we added to the environment.

The same architecture can be built in AWS using a combination of different functions. The entire concept is about registering the hostnames of resources (such as the EC2 instances) with your domain name in Route 53. This is preferred by some operators who do not want to work with AWS auto-generated names such as xyz.internal and is particularly useful in an environment like a public cloud where the IP addresses change frequently.

- To design and implement such a solution, you need to get creative, and there are a few ways to do so.
  - One approach is to leverage CloudWatch Events to detect instance launched/terminated events in conjunction with Lambda functions to make the necessary changes to the Route 53 zones.
    - When the new instance is moved into the running state, a Lambda function developed in languages such as Python or Java can be triggered to create a record in the appropriate Route 53 zone.
    - If needed, once the instance goes down, another function can take care of removing the record from the zone.

Split-View DNS (Split-Horizon DNS) for Corporate Networks

Many companies need to use the same domain name for computing within VPC and access from the outside (internal access vs. external access). For instance, your external website can be accessed via www.goldentstatenetworks.com, while your intranet is accessed via intranet. castlencia.com. This behavior is supported and called Split-view or Split-horizon DNS; when deployed, you can have an internal version of your external website using the same domain name.

- The Split-view works when you have a public hosted zone (publicly registered domain) and a private hosted zone (attached to VPCs), both with the same name.
- The source of the queries (the Internet vs. VPCs) would be looked at to determine whether the response record should come from the private or public hosted zone that both have the same name. If the query is received from within AWS, the private address, and if it's coming from the Internet, the public address will be supplied.
- Some companies might still prefer to use external DNS providers for their public zones instead of using Route 53 pubic-hosted zones. The Split-view DNS supports that setup as well.

§*Exam Tip: In contrast to how it might sound, split-view scenarios are pretty common in real life. Hence, I wouldn't be surprised if they also showed up on the exam.*

DNSSEC and the challenge of protecting DNS messages

I talk to the operators of the largest enterprise and service provider networks in North America, and surprisingly up until recently, this important security gap was not a huge concern to many architects or decision makers. Probably verifying DNS responses received by your resolvers to make sure they have not been tampered with is not one of your top priorities either, but it must be, especially if you are required to adhere to strict regulatory mandates.

In late 2020, the support for Domain Name System Security Extensions (DNSSEC) was added to Route 53 to provide data integrity verification and data origin authentication for the messaging mechanism of DNS. After enabling DNSSEC signing for a hosted zone in Route 53, every response for the zone is signed using public key cryptography. Once you have provided such signed responses to your DNS resolvers, who are trying to resolve your domain name, they can validate to ensure all the messages have indeed come from Route 53 and have not been tampered with in transit.

- The DNSSEC is a feature that authenticates responses for the look up attempts against your domain name.

- It does not provide encryption, but by validating the responses, it can prevent unauthorized 3rd parties from manipulating the response messages to DNS queries.

- Although in most commercial use cases DNSSEC is still optional if you are required to comply with the FedRAMP, according to section 4.1 of the Mandate Readiness Assessment Report, your implementation must support DNSSEC: "Does the system's external DNS solution support DNS Security (DNSSEC) to provide origin authentication and integrity verification assurances?"

- Although different implementations of DNSSEC have slightly different details, Route 53 primarily works based on two types of keys to implement the public key cryptography:

  - *Key Signing Key (KSK):* It is the customer's responsibility and can be managed in AWS KMS.

  - *Zone Signing Key (ZSK):* It is the cloud provider's responsibility (AWS).

- With DNSSEC enabled, Route 53 cryptographically signs the records in your hosted zone.

- The ZSK is made of two keys: a public key and a private key.

  - The private key part of ZSK is used to sign the regular DNS records in the zone, such as the A and AAAA records.

  - The pubic key part of the ZSK is placed in a new DNS record type called DNSKEY and is shared with the querying DNS resolver.

- Once the two keys function together, you can provide your querying resolvers with 3 crucial pieces of information: the records, the signed records using the private key, and the DNSKEY containing the public signing key. Then the resolver can use the public key to verify the authenticity and integrity of the DNS response.

- But how do you make sure the public key (DNSKEY record) of the ZSK has not been tampered with?

    - This is where KSK comes into play. The private key part of it signs the public key part of ZSK (the DNSKEY record).

    - The public key part of the KSK is published by the DNS server in the form of DNSKEY record and is used to validate the public key (DNSKEY record) of the ZSK.

    - Hence, it is fair to say, the public KSK and public ZSK are signed by the private KSK

Finally, if you recall from the foundational courses, DNS has a hierarchical model. For example, in terms of the global name resolution system, at the top of the pyramid, there are the root name servers, which *delegate* responsibility (authority) for each top-level domain (TLD) to its own servers, such as the ones responsible for .com, .org, .net, etc. and the authority for each company's domain is delegated to the next tier where for example the DNS servers of the Castlencia company route traffic to www, mail, app1, app2, etc. under Castlencia.com. Delegation at each layer is done by adding an NS record to the *parent* tier pointing to the child servers responsible for the name space[5].

But now, in the context of DNSSEC, how is the same trust transferred from the parent to the child zone?

- DNSSEC added support for a new DNS record called the delegation signer (DS) to implement the transfer of trust from a parent to a child zone. It contains the hashed DNSKEY record, which in turn contains the public KSK. This new record is placed in the *parent* zone.

- Once fully implemented, when a resolver is querying a child zone, in addition to the referral, the parent also provides the DS record showing the child zone also supports DNSSEC.

- When the querying resolver receives the response (referral) from the DNS server hosting the parent zone, it needs to check the validity of the child zone's public KSK. This is done by hashing it and comparing the result to the DS record received from the parent. A match would mean a successful verification.

§*Exam Tip: I have been around the corner long enough to understand when a topic goes out of the general network engineering's comfort zone. DNSSEC is one of them. As usual, I don't believe in shortcuts. Please go through the section a few times and draw up a few hypothetical scenarios with different record types. Go back and review them several more times until you feel absolutely confident that you've grasped the details and flows. It's not complicated, trust me.*

---

5. Also, likely an A record to resolve its IP address from the name.

The Challenge of connecting IPv6-only workloads to the world of IPv4

I have written blogs and given talks on our journey as an industry toward IPv6. Although, the reasons behind our seemingly slow migration are outside the scope of this book, but the outcome of the project is not. I still remember we had meetings in early 2000 to discuss expedited migration plans and probably most readers of this book will retire before the last IPv4 disconnects from our networks. Hence, we need "bridging" solutions to get us from where we are today to the tail-end of the journey where everything only relies on IPv6.

In a series of updates between 2020 and 2022, AWS added certain IPv6 capabilities to the VPCs. One capability that stands out and you need to be familiar with for the ANS-C01 exam, is how an IPv6-only subnet communicates with various IPv4 resources outside a dual-stack VPC. This feature is enabled by the enhancements made to two key services of Route 53 resolver and NAT Gateway.

There is a reference architecture at the end of this chapter but there are two main issues with IPv6 hosts on AWS when they try to connect to the outside world:

- Name resolution using Route 53 resolver
- Routing to IPv4 destinations

The name resolution process is an issue because when the IPv6 only host contacts the CIDR+2 resolver to get the IPv6 address of its target (i.e., Castlencia.com), it might receive the IPv4 address (the A record). So, the right logic is built into the Route 53 resolver to return the AAAA record is one is available. But what if there is none? In that case, the resolver synthesizes the outcome by prepending the well-known prefix of 64:ff9b::/96 as defined in RFC-6052. This somehow reminds me of the old days when the firewalls who do DNS doctoring!

- As a result of the synthetization process the IPv4 associated with the A record turns into an IPv6, that is consumable by the inquiring IPv6-only host. For example, 64:ff9b::10.1.1.100 turns into 64:ff9b::a01:164.

The next issue happens when the host attempts to actually use the synthesized address (in our case 64:ff9b::a01:164) to communicate with the IPv4 destinations, including those in other VPCs. This is the DNS64 process.

The routing part is a different issue. How do we route an IPv6 packet through the NAT Gateway to its IPv4-only destination?

- Enhancements have been made to the NAT Gateway to identify the 64:ff9b::/96 range (DNS64) and use its own IP address as the source and the IPv4 address as the destination after truncating the 64:ff9b:: part. This is the NAT64 process.

Health checking with Route 53

Route 53 supports a range of health checks to monitor the status of resources. You can monitor the status of an endpoint such as a Web server by its IP address or domain name.

- To further test a Web server, the health check can be created to reach certain ports or pull specific web pages or URL paths to ensure they are available.

- The checks can be done at the rates (intervals) and thresholds you specify.

- You can monitor the status of a group of other health checks:

  - If all the health checks are passed (e.g., all the servers are healthy)

  - If any health check is passed (e.g., at least one server is healthy)

  - If a minimum number of checks is passed (e.g., a certain number of servers are healthy)

- You can monitor any change in the state of your existing CloudWatch alarms created in other regions.

  - If the CloudWatch alarm moves to the INSUFFICIENT_DATA state, the health check can be configured to be healthy, unhealthy, or remain in the last known status. This could be due to several reasons, such as lack of data and not having enough time since the starting point.

- There is one exception to this process when you are creating health checks in Route 53. If your records are alias records, you have the option to enable "Evaluate Target Health," a health check mechanism exclusively available to alias records. This option replaces the creation of health checks that you normally do for the other types of records.

  - For example, if your alias record is pointing to a load balancer, the Evaluate Target Health feature considers the alias record healthy as long as all the target groups of the ELB are healthy. To be a healthy target group, it must have at least one healthy EC2 instance.

- One of the benefits of monitoring the health of DNS records in AWS is the ability to deploy failover models.

  - Simple health check model for DNS failover: You can monitor the health of your records and have Route 53 decide how to route traffic based on their status. This is helpful when you have a number of resources, such as frontend Web servers.

    - For alias records, this will be done by the "Evaluate Target Health" feature.

    - For non-alias records, this will be done through the creation of regular Health Checks.

  - Complex health check model for DNS failover: You can create a decision tree with a mix of alias and non-alias records. Then you can also take advantage of another unique feature of alias records that allows them to point to other Route 53 records.

    - For instance, at the global level, you can define several alias records in each region. These alias records are, in turn, pointing to a number of A records pointing to your EC2 instances. You can create a complex monitoring model by enabling the "Evaluate Target Health" feature for the alias records and enabling the regular health checks for the A records to check the status of the actual EC2 instances underneath them.

Use Route 53 Resolver Query Logs (RQL) to monitor DNS queries

In summer 2020, AWS introduced the Route 53 RQL to log DNS queries made to the internal DNS server (i.e., Route 53 Resolver or CIDR+2) within a VPC.

Very similar to logging any DNS interactions in traditional environments, this feature has certain benefits, including:

- Meeting regulatory and compliance requirements: Several government-level mandates require network operators to store such queries.

- Application troubleshooting. This includes queries made by EC2 instances, Lambda functions, or any application you might be running in a container in environments such as ECS or EKS (which I will introduce later in the book).

- Breach investigations and postmortem procedures. Having access to all the DNS queries made by compromised systems and applications could be an integral part of any investigation.

The Resolver query logs can be sent to three different types of destinations:

- *Amazon S3 buckets:* Suitable if you are simply required to store the queries by your regulatory organization. You may not go back to these for months, but when the time comes and you don't have them, there could be huge fines involved.

- *Amazon CloudWatch Logs:* Suitable if you wish to have the same look and feel to store and look up logs as many other services for day-to-day operations and consumption.

- *Amazon Kinesis Data Firehose*: Similar to any large-scale real-time stream processing, this is a suitable option if you have plans to receive and take actions in real-time or simply wish to feed the data to other downstream systems such as your expensive Splunk deployment!

§Exam Tip: *Although RQL might not be the first thing to configure in a lab but in most production networks, it is involved. My warning about hefty fines and significant financial damages in case one fails to log data properly is indeed a real concern in many countries.*

Reference Architecture(s)

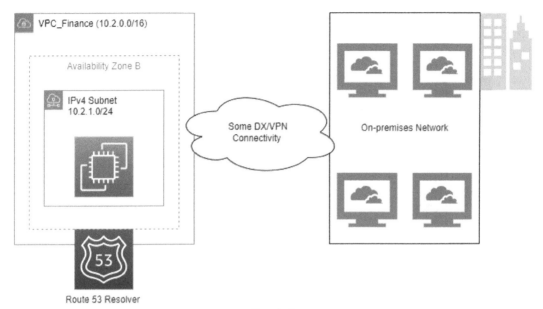

Figure 42

Here is every junior architect's idea for hybrid environments that actually does NOT work! In this INVALID architecture, the hosts located in the physical data center are trying to resolve the hostnames of the EC2 instances by contacting the Route 53 resolver service that in this case sits at 10.2.1.2 (CIDR+2). The resolver service won't respond to such queries over Direct Connect or VPN. You would need an intermediary service such as DNS forwarders on both sides. Keep in mind, this solution would not work even if they deployed a BIND or Microsoft Active Directory service only in the physical data center. In that case too, the request would still be coming from an external source over the VPN or DX.

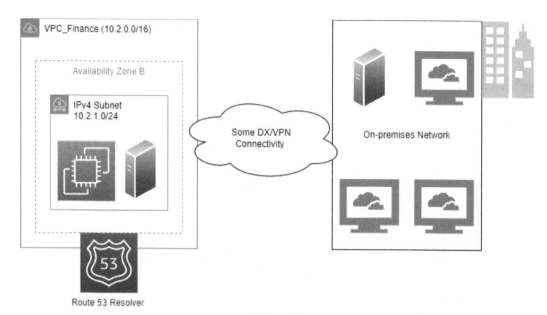

Figure 43

The previous generaion of a working architecture for hybrid designs. The architect uses two servers to implement some forwarding logic as the intermediaries. This solution works, however; the teams will be responsible for deploying, managing and maintaining extra services such as Microsoft Active Directory or Linux BIND. In this case, you would need to configure conditional forwarding rules on each side to decide "what to resolve locally? vs what to forward to the other side?". The CIDR+2 resolver accepts the queries sent to it via the DNS server placed in VPC Finance. It would reject them if they came directly from the on-prem servers or clients over the Direct Connect or VPN.

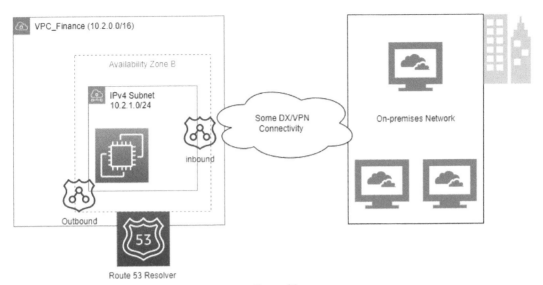

Figure 44

The most recent working architecture using the resolver inbound and outboudn endpoint. The customer deploys the inbound and outbound resolver endpoints in their AWS footprint. Although they play a similar role as the previous intermediary servers, they are managed by AWS, and as you saw in the lessons have fine-grained forwarding features. The on-prem requests to resolve the EC2 hostnames, by the on-premises DNS server (not shown here) are forwarded to the *inbound* resolver endpoint to get to the Route 53 resolver. In the opposite direction, when the EC2 resources make name resolution requests for on-premises resources, they take the path via the *outound* endpoint after hitting the CIDR+2 resolver to get to the on-prem DNS service.

Hence the traffic flow for the DNS queries would be:

On-prem resources resolving AWS-based hostnames

- On-prem client -> on-prem DNS resolver/forwarder -> DX/VPN -> Inbound endpoint -> CIDR+2 resolver -> Private Hosted Zone

AWS-based resources resolving on-prem hostnames

- AWS-based resources (e.g.,EC2 instances) -> CIDR+2 resolver -> Outbound endpoint -> DX/VPN -> On-prem DNS resolvers

CHAPTER 12

Foundations of Elastic Load Balancers

Similar to traditional on-premises networks, you can deploy different types of load balancers in AWS. This construct helps you spread the load across a group of resources (also known as targets). At a very high level, you will have a Virtual IP (VIP or, in fact, a DNS hostname) that is seen by your users. Also, a group of backend servers is sitting behind the load balancer. The Elastic Load Balancer also has a process running on it called a listener awaiting connection requests for the ports and protocols you define. Although you can deploy non-AWS load balancers on EC2 instances and implement features unavailable in AWS, the native load balancers remain popular among many customers. For instance, if the customer has developed extensive iRules[6] for their fleet of F5 load balancers, they might prefer F5 on EC2 over ELBs.

- Elastic Load Balancers can be architected in two different scenarios:
    - Internal: Routing traffic from the clients to servers using private IP addresses
    - Internet-facing: Routing traffic from the clients on the Internet to the servers

AWS currently supports 4 different types of load balancers:

- **Classic Load Balancer**
    - The traditional type, which has been around the longest. It is the grandfather of the family.
    - In addition to regular VPCs, it supports EC2-Classic.
    - Can work as a Layer 4 load balancer (with very limited L7 capabilities)
        - Layer 4: Can distribute traffic just based on basic TCP information
        - Layer 7: Can distribute traffic based on application layer information such as those required to spread load across Web servers
    - Supports SSL/TLS offloading: Hence, you can perform the resource-intensive SSL/TLS termination process on them.

---

6. A unique feature of F5 load balancers to script custom actions such as header checks and decisions.

- Does not support some newer features, including Websockets and Load Balancer deletion protection

    - Deletion protection is a safeguard mechanism that, if enabled, does not allow the user to delete the load balancer, potentially inadvertently. The feature has to be turned off before the load balancer can be deleted.

- Although it supports HTTP/HTTPS, load balancing still does not support host-based and path-based routing

    - This would help send traffic to different target groups based on the URL paths or the host address entered by the Web users. This feature is currently only available in Application Load Balancers.

- Does not support load balancing to multiple ports on the same instance. You need individual servers or instances.

- Supports HTTP, HTTPS, TCP, as well as load balancing for SSL over TCP

§*Exam Tip: Over time, our Classic friend is losing its popularity. Having said that, it is still part of many production networks.*

- **Network Load Balancer**

    - The flagship high throughput layer 4 load balancer

    - Distributes traffic based on layer 4 information of the incoming packets.

        - Although you would not have the opportunity to make decisions based on Layer 7 content, this leads to extreme performance where millions of sessions just need to pass through the load balancer with minimum handling.

        - This also provides an opportunity to honor and maintain end-to-end encryption and mutual authentication between the users and the server.

    - Supports a wide range of features, including Websockets and Deletion protection.

    - It was only in 2019 that AWS added SSL/TLS offloading (TLS termination using TLS listeners) to its supported features for Network Load Balancers.

        - Having said that, if you need detailed Web traffic load balancing, most likely Application Load Balancers would be a better choice.

    - Does not support Lambda functions as its target type (only IP or EC2 instance ID are currently the valid targets).

    - Supports TCP, UDP, TCP_UDP, and TLS.

        - TCP_UDP is an AWS notation to show support for both TCP and UDP protocols for the same ports.

            - DNS TCP_UDP 53 is a perfect example. A DNS server can use both in different situations such as queries, retries, and zone transfers.

- As we will see, unlike ALBs, Network Load Balancers do not support security groups for inbound and outbound traffic.

§*Exam Tip:* *When someone at work or a question on the exam says, "millions of sessions", "light-weight processing", "only L4 processing", "no L7 inspection", "minimum processing", your brain should at least consider the NLB as the first choice.*

- **Application Load Balancer**
  - The flagship layer 7 load balancer
    - Ideal for distributing traffic across a number of backend Web or application servers.
    - Is effectively a layer 7 proxy that receives the inbound sessions from the clients and establishes outbound sessions to the backend servers (the targets) on their behalf. This is a key difference between the ALB and NLB and essentially why the source IP address of the requester is changed.
  - Supports a wide range of Web-related operations, including SSL/TLS offloading, host-based routing, path-based routing, header-based routing, Websockets, HTTP2, and Google gRPC.
    - You can define complex policies to inspect the Layer 7 header of your HTTP requests from the users and decide how to route them and to which one of your target groups. For instance, you can have different target groups for mobile.example.com and desktop.example.com or different target groups for example.com/fr and example.com/en. We have many more examples on this key feature.
    - Supports integration with Amazon Certificate Manager (ACM) for TLS offloading
  - Supports Deletion protection. So you can't just randomly delete the ELB!
  - Supports HTTP and HTTPS protocols.
  - As it scales automatically, the IP address of the ALB changes (i.e., it is not static in contrast to the IP address of an NLB). This could lead to some interesting issues that were mostly resolved, as we will see later in this chapter.
  - Supports security groups for IPv4/IPv6 inbound and outbound traffic (which is a big deal!) Be very careful here, as any misconfiguration here could turn into a long troubleshooting process.
    - *Inbound*: The traffic coming into the ELB and received on the listener ports
    - *Outbound*: The traffic leaving the ELB toward the backend targets, including production or health check traffic streams.
  - Supports integration with AWS Web Application Firewall (WAF)

- The goal here is to stop Layer 7 attacks against the Web servers behind an ALB
- The most common types of attacks are SQL injections and cross-site scripting (CSS)
  - For example, when a user includes specially crafted SQL queries in their requested URLs
- I have more details on the WAF service later in the book

- **Gateway Load Balancer**
  - Architecturally and conceptually different from the other types of Elastic Load Balancers or any traditional load balancer.
  - Introduced in 2020 and is primarily aimed at the growing market of security appliances and how other VPCs can leverage the security inspection appliances located in a shared services VPC. In fact, it can be considered a major enhancement to the concept of VPC Ingress routing introduced earlier in the book.
  - For example, a network operator needs to inspect inbound or outbound traffic before sending them to the next destination (e.g., proxy, etc.)
    - This applies to inbound traffic from the Internet before it hits the EC2 servers. Also, it similarly applies to the traffic outbound to the Internet originating in one of the spoke VPCs. In both cases, the architect can intercept the traffic by editing the route tables and directing them to a VPC endpoint.
    - The endpoint (which acts like a pipe) uses AWS PrivateLink technology to send the traffic to the destination VPC, where the security appliances are sitting behind a Gateway Load Balancer.
    - The return traffic will take the same path via the endpoint, and the route table associated with the endpoint will determine where the traffic will land.
  - The architecture described includes three main components:
    - The Gateway Load Balancer: Behind which and in the same VPC, you have your security appliances.
    - The VPC Endpoint: Provides an entry point for the intercepted traffic by the custom route added to the routing table.
      - For instance, when 0.0.0.0/0 points to vpce-xyz the traffic bound for the Internet Gateway is now taking the path via the VPC endpoint to the Gateway Load Balancer and its security appliances.
      - You may have multiple VPC endpoints, one for each spoke VPC
    - Secure Connection using AWS PrivateLinks across VPCs
  - Gateway Load Balancer endpoint (Powered by PrivateLink)

- Is similar to interface VPC endpoints with a private IP address from the IP range allocated with the subnet

- Works in conjunction with the new Gateway Load Balancers

- Is used as the entry point for intercepted flows to feed them to another part of the network configured with a Gateway Load Balancer

  - This is a common architecture for firewalls and security appliances where traffic needs to be redirected for a particular operation

- Private DNS names are not supported

Session Persistence (Session Stickiness or Session Affinity)

Session persistence or stickiness is a *target-group level* technique to create affinity between your end users and the targets in the target groups in AWS (as you will see, slightly different in Classic Load Balancers). In other words, for a specific time, you can guarantee that the user is served only by a particular backend instance and will not be sent to random destinations each time.

Without sticky sessions, each incoming request is treated independently by the Elastic Load Balancers and can land on one of the registered backend servers selected by the algorithm and create a new session object. The sticky sessions can be helpful if you are trying to limit the session objects to one backend server for a session, eliminate the need for the servers to share the session object details, and eventually better responsiveness.

Load balancers and applications use Cookies to enable the session stickiness mechanisms:

- In the context of AWS load balancing, an HTTP cookie is a small encrypted text file that stores information about the binding between the client and instance.

- The cookie file lives on the client device but includes information in the HTTP request headers.

- When the header is processed by the load balancer, the cookie field helps the load balancer send the traffic to the same instance as before.

- Each cookie has an expiration time (i.e., duration or validity period), and once expired, the session is no longer sticky.

- The cookie name for the Application Load Balancers is AWSALB, and the cookie name for the Classic Load Balancers is AWSELB.

  - These names cannot be changed.

- Note the Network Load Balancers' sessions are essentially sticky, so the topic of cookie files does not apply to them. Network Load Balancers for the entire life of a session route it to a specific target.

There are generally two types of cookie-based session stickiness:

- Application-controlled session stickiness

- The application (such as ASP) creates and manages its own cookie.
- The ELB also creates a cookie but the expiration time follows that of the cookie generated by the application.
  - Hence if the application's cookie expires, the session won't be sticky anymore.
- Initially supported by Classic Load Balancers and, as of 2021, also supported by Application Load Balancers.
- Duration-based session stickiness
  - The ELB generates and manages the cookie.
  - The ELB is also responsible for the expiration time.
  - It is supported by the Application, Network, and Classic Load Balancers.

§*Exam Tip: Before diving into the details, if you have not passed the Associate and Professional exams, I would like to encourage you to go back and have a look at the concept of Auto Scaling in EC2 as it relates to ELBs. This is an important topic, but the assumption is when the candidate makes it to this level, they already know how they work in great detail. In the rest of this chapter, I assume you are familiar with the topic.*

Where could stickiness go wrong?

- While stickiness offers several benefits, including consistent user experience and easier resource management, using cookies and sticky sessions could also lead to certain performance issues such as unbalanced load on the backend servers.
  - This can happen randomly due to a scenario where users with longer sessions over time are stuck to specific backend instances.
  - This also can surface in scenarios where NAT and sticky sessions coexist. Depending on the architecture, you might end up pinning all the requests coming from a source NAT IP address with thousands of users behind it to a single backend resource.

CHAPTER 13

Advanced Topics in Elastic Load Balancers

Source IP address preservation; the million-dollar question

§Exam Tip: Read this section very carefully. It's an integral part of most job interviews and production networks; also an absolute fair game for the ANS-C01 exam.

Many network operators would like to see the actual source IP address of the visiting clients in their servers' access log files instead of the private IP address of the load balancer, for instance, due to security reasons and investigations that you might want to conduct later on. This issue has existed for a long time, and there are several solutions to preserve the source IP address of the clients, although, in the context of AWS, it chiefly depends on the type of Elastic Load Balancer used.

Given the types of Elastic Load Balancers and how they are architected, several scenarios may be encountered, including:

- Network Load Balancers (with registered instances as targets)
  - The source IP address will be preserved and no further action is required.
- Network Load Balancer (with registered IP addresses as targets)
  - If configured with TLS or TCP listener: The source IP address can be preserved if the load balancer using proxy protocol version 2 attaches a proxy header to the TCP data. The header preserves the actual IP address of the client.
  - If configured with the UDP or TCP_UDP listeners: The source IP address will be preserved and no further action is required.
- Application Load Balancers
  - The source IP address can be preserved if the X-Forwarded-For request header is used. The load balancer uses the header to store the IP address of the visiting client and it is handed over to the Web server.

- Classic Load Balancers
  - The source IP address can be preserved if the X-Forwarded-For request header is used. The load balancer uses the header to store the IP address of the visiting client and it's handed over to the Web server.

SSL/TLS offloading (SSL/TLS termination)

§*Exam Tip: Another critical topic that is also in use in many production networks out there. If I were to design the exam, I'd seriously quiz you on this topic because several interesting scenarios can be built just based on what follows. Check out the mock exams in the book for some examples.*

In traditional data centers, although it was possible to establish end-to-end SSL/TLS sessions between clients and Web servers, it became increasingly difficult and costly to constantly scale up and upgrade the Web servers beyond the requirements of their main mission to accommodate SSL/TLS encryption processing at scale. The same logic applies to even today's capable servers and EC2 instances.

The solution was to terminate the SSL/TLS sessions on devices such as Load Balancers, where you had specialized pieces of hardware for SSL/TLS processing, such as expansion modules. The same concept exists in AWS Elastic Load Balancers, where they can perform SSL/TLS termination. The session remains encrypted based on the SSL/TLS settings between the clients and the Elastic Load Balancer. After terminating the original session on the load balancer, if needed, an encrypted session can be established between the load balancer and the backend server.

- To perform SSL/TLS offloading with Application Load Balancers, you would need to deploy at least one X.509 server certificate on the HTTPS listener.

- In order to perform SSL offloading with Network Load Balancers, you would need to deploy one X.509 server certificate on the TLS listener.
  - You can have the traditional end-to-end SSL/TLS encryption behavior without any offloading by using the TCP listeners. This will give you a pass-through experience.

- To perform SSL/TLS offloading with Classic Load Balancers, you would need to deploy at least one X.509 server certificate on the HTTPS listener.
  - You can have the traditional end-to-end SSL/TLS encryption behavior without any offloading by using the TCP listeners.

- Some companies with strict regulatory requirements may have to carry the SSL sessions all the way to the servers. In those cases, offloading (and keeping the backend session unencrypted) is not an option. Instead, you can have a TCP listener on the Elastic Load Balancers (for example, an NLB) and leave the SSL/TLS processing and termination to the backend servers, similar to the traditional on-premises model.

Elastic Load Balancers and their targets

- Network and Application Load Balancers can have EC2 instances as well as private IP addresses as their targets.

  - The key benefit of this flexibility is expanding the scope of backend servers from AWS to on-premises over Direct Connect. With private IP addressing, you can have on-premises and AWS-based servers behind a load balancer.

  - At this stage, the Application Load Balancer remains the only type that supports Lambda functions as its target. Hence, you can develop a Lambda function (for example, those developed in Python) and feed it through the ALB.

  - As you will see later in this chapter, the ALBs can be registered as your NLB's targets!

Elastic Load Balancers and their target selection algorithms

- Application Load Balancers

  - At the target group level, by default, it uses Round Robin but can be changed to the Least Outstanding Requests algorithm.

- Network Load Balancer

  - Similar to the traditional concepts of network engineering such as ECMP, to spray the traffic across its targets, it gathers some key parameters of a session such as the source and destination IP address and port number as well as the protocol and TCP sequence number to generate a hash code and use that to choose the next target.

- Classic Load Balancers

  - Uses Round Robin for the TCP listener and the Least Outstanding Request algorithm for the HTTP/HTTPS listeners.

Elastic Load Balancers and the challenges of multi-tier architectures

While in some large-scale architectures, you need to have more layers of load balancers, you could also face unique challenges. In multi-tier designs, you can have other services such as cache servers or vendor-specific load balancers between the two tiers of AWS Elastic Load Balancers:

- Tier 1 Elastic Load Balancers, where your load balancers are facing the clients

  - You might favor Network Load Balancers to have more flexibility in preserving the source IP address of the visiting clients. You might also favor Network Load Balancers to achieve very high throughput at tier 1. This is especially true if you have caching solutions between the two tiers. While it would reduce the load on Tier 2, your Tier 1 would still have to potentially handle millions of sessions.

- Tier 2 Elastic Load Balancers, placed between cache or vendor-specific load balancers to the north and backend EC2 instances to the south
  - The cache solutions and other third-party services that sit between the two tiers of Elastic Load Balancers may have issues with forwarding traffic downstream to an FQDN or CNAME; they might constantly try to resolve the names to IP as the next hop, or might not even be able to support names for those next hops, to begin with. In such cases, since currently, the Network Load Balancers are the only type that can have a static or Elastic IP address, they make the best choice for Tier 2. They can be easily pointed at by those third-party solutions that only take IP addresses or support them better than hostnames as the next hop.

If your multi-tier solution must support sticky sessions at both layers building both tiers using Application Load Balancers or Classic Load Balancers due to the naming convention of cookies in AWS could cause issues and should be avoided.

- Application Load Balancers use the cookie name of AWSALB and Classic Load Balancers use the cookie of AWSELB. For an efficient multi-tier sticky solution, you can create the tier 1 using one and the tier two using the other type (ALB/CLB or CLB/ALB), which would result in cookies with different names and prevent any confusion.

Elastic Load Balancers and the challenges of multi-AZ architectures

With all the different types of Elastic Load Balancers, you have the option to enable or disable a feature called cross-zone load balancing:

- If enabled: The load will be distributed across all the targets in all the AZs defined in your architecture.
- If disabled: The load will be distributed only across the targets in the same AZ
  - This could result in some complicated troubleshooting scenarios where some of your seemingly-identical servers (targets) might be receiving more traffic than the others just because of the AZ they are located in. For instance, if you have only one target in one AZ and 100 targets in another; with two dedicated ALBs in each AZ, the load on each target in AZ2 can be 100 times more than the load on the single target in AZ1 – If both load balancers are roughly fed the same amount of traffic by Route 53.

Elastic Load Balancers and the attempts to achieve the best of both worlds

Let's face it. Although the ALB and NLB offer similar functionalities, they still have several fundamental differences. In fact, sometimes, the process of choosing the right load balancer on any public cloud provider as one of the most challenging decisions that need to go through extensive Proof of Concept (PoC) testing before going into production. AWS networking is no exception. The NLBs are slated for taking millions of sessions per second, support static IP addresses in each AZ, and, as you saw earlier in this book, work closely with PrivateLinks (endpoints) to implement SaaS applications. None of these features today is supported by ALBs.

On the other hand, the ALBs support best-in-class Web traffic routing and categorization based on certain criteria such as hostnames and paths, WAF, and HTTP2 routing.

But what if, in our architecture, we need the best of both worlds? For example, we need to implement a SaaS service with multiple backend Web servers, each designated to process certain URL paths in our SaaS hosting VPC? This can only be done using ALBs while, as I showed you, currently, AWS only supports NLBs for this particular architecture.

- Up until 2021, there was no straightforward way to combine the two Elastic Load Balancers in one architecture with one set of targets.

- Many architects would deploy 3rd party solutions such as NGINX or F5 load balancers to achieve their special requirements.

- Now, in addition to the traditional target types of instances, IP addresses, and Lambda functions, you can define an ALB as the target. This is a key feature. Check out the reference architectures for more details.

  - Once implemented, the NLB will receive the TCP traffic (all ultra-light layer 4 processing) and forward it to the ALB as its target. You take advantage of the ability to receive millions of sessions right at the "door" and can have architectures such as the SaaS applications with PrivateLinks. At the same time, on the ALB, you have access to a wide range of possibilities to process the HTTP headers, do WAF, and choose the best backend target to send the session to.

- Although it is obvious but still worth noting that since the ALBs support security groups for inbound and outbound traffic; if you enabled those on an ALB sitting behind an NLB as its target, it would require an appropriate set of rules. We have an interesting question on this in the mock exams.

  - *Inbound (into the listener)*: If the traffic is coming into the ALB from an NLB the source IP address will NOT change to the IP address of the NLB and will remain the same. For example, this could be the CIDR block of the consumer's VPC. Also, you need to allow any health check traffic in.

  - *Outbound (out to the targets)*: Similar to the previous cases, there are two types of traffic leaving the ALB and both need to be permitted; the health check traffic going out toward the targets and the production traffic leaving the ALB toward the targets.

§Exam Tip: There is a reference architecture on this topic in the book but I expect everyone to know that an ALB can be an NLB target in a wide range of scenarios. Two main use cases are the simple designs where one customer runs both to benefit from the advantages of each and a more complex use case is where the customer deploys them in a SaaS model with endpoints. This is the case that we discussed previously and the reference architecture covers. Either way, the overall architecture never changes. And you sill need to be aware of the details of the security groups on the ALB and the fact that the NLB might have other targets at the same time (in addition to the ALB).

Elastic Load Balancers and the challenges related to hosting multiple Web sites and their TLS certificates on one ELB listener

In the most traditional on-premises architectures, you had one HTTP Web site running on one Web server with one dedicated IPv4 address. Many years ago, we enhanced this model and allowed the hosting of multiple HTTP Web sites on one IP address. But this never resolved the issue for TLS-based (HTTPS) Web sites, and for those, we had to use separate IPv4 addresses.

Why? Because if you hosted dedicated TLS certificates for each Web site, how would the server know which certificate to provide to the client right at the TLS handshake; well before the HTTP session has formally started (i.e., before the client tells the server what Web site it is interested in)?

This issue was resolved by introducing the Server Name Indication (SNI) extension of TLS, which enabled the client to choose a particular hostname and receive its certificate right in the first part of the TLS handshake when the Client Hello is sent to the server. In other words, with the SNI, the client's browser during the TLS handshake uses the SNI field to specify the hostname (e.g., SNI=castlencia.com) that it's interested in. This allows the server to return the right TLS certificate designated for Castlencia.com in response and facilitate the next steps in the HTTPS session.

- The SNI was first added to ALBs in 2017 and to NLBs in 2020.

- With the SNI, now you can have multiple certificates for multiple Web sites on one TLS listener.

- If the hostname provided by the client's browser matches multiple certificates on the ELB, the ELB chooses the best certificate by looking into different criteria, including what is supported by the client. This happens when you bind more than one certificate to a Web site. This feature is called smart certificate selection in the context of the SNI.

- Currently, with the SNI, AWS supports up to 26 certificates (including the default certificate specified when you created the listener) on each load balancer.

- The default certificate is used if the browser is very old, such as the early version of Windows XP or Android, and does not support the SNI.

- The SNI has full integration with AWS Certificate Manager (ACM), and you can use certificates provided by ACM. The same integration is also supported with AWS IAM.

Elastic Load Balancers to support IPv6 backend servers

Some 20 years ago, I was standing in a conference room and presenting the new bizarre form of IP addresses that were supposed to replace IPv4. I still remember the facial expressions when we discussed the compression and expansion rules for those strangely long addresses. That is normal, I suppose. But what is not normal, is the fact that everyone was warned to start planning their migration project to prevent losing access to the Internet.

Well, the sky never fell as we were expecting but gradually, more and more services do support IPv6 addresses. Today, at least in North America, many governments contract require various types of IPv6 addressing. I still write and give talks about the reason why we were (and are) so slow, but that is really beyond the scope of this book.

During the years of 2020 and 2021, AWS took long strides toward supporting IPv6 on NLBs and ALBs. Although it is still not possible to run everything based on IPv6, with dual-stack load balancers, it is now possible to have end-to-end Ipv6 sessions, from Ipv6 clients to Ipv6 backend servers on AWS.

- The NLB and ALB configuration options now support IP address types with the following two options determining what type of connections is accepted by the ELB:
    - *Ipv4:* To support Ipv4 only clients
    - *Dual-stack:* To support Ipv4 and Ipv6 clients. As of November 2021; this type is available to both internal and Internet-facing architectures.
        - Currently, on NLBs for UDP or UDP_TCP architectures, you must choose the Ipv4 type
            - In this architecture you must have dual-stack subnets
- As for the target groups, out of the four possible options, currently, only the target type of *IP addresses* supports IPv6 targets:
    - *Instances*
    - *IP addresses*: Supports IPv6 architectures and targets.
    - *Lambda function*
    - *ALB (as a target for an NLB)*
- You cannot mix the two types of IPv4 and IPv6 targets in the same target group
- Once the IPv6 target groups are created, you can create a listener for the ELB and point to the IPv6 target group.
- Hence to summarize the traffic flow as of mid-2022; an IPv6 client sends a request to the listener of a dual-stack NLB or ALB with IPv6 target groups, and the load balancer balances the traffic among the IPv6 targets of a dual-stack subnet in an IPv6 target group! This can be done both internally or from the IPv6 Internet to internal or Internet-facing ELBs. And as you saw, the target group must only have IPv6 targets.

Monitoring and logging for Elastic Load Balancers

§Exam Tip: *Similar to my comment about DNS logging, ELB logging is just as crucial. In addition to the ANS-C01 exam, you might need them for compliance reasons, troubleshooting scenarios, or complex forensics.*

A few different monitoring and logging options are available to both types of load balancers that can be utilized for different use cases:

- **How to monitor and log activities on a Network Load Balancers?**
  - *CloudWatch*: Similar to the other use cases of CloudWatch critical data points about your ELBs and their targets are published to Amazon CloudWatch in the form of time-series data (i.e., metrics). This includes detailed statistics on the flows, packets, and bytes processed by the NLB. The CloudWatch data for NLB also include the number of healthy and unhealthy targets.
    - This is classic NLB level data that can be used to evaluate the load and status of the load balancer itself and its available targets.
  - *Access logs:* If the NLB has TLS listeners, you can enable capturing access logs for the TLS requests.
    - The outcome is compressed and stored in S3 buckets.
    - You can use the server-side encryption feature of S3 to automatically encrypt and decrypt the stored access logs.
    - The access logs include several key pieces of information about the TLS requests, including the resource ID of the NLB, listener that is engaged, the IP address and port number of the client, and the destination it is trying to reach (i.e., the listener or an endpoint), protocol details and the count of bytes sent or received for the request.
    - In contrast to the metrics exposed by CloudWatch, the Access Logs feature gives you visibility into the TLS requests.
    - Currently, NLB only supports Access Logs for TLS.
    - The log files are published every 5 minutes.
- **How to monitor and log activities on an Application Load Balancer?**
  - *CloudWatch*: Similar to the offering for the NLBs but with several key differences in terms of the metrics. This makes perfect sense, as an ALB technically is a proxy and, unlike an NLB, receives an HTTP/HTTPS request and establishes a connection to the backend targets. So, the metrics are designed to provide information about HTTP/HTTPs sessions.
    - In addition to the regular IPv4 byte count data, you can also monitor other key metrics, including IPv6 byte and request counts, rejected/new connections, HTTP error codes, and the number of gRPC requests.
    - Similar to the NLB metrics, here, too, you can monitor the number of healthy targets behind your ALBs.
    - This is classic ALB-level data that can be used to evaluate the load and status of the load balancer itself and its available targets.
  - *Access Logs:* The Access Logs feature for ALBs is much more liberal and not limited to one type of request as it is with the NLBs.

- The outcome is compressed and stored in S3 buckets.

- The access logs include several key pieces of information about the requests processed by the ALB, including the server responses, client's IP address (i.e., source address), request paths in the header, latency details, and all the relevant timestamps.

- The log files are published every 5 minutes.

- AWS works with several major vendors, including Splunk to receive and digest the logs. Splunk is known to have an expensive licensing structure; you need to have a strong case to process the logs to justify a paid subscription such as Splunk. You can always find other more affordable solutions.

- Enabling the Access Logs feature for both types of load balancers is free of charge.

Okay. At this point, I am confident that I have covered everything you would need to be successful on the ANS-C01 exam from an ELB perspective. Yet, since the book comes with an extra chapter on Containers, I thought it won't do justice to the readers unless the ELB part of the containers is briefly reviewed here too. As you saw in the introduction of the book, you can find a lot more details on container networking in the attachment of this book. But here goes the ELB part of it, as this is called out as an exam topic.

The AWS Load Balancer Controller add-on for Amazon Elastic Kubernetes Service

One of the topics that the exam guide has specifically called out is the AWS Load Balancer controller or formerly called the AWS ALB ingress controller. While the topic by itself, just like the rest of the EKS chapter in the attachment, is fairly easy to understand, since it has many dependencies on non-AWS topics, we limit the scope to what an AWS-focused network architect or an ANS-C01 candidate needs to know without getting into too much configuration details. I selfishly decided to cover the topic here as we are talking about the ELBs than in the separate section of containers. Let's call a spade a spade; after all, it's about building and managing ELBs, and this is the ELB section of the book.

Exposing EKS-based services to external clients

- Many application owners, in addition to in-cluster access requirements, also need their applications to be accessed by external users; in most cases, those coming from the Internet.

- In production environments, this type of access to services hosted in containers needs to go through a load balancer to provide traffic distribution and health monitoring.

- There are two main architectures in Kubernetes on AWS that you can use to expose services to external clients through a load balancer:

  - Exposing services through an Application Load Balancer

    - Suitable for HTTP and HTTPS applications

- Exposing services through a Network Load Balancer or a Classic Load Balancer

- In both architectures, you need to install an AWS Load Balancer Controller to manage the load balancers for a Kubernetes cluster

  - There are different ways to install the controller, including using Helm, which can perform package management for Kubernetes: "*helm install aws-load-balancer-controller.*"

- Once the controller is installed, the architect can decide what type of load balancer better fulfill the requirements. Each type, as mentioned above, needs a different approach to deploy in EKS.

Exposing EKS-based services through Application Load Balancers (ALB)

AWS automatically provisions an ALB when you create a special type of Kubernetes resource called an Ingress object or resource.

- The ALB created by this process supports both EC2-based nodes and AWS Fargate. Both types of pods can receive traffic from an ALB.

- You need two subnets in two different AZs. In each subnet, you need to have at least 8 IP addresses.

  - Depending on your architecture, you can have public or private subnets.

But you might be asking yourself how the Kubernetes administrators create resources such as Ingress objects.

- Very similar to your traditional Ansible playbooks. You create a file and apply it.

- Generally speaking, to create objects and resource in Kubernetes, we create a (text) file called the manifest. Once applied using the kubectl command, this file causes Kubernetes to create the object described in the YAML or JSON format. This applies to a wide range of Kubernetes resources such as the Ingress object, as you saw above.

  - If you recall from the previous sections, running this command on your administration station would talk to the control plane of EKS and that in turn will make the required changes to the cluster.

- Below is a partial manifest YAML file used to trigger the creation of an ALB in a public subnet (Internet-facing). This Ingress object will receive HTTP traffic and route it to the targets as specified by the rule:

```
apiVersion: networking.k8s.io/v1
kind: Ingress
metadata:
  namespace: CorpApp
  name: ingress-Resource-CorpApp
  annotations:
    alb.ingress.kubernetes.io/scheme: internet-facing
    alb.ingress.kubernetes.io/target-type: ip
  spec:
```

```
    ingressClassName: alb
    rules:
     - http:
       paths:
       - path: /
         pathType: Prefix
         backend:
           service:
             name: service-CorpApp
             port:
               number: 8080
```

Exposing EKS-based services through Network Load Balancers (NLB)

- Unlike the manifest file for an Ingress resource that would automatically provision an ALB, in order to create an NLB, you would need a manifest file for a Kubernetes service with the type of Load Balancer as shown below:

```
apiVersion: v1
kind: Service
metadata:
  name: CorpApp-service
  namespace: CorpApp
  annotations:
    service.beta.kubernetes.io/aws-load-balancer-type: external
    service.beta.kubernetes.io/aws-load-balancer-nlb-target-type: ip
    service.beta.kubernetes.io/aws-load-balancer-scheme: internet-facing
spec:
  ports:
    - port: 80
      targetPort: 80
      protocol: TCP
  type: LoadBalancer
  selector:
    app: CorpApp
```

- Similar to the previous partial YAML file, in this case, too applying the manifest using the kubectl command from your administration station would create an Elastic Load Balancer, but an NLB.

- With NLBs, you can get away with only one subnet, but still, the subnet needs to have at least eight available IP addresses.

- You can designate your NLB targets by their IP address or instance IDs if the pods are hosted on EC2 servers, but if you're using Fargate to launch your pods, the targets must be identified by their IP addresses.

- The previous generation of the controller, called the AWS cloud provider load balancer controller, could create Classic Load Balancers, but this functionality no longer exists in the AWS Load Balancer add-on.

Final thoughts:

- Load balancers of either type can have a wide range of configuration options. If you check the Kubernetes documentation for AWS, you will find various "annotations" that can be used to fine-grain your load balancer's configuration details.

  - For example, service.beta.kubernetes.io/aws-load-balancer-healthcheck-healthy-threshold can be added to the manifest to specify the acceptable threshold for health checks. And there are many more.

- In contrast to what some people think, you must keep the AWS Load Balancer Controller running in your cluster to control and manage the Elastic Load Balancers. It is not an "initialization script"!

- Last but not least, monitoring containerized solutuions in AWS including EKS and ECS clusters is done through CloudWatch Container Insights. The service collects and logs details on a per container basis for all sort of resources such as CPU, network, memory and disk and can make them available in JSON format.

§Exam Tip: *What if you understood a little about the EKS load balancing the first round? Don't worry. Review the containers sections of the book for a lot more details. And keep in mind, although I hate to admit it, K8s administration is not a big part of the blueprint.*

Reference Architecture(s)

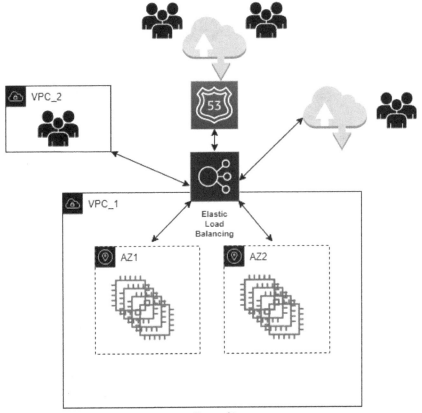

Figure 45

The most simplistic architecture for AWS elastic load balancers. For better availability, the targets are placed in two different AZs. Depending on the load balancer's public or private configuration, the targets can be accessed by users on the Internet and in other VPCs.

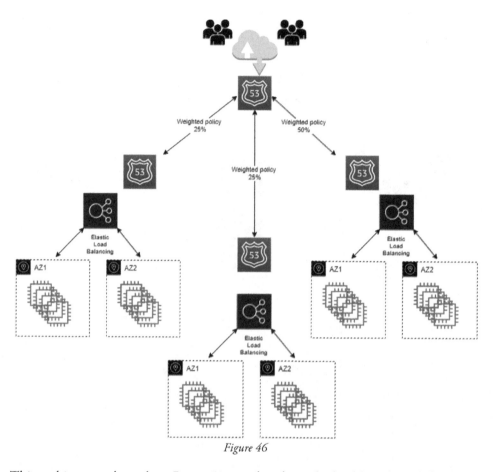

Figure 46

This architecture shows how Route 53 can distribute the load based on defined portions among multiple destinations, in this case, elastic load balancers. In turn, the ELBs distribute the load among their own targets, which, as shown here, can be located in multiple-AZs.

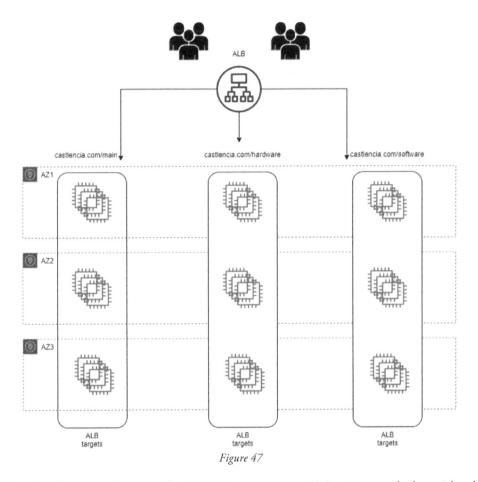

Figure 47

Classic reference architecture for ALBs. You can use an ALB to inspect the layer 7 header of the packets. In this case, the architect is using an ALB to decide how to route various requests coming from the Internet based on their URLs. Their ultimate goal is to have a different set of targets (potentially web servers) located in redundant AZs respond to each customer request.

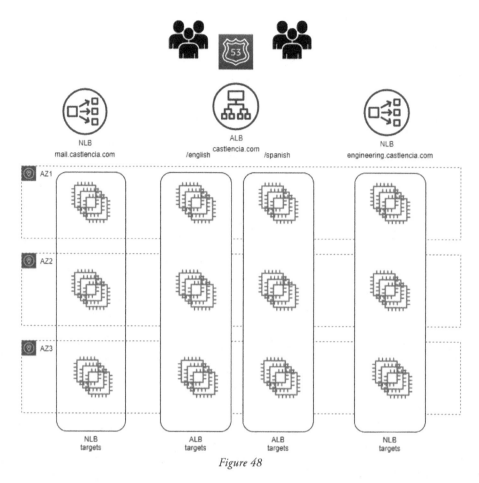

Figure 48

Here the architect is using two different types of elastic load balancers. The high-throughput NLBs are used to process requests for the two DNS names of mail and engineering. There is no layer 7 processing involved. The architect also has an ALB to discriminate between the URLs by inspecting the L7 headers for Castlencia.com. If the directory is /english, the ALB rule uses one set of targets spread across three AZs, and if the directory is /spanish, another set of targets is used. This can be critical when architecting at a scale where you need to have specialized servers to respond to very specific requests by inspecting the incoming HTTP headers.

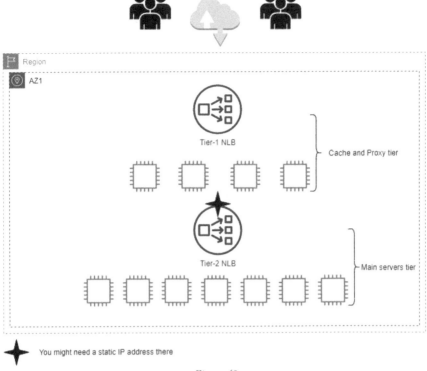

Figure 49

This architecture shows a simple sandwich deployment with two tiers of NLBs. Between the two tiers, the architect can insert any set of firewalls or cache engines. As you will see in the following designs, the choice of ELB for the second tier will be limited to NLBs in certain scenarios. For example, if the servers or firewalls can only address their next hop by its IP address.

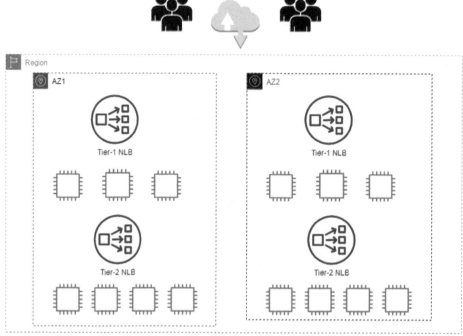

Figure 51

Reference architecture for a simple high-throughput design. While there will be no Layer 7 processing, the architect can handle millions of sessions. The architect needs to pay close attention to the capacity planning process for the servers between the two tiers of ELBs. They can easily turn into a bottleneck.

Although it's beyond the scope of this book, for such servers, you need to take some extra steps. This topic is extensively discussed in Linux-related training courses, where we show how to optimize high-throughput cache servers.

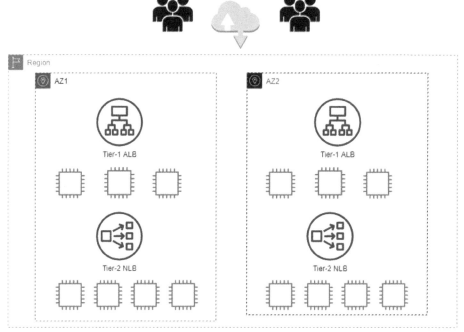

Figure 52

This reference architecture shows a dual-AZ sandwich model for load balancing. Here, the architect is inserting some logic such as caching or firewalling between the two tiers. Once the processing by the caching engines or firewalls is complete, the traffic is sent to the second-tier load balancers. Two key points stand out in this architecture: (1) deployment of an NLB at the second layer because currently, it's the only type of ELB that can be addressed by the cache servers by its static IP address, if needed (2) if stickiness is required in both tiers, the architect cannot deploy two lines of ALBs or two lines of CLBs. It's strongly recommended to deploy a mix where the cookie names would be different. This topic is covered in the mini-scenarios.

The choice of ALBs is usually based on the customer's potential layer 7 requirements. Do they need to inspect the HTTP header to make any decisions? Do we need separate routing strategies for different URLs? Etc.

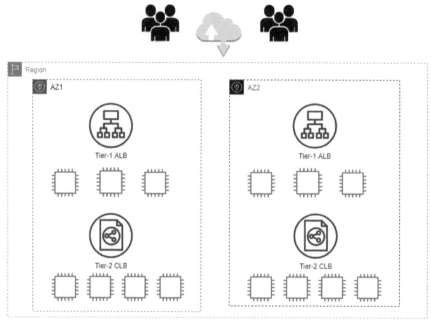

Figure 53

Reference architecture for a sandwich ELB design. Here the architect deploys a number of firewalls or cache engines between the two tiers of load balancers, but since they absolutely need sticky sessions everywhere, they would need different cookie names. The use of two different types of load balancers with two different sets of cookies satisfies this requirement. There are multiple mini-scenarios in the book to get to the bottom of this issue.

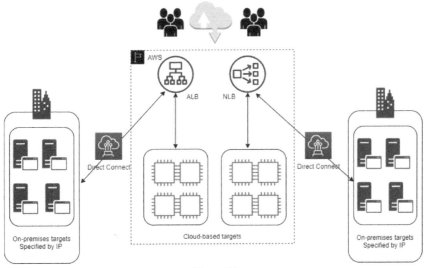

Figure 54

The reference architecture presented here demonstrates the fact that both NLB and ALB elastic load balancers can have targets registered by their private IP addresses. In addition to architecting for microservices, this feature comes in handy when the targets are split between AWS and on-premises. This might be for a range of reasons, including an ongoing migration project.

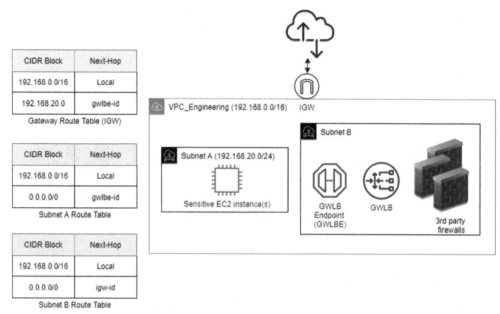

CIDR Block	Next-Hop
192.168.0.0/16	Local
192.168.20.0	gwlbe-id

Gateway Route Table (IGW)

CIDR Block	Next-Hop
192.168.0.0/16	Local
0.0.0.0/0	gwlbe-id

Subnet A Route Table

CIDR Block	Next-Hop
192.168.0.0/16	Local
0.0.0.0/0	igw-id

Subnet B Route Table

Figure 55

Reference architecture for a basic GWLB deployment. Two obvious components: (1) GWLB endpoint (2) GWLB. This solution was an enhancement to the simple VPC ingress routing that came out about a year before that. The ingress routing feature, as seen in the gateway table, is still extensively used. As you will see later, this architecture also provided a bridge from simple deployments to AWS Network Firewall.

Figure 56

Reference architecture for a sample deployment with a centralized GWLB data plane. The architects allocate a dedicated VPC to the firewalls stack and their GWLB, then drop the endpoints in each of the protected VPCs to suck in the traffic and route it back to the central VPC. As you saw before, the endpoints cannot be placed in the same subnet as the protected hosts, or the traffic cannot be routed "into" the endpoints.

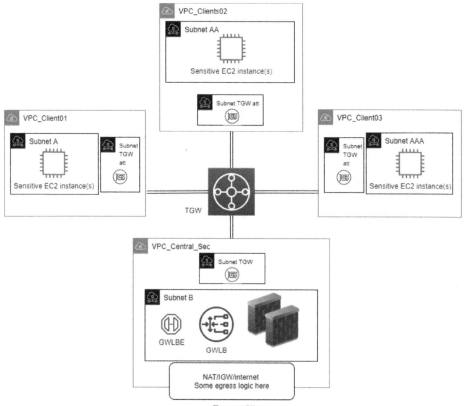

Figure 57

Reference architecture to show further enhancements using transit gateways. Also, as shown here, you can add a NAT construct to the design for more secure north-south traffic flow. A similar architecture with minimum changes can be used to inspect the east-west traffic between the VPCs. The architect needs to keep in mind that currently, the maximum bandwidth per VPC connected to the transit gateway is around 50Gbps. Although this might not be an issue for VPC_clientX needs to be carefully studied for VPC_Central_Sec.

Now, let's talk about something more important.

§Exam Tip: *The traffic flows discussed here form some of my favorite parts of job interviews. Also, as a new key feature compared to the ANS-C00 days, it's fair game to show up on the ANS-C01 exam.*

What if we cared more about availability and built more than one security pod in VPC_Central_Sec in two different AZs? We could also have different AZs in our client VPCs. Wouldn't that be nice?

It would be a great idea but let's follow the flows and see where it might fail. As a network or cloud architect, you are expected to predict and avoid situations similar to this:

Host1 in AZ1 part of VPC_client01 is trying to establish a session with Host2 located in AZ2 part of VPC_client02. This is absolutely normal. The packets leave the host and make it to the TGW. Then, since we're inspecting the east-west traffic, the packets are sent to the central VPC, but you have two security pods in AZ1 and AZ2 and need to decide which path to take. The TGW, by design, favors the pod in AZ1 to keep the traffic local within one AZ; from AZ1 to AZ1. All good, we're smart and minimizing our data transfer charges. Subsequently, the packets pass the inspection process and eventually make it to Host2 in AZ2.

One leg of the mission is accomplished.

Host2, replies by sending its response back to the TGW. The TGW, again dutifully, favors the same AZ and sends the traffic to the pod in AZ2 for inspection. The stateful firewall has no trace or precedence of this session and drops the packets. You didn't get lucky in this particular case, but you could have.

We need a deterministic and reliable behavior.

The TGW Appliance Mode addresses this particular issue with asymmetric routing by sending the traffic to the firewall that has been working on the session and not to a random firewall just because it's located in the same AZ as the sending host.

There are quite a few scenarios in this book to discuss the details of this issue.

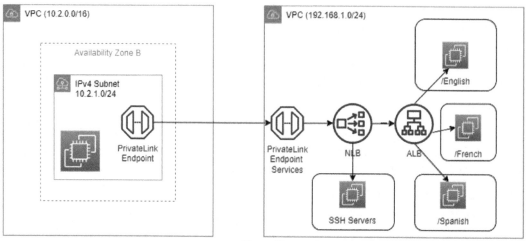

Figure 58

A reference architecture for one of the most important use cases that was made available after the introduction of ALB as an NLB target. Here, the architect is leveraging the NLB to load balance traffic among a number of SSH servers (TCP 22) while the ALB as one of its targets has its own set of targets, in this case a group of Web servers. It is evident that the architect is using the ALB for path-based routing. This designs, as we discussed in the lessons, offers the best features of both types of load balancers.

CHAPTER 14

Global Accelerator and Global Customer Demand

Globally available applications and their challenges

Let's take a California-based start-up called Castlencia with a promising product as an example. Our start-up initially makes its application available to the users in California by hosting it in the us-west-1 region in North California. The application team receives extremely positive feedback for the great performance of their application and the quick turnarounds as users perform different actions in the applications. Also, since the application is deployed on two sets of servers in two different Availability Zones, the recorded uptime also remains pretty impressive.

As their application gains popularity, they start offering services to the users in the entire North America. To keep everyone happy, they deploy the same service in the us-east-1 region in Virginia, and more or less, the user experience remains acceptable. Now they have 2 public IP addresses for their Elastic Load Balancers, and for the most part, Route 53 directs the users to the closest location. Although overall, the service is still solid, the IT team notices emerging patterns in user complaints, especially those filed by sensitive customers. The latency is less predictable and varies as the users take the path via the public Internet to hit one of the two regions on the east or west coast of the United States. Also, when one of the IP addresses fails (for example, in the case of ELB maintenance), the latency to picking the next healthy node and redirecting the traffic toward that IP takes some time.

Not a major issue, yet. Six months later, they make their application available globally by adding more capacity, this time in the eu-west-2 region. Now they have 3 public IP addresses associated to their URL. At this point, the issues noticed earlier are much more pronounced. Their user experience has officially deteriorated. One of their network architects best described that the performance and even availability of their application are, first, at the mercy of the service providers of their users and how they route the requests to the right endpoint, and then how long the DNS entries are cached at different levels.

After a stressful internal meeting, the network engineering team of Castlencia summarizes the ideal solution as, although the ELBs provide great load distribution within one region, we need a solid multi-region load distribution mechanism as described below.

1. We need to make sure the users are routed to the most optimal group of servers based on performance

2. We need to be able to detect unhealthy regions in less than one minute and redirect users to the closest healthy ones (blackout situations)

3. As we go through planned or unplanned maintenance windows for the ELBs or servers behind them, we need to be able to make a region and possibly its resources less attractive

4. They need to have a short and fixed list of IP addresses regardless of the number of new regions that they might want to launch in the future or what might fail or be replaced by the application teams

5. The performance (including latency and jitter) plays a major role in user experience. It needs to be deterministic and as much as possible decoupled from the variations of those parameters in the public Internet with all its congestions and path outages.

The AWS Global accelerator service does exactly what is described above, in addition to a few other things.

§*Exam Tip: A really big part of answering GA questions is understanding the "Why GA?" questions. In real life and on the exam, you should be able to digest the requirements and identify whether GA is the right way to go compared to other seemingly similar solutions such as CloudFront or ELBs. Hence the story above.*

Standard vs. Custom Global Accelerators

The Global Accelerator service can be implemented in two different types. Each type is suitable for certain use cases:

- Standard Global Accelerators
  - They do what was described in our scenario
    - Ideal for situations where a global audience needs to consume a service located in one or more AWS regions with all the concerns mentioned above.
    - The target endpoints can be:
      - NLBs: Internet-facing only
      - ALBs: Internet-facing or Internal
      - EC2 instances: Only certain regions and instance types
      - Elastic IP addresses
    - They support TCP and UDP sessions

- Custom Global Accelerator
  - They are ideal for special use cases where a number of users need to be pinned (mapped) to specific destinations somewhere within the AWS global fabric and not just the closest endpoint.
    - For example, gaming servers where it matters if a group of users or players are connected to the same server providing the same experience to everyone involved.
    - The target endpoints can't be as diverse as they were with the Standard type
      - Currently, in 2022, the only acceptable form of endpoint group for the Custom type is VPC subnets that can contain one or more EC2 instances as the final destinations
    - They support TCP and UDP sessions

The High-level architecture of standard AWS Global Accelerators

- Makes the AWS worldwide infrastructure with its vast edge network available to the customers as a global fabric
- Provides the customers with 2 fixed public IP addresses. These IPs are used as the entry points into the fabric and are anycast to the world by the AWS edge network
- When requests are made from the users to access applications hosted in one or multiple regions, instead of relying on the public Internet, the traffic uses the closest entry point into the fabric
- The request lands on one of the listeners of the Global Accelerator (could be TCP, UDP, or TCP_UDP – remember the DNS example?).
- At a macro level, a new request is created by the Global Accelerator and sent to the closest healthy endpoint in the best region serving the application (e.g., an Elastic Load Balancer in the eu-west-2 region)
- The endpoint could even be a load balancer (NLB or ALB) to further spread the load at a micro level within the selected region
- If an endpoint becomes unavailable, the situation is detected in less than one minute, and the requests start being redirected to the next most optimal destination within the fabric

The High-level architecture of custom AWS Global Accelerators

- Makes the AWS worldwide infrastructure with its vast edge network available to the customers as a global fabric
- Provides the customers with 2 fixed public IP addresses. These IPs are used as the entry points into the fabric and are anycast to the world by the AWS edge network
  - Here is where things start to diverge from the Standard type of Global Accelerators.

- When requests are made from the users to access applications hosted behind the Global Accelerator service, instead of relying on the public Internet, the traffic uses the closest entry point into the fabric

- The request lands on one of the listeners of the Global Accelerator

- Right at the edge, a mapping (pinning) forms for the request. Each new request creates a mapping entry that ties the IP address and port number of the Global Accelerator's listener to the IP address and port number of the backend EC2 server fulfilling the request.

  - Hence the requests are not spread across multiple regions to achieve higher performance, rather specific groups of clients always go to (are pinned to) a very specific EC2 server

- If an endpoint becomes unavailable, the situation cannot be detected by Global Accelerator, and the health check and fail-over processes need to be built into the application.

Global Accelerators and IP Addressing

- With both Standard and Custom Global accelerators, the two public IP addresses are fixed and anycast to the world by the AWS edge network. Hence, any users located anywhere in the world will hear about them from their closest AWS edge location, and that's where they'll go when they need to visit the service.

- The two IP addresses can be supplied by the customer from their own range of public addresses (BYOIP). The usual rules apply, including the customer, who obviously, should stop advertising those IP addresses to the world from their own edge network.

- In the case of Custom Global Accelerators, the endpoint VPC subnet size can be between /17 and /28

  - Once again, as a reminder, the custom Global Accelerator pins the traffic of certain users to a very specific EC2 instance in the VPC subnet specified.

Global Accelerators and TCP Termination at the Edge

Since March 2020, and by default, to improve the performance of TCP sessions, Global Accelerator has been modified to play a man-in-the-middle role. So that, for example, instead of having one long-haul TCP session between a client in India making an API call to an application server in the us-west-1 region (~200ms), the client establishes a TCP session to the closest AWS edge location (say in Mumbai ~5ms), the Global Accelerator terminates that session and immediately establishes the second leg from Mumbai edge to the us-west-1 in California. The most obvious advantages are:

- The client's perception of TCP session establishment (the handshake process) is now much better as it's done with significantly lower round trip times

- The overall experience is enhanced, too, as the longer leg of the connection is established over the AWS private network instead of the public Internet

Finally, similar to the port overriding behavior with Elastic Load Balancers with Global Accelerator, too, you can receive a connection for port TCP 80 of a server at the edge, but send it to port TCP 8080 of the backend server.

Service Preference with Standard Global Accelerator

With Standard Global Accelerators, you can manipulate how the traffic is routed to its final destination. In production networks, this capability could be useful in a number of cases:

- At a global level, you can use the dial feature to make certain regions more or less attractive.
  - This could be a gradual migration scenario from one region to another or simply a diminished capacity situation where a region cannot handle the entire load that it's supposed to
  - The units are in percentages
- At a regional level, you can use the weighted routing feature to make certain endpoints of an endpoint group more or less attractive.
  - Similarly, this could be a scenario where an ELB in an endpoint group has more horsepower behind it compared to another ELB in the same endpoint group.
  - The units are the weights, and it is measured as the relative value to the sum of the weights for all endpoints
    - ELB1: 5, ELB2: 10; ELB2 attracts twice as much traffic within the same endpoint group

Additionally, similar to the concept of stickiness in ELBs, with Global Accelerators too, if you are running a stateful application that needs to see all its traffic from one source IP go to the same endpoint resource, it is possible by using another knob called Client Affinity.

- By default, this is set to none meaning the incoming traffic is spread across all the endpoints in the endpoint group.
- The value can be modified to Source IP to use a hash value of the source and destination IP addresses to ensure stickiness to the same endpoint
  - Needless to say, there are scenarios such as fail-overs where the stickiness to the same destination can no longer be maintained

Hardening VPC Subnets for Custom Global Accelerators

When creating Custom Global Accelerators, the user first defines the endpoint groups and then adds endpoints to them. As mentioned before, the only acceptable type of endpoint for Custom Global Accelerators is VPC subnets.

But how do you expose a subnet to the users as an endpoint?

- By default, when a VPC subnet is selected for a Custom Global Accelerator, the field subnet traffic is set to "Deny all traffic."
  - This prevents any custom Global Accelerator traffic from getting into the subnet and provides maximum security but makes the subnet non-functional
- The least secure option is to set the subnet traffic value to "Allow all traffic."
- The recommended choice, however, is the option of "Allow traffic to specific destination socket addresses."
  - By selecting this option, you can individually pick the EC2 instances by their IP addresses and choose the ports that you want to expose.

Global Accelerators and the Name Resolution Process

- By default, for both Standard and Custom Global Load Balancers, AWS automatically creates a DNS hostname such as xyz.awsglobalaccelerator.com for the two fixed IP addresses it assigns to your Global Accelerator.
- Although this random name might work for the customers who want to use the name in their codes, it won't be convenient for many other customers
  - The ideal solution for most customers is to use their own publicly registered domain names to reach their applications, either in the form of domain apex/root such as Castlencia.com or a hostname such as application.castlencia.com.
  - With both types of Global Accelerators, this can easily be done by creating an alias record and linking it to the random hostname created by AWS.
    - We explained the alias record types in the Route53 section. Remember, it is an absolutely important topic.

Source IP preservation with Global Accelerators

§*Exam Tip*: *Now that you are here, can I trouble you for a second and ask you to go back and review the same section in the ELB part of the book?!*

If you recall from the previous chapters, we investigated various options to preserve the client's IP address with Elastic Load Balancers. The concept there was about preserving the original source IP address between the client and the server behind a load balancer. The topic here is about preserving the source IP address between the client and the endpoint – which could be an ALB.

First and foremost, with Global Load Balancers, the IP address of the client can be only preserved with two types of endpoints:

- Application Load Balancers (ALBs)
  - Internal ALBs: The client IP address presentation is always on

- Internet-facing ALBs: On by default but can be turned off when you create one afterward
- EC2 instances
  - The client IP address presentation is always on

Regardless of the endpoint type, the Global Accelerator Service drops an Elastic Network Interface in each subnet used by the endpoint. As you might expect, it's the architect's job to ensure enough IP addresses are available in those subnets.

- Protecting your resources while preserving the original client's IP address is done by permitting those IPs and ports within your network.
  - Most notably, if you are using NACLs for the subnets, you must take into account the inbound and outbound traffic, which may include the ephemeral ports, as explained in earlier chapters.

CHAPTER 15

SD-WAN and a Long Journey Ahead

But what is Software Defined Networking (SDN) anyways?

SDN or Software Defined Networking is an attempt to separate (technically decouple) different planes involved in complex networking technologies. Although the initial versions of the idea from the mid-2000s were more focused on decoupling control and forwarding planes, in modern networks, we can go after a lot more, including separating the management, data, control, and orchestration planes. The most obvious benefit of this architecture is modularity, and the flexibility offered to network designers to scale at an unprecedented level without having to worry much about the capabilities of every networking node. I understand this sounds a bit complicated but bear with me. In reality, it is simple.

So now, what is SD-WAN?

We managed very large Wide Area Networks (WAN), including hundreds and sometimes thousands of routers manually for decades with models such as hub and spokes. The spokes, in most cases, were the branch offices. Between the two words, we had a fabric made of some WAN (and its circuits) that could be anything from Direct Internet Access (DIA) and Layer 2 or 3 MPLS connections to dark fiber and various types of leased lines or wireless connections. Then at each location, we would place one or more edge routers and connect them using a mesh of some sort of overlay. The overlay network could be made of IPSec tunnels or LSP paths defined by the MPLS service provider.

While on paper, the design doesn't sound complicated, maintaining such infrastructure was indeed a difficult task. Just imagine, you had to configure thousands of devices, maintain their operating systems, ensure the right Quality of Service (QoS) settings on them, and worse of all, have some sort of mechanism to detect bad or lossy circuits and switch traffic over to healthier circuits and potentially back to the primary circuits. I am sure some readers remember making such traffic shifts in the middle of the night! I do.

Very briefly, SD-WAN is an attempt to address most if not all of the issues discussed there. Once fully implemented, your sizable WAN environment will look like a giant fabric made of some proprietary overlay that can be managed from a central point. The edge devices will usually be made by the same vendor and receive configuration, commands, operating system settings, and updates from a central location. All you need to do is to deploy the edge devices at one of your sites (either data center or branch) and simply onboard them to the management tool. Cisco SD-WAN solution (formerly called Viptela) offers one of these architectures with separate control, management, data, and orchestration planes.

But what does this all have to do with the cloud?

Long story short, your cloud footprint is one of your "sites." You might have 120 VPCs and a wide range of workloads, but they are all collectively part of your cloud footprint and, just like any traditional data center, need to connect to the rest of your SD-WAN global mesh. There are different architectures, but this is the most straightforward way to picture the technology.

The classic way to architect SD-WAN in the cloud

Imagine all of your branch offices and data center have received their own SD-WAN edge devices. Now to connect the cloud to the same fabric, you have a (virtual) SD-WAN appliance to install on one or two EC2 instances. Traditionally, through the Marketplace, we would load the right image onto the EC2 instances and run IPSec tunnels between them and the cloud routers (also known as Transit Gateways!). The traffic could be routed using simple static routes. Needless to say, such architecture, although quick to implement, opened the gates to several more fundamental issues, such as low throughput (as a result of heavy IPSec operations) and lack of flexibility (as a result of static routing). Technically, it is always possible to implement this, but it is definitely not recommended after the changes AWS made to the offerings in 2020.

The right way to extend SD-WAN into the cloud

In 2020, AWS introduced a new attachment type for Transit Gateways. By leveraging the Connect attachment type, you can natively attach your SD-WAN appliances to the Transit Gateway and run a GRE tunnel over the attachment. Once the tunnel is established, you can easily configure BGP and enjoy all the flexibility of dynamic routing between the appliance and Transit Gateway. This overlay architecture not only enables extending various SD-WAN deployments into the cloud but also makes it possible to extend other network virtualization solutions such as VRF-lite into AWS.

A key point that some students do not properly understand is that the new attachment type cannot exist all by itself. In fact, it is built on top of another attachment type, which could be Direct Connect and VPC, while the underlying attachment is called Transport attachment.

These two choices (DX vs. VPN) are not to be taken lightly, as each represent one main type of architecture supported by the AWS SD-WAN integration solution:

Two main supported SD-WAN architectures

- The SD-WAN appliance resides in the customer's physical data center
  - The Connect attachment is built on top of an existing Direct Connect attachment
    - Ideal for customers with on-premises SD-WAN appliances who also have Direct Connect between their data centers and AWS.
- The SD-WAN virtual appliance is deployed on EC2 and resides on AWS
  - The connect attachment is built on top of an existing VPC attachment
    - Ideal for customers with virtual SD-WAN solutions deployed in a dedicated VPC on AWS

How to implement the solution?

1. Decide your architecture. If you are bringing a virtual SD-WAN solution to the cloud, you would need a dedicated VPC with separate subnets for each appliance. The SD-WAN VPC subnets would have a minimum of two routes to the outside world; a default route to the Internet (via an IGW), and a route to the TGW (via its attachment).

2. Make sure your Transit Gateway has a CIDR block assigned to it. You probably haven't done this before in other architectures, but now it's critical, so the gateway would need local IP addresses to peer with the SD-WAN appliance over GRE. This concept is similar to assigning IP addresses to router interfaces in traditional networking.

3. Create the Connect attachment on top of either a VPC or Direct Connect attachment. For SD-WAN appliances on EC2, you need the former while the latter is used when your SD-WAN appliance is installed in your data center.

4. Define the GRE addresses for the Transit Gateway and its peer (the SD-WAN appliance). Here you will also need to enter the BGP "inside" CIDR block, which is the range used for BGP peering inside the tunnel.

5. Specify the peer's AS number for BGP

Key SD-WAN in AWS architecture points

- If the SD-WAN appliance is located in the customer's data center, the transport layer must be a Direct Connect attachment (and not VPN)

- GRE is a much lighter solution compared to IPSec and when encryption is not required (or done somewhere else). It can make a great encapsulation (overlay) choice. This results in higher bandwidth rates between the SD-WAN cloud and AWS.

  - If the customer has security concerns around the second architecture and lack of encryption over Direct Connect, there are other solutions to address the issue, such as MACsec.

- Previously with the IPSec tunnels between the SD-WAN appliances and TGW, we were limited to 1.25Gbps per IPSec tunnel. Now by leveraging the GRE tunnels, you could reach 5Gbps per tunnel.

- It is possible to run 4 GRE tunnels on one transport attachment to reach around 20Gbps – which is significantly higher than the original bandwidth attainable using IPSec tunnels between the SD-WAN appliances and TGWs.

- You need to clearly understand the difference between the outer and inner IP addresses.

  - The outer addressing is used for the two ends of the GRE tunnel, and that's what's used for the addresses in the GRE header – our overlay. This address comes from the CIDR block you define for the TGW.

  - The inner addressing is used by the BGP peers to communicate over TCP 179 and establish the BGP neighbor relationship.

- The AS numbering also plays a major role in how the SD-WAN architecture is implemented.

  - If you use the same AS number for the TGW and the SD-WAN appliance, the neighbor relationship would be iBGP (internal), and if the AS numbers are different, it would be eBGP (external). As you will see later in this chapter, this choice has consequences.

  - If you have IPv6 routes to exchange between the TGW and SD-WAN appliance, the right BGP address family would be Multi-protocol BGP (MP-BGP) – which makes sense as we did for years in traditional networks.

- It is possible to deploy more than one SD-WAN appliance in AWS or physical data centers. The architecture remains the same, with the only difference that, in that case, you would need two GRE tunnels, one to each appliance.

  - Once implemented, since you are running BGP over the two GRE tunnels you can use your regular BGP knobs to engineer the traffic and define your routing strategies, such as active-passive.

    - I am sure more experienced network engineers now appreciate the value of using different AS numbers to have eBGP here. With eBGP neighbors, now you have powerful tools such as AS_PATH prepending to influence the traffic to choose your active and passive links (and SD-WAN devices).

§*Exam Tip:* *I understand we covered a lot of details here. But it's worth it, and I did my best not to overlook any aspects of the design. If I were you, I'd go back and again design my own hypothetical scenarios and practice at least 5 times.*

CHAPTER 16

AWS Security Tools and Services

AWS CloudTrail

- It is a service to record activities within your AWS footprint at the API level

  - The data is stored in an S3 bucket.

  - The data includes key information about the users, their source IP address, the nature of the API, and the results of calling the API.

  - This comes in handy when you are investigating cases such as unauthorized access to your account, unexpected changes to your cloud architecture, or tracking what the intruders might have done to your environment after a potential breach.

    - Each action will result in a number of API calls recorded by CloudTrail

§Exam Tip: The key term for the exam would be "API-level" tracking meaning the system logs the API calls for various actions. This is different from other types of logging that you have seen so far.

AWS Config

- It is a service used to gather an inventory of your existing AWS resources, their configuration, and how/when they have been modified.

  - Uses the concept of Config Rules to track and evaluate your current compliance against a set of desired configurations.

  - It is a perfect tool if you need to have reference configurations for your resources and track any divergence from them.

  - This comes in handy when you are subject to regulatory compliance and need to store configuration history details and changes to them.

  - If you need detailed API level change tracking, AWS CloudTrail would be the right choice.

AWS GuardDuty

- It is a fully managed threat detection through continuous monitoring service that consumes data from the following resources and applies various techniques such as machine learning (ML) to detect potential anomalies:

  - VPC flow logs covering (most) IP traffic sent and received by the NICs

  - AWS CloudTrail event logs, including the API calls it has logged and the source IP address making such calls, and its timestamp. AWS CloudTrail management (control plane) events such as routing and subnet changes as well as IAM modifications, and finally, AWS CloudTrail events for S3 such as Get, Put and Delete objects; representing the data plane.

  - DNS logs can be consumed as a data source for GuardDuty only if you use AWS DNS resolver. Currently, any other 3rd party DNS solution would be considered under the radar.

  - Kubernetes (EKS) audit logs can be used as a source once Kubernetes protection is activated in GuardDuty. The audit logs include activities such as the control plane actions as well as the users' and applications' interactions through the API.

- The console identifies the affected instances as well as the threat types such as unauthorized access, backdoors, reconnaissance attempts, penetration testing attempts, or activities related to potential trojan horses

- The GuardDuty data can also be accessed through CloudWatch

  - This can be useful if you need to create SNS notifications and send email or SMS to a group of recipients about the findings.

- When properly configured, GuardDuty can be useful in detecting many scenarios, including:

  - Unauthorized cryptocurrency mining – which would require communication with certain destinations

  - Unauthorized privilege escalation attempts

  - Unauthorized deployments such as spinning up instances

  - Authorized and unauthorized penetration testing that are running to identify weaknesses such as overly-permissive security groups

AWS Inspector

- It is an automated security assessment and vulnerability scanning service that can evaluate if any Common Vulnerabilities and Exposures (CVE) are filed against your cloud resources, such as the operating systems of your compute instances.

  - The service supports continuous security assessment scans, and it automatically discovers EC2 instances and containers

- The service also supports other rule packages such as Security Best Practices or recommendations based on Runtime Behavior Analysis, including unused risky ports

- Each finding includes the severity level, a brief description, and an actionable section called recommendation that can be as simple as a change to the Linux configuration files or Windows services

- The service can also work with an AWS-developed optional agent that is installed on Windows and Linux instances

- You can link the service to a Lambda function using SNS. In this configuration, the code defined in the Lambda function can take various actions

AWS Macie

- It is a managed service that helps you discover and protect sensitive and potentially personal data in S3 buckets.

  - The service uses machine learning and pattern matching to look for sensitive data such as names, social security numbers, or other custom patterns and data types that you define.

  - If required, Macie can send the findings to Amazon CloudWatch

AWS Detective

- AWS offerings such as CloudTrail, GuardDuty, and VPC Logs help you gather large amounts of logs and data that can be studied by security teams to narrow down investigations and potentially identify the root cause of security incidents. AWS Detective is a service that uses machine learning (e.g., to identify normal vs. abnormal behaviors), graph models, and other techniques to assist cloud operators in their security investigations

  - The tool consumes the data collected by CloudTrail, GuardDuty, and VPC Logs to analyze and detect the root cause of suspicious security activities. A hint to the root cause could be something as simple as an unusual use of an API call or a login attempt.

AWS Trusted Advisor

- AWS Trusted Advisor does a lot more than just security evaluation but I felt this would be an appropriate section to bring it up as security and availability are some of its key deliverables.

- The trusted advisor is a service used to evaluate whether your implementation follows a group of 10s of best practices across 5 main categories of cost, performance, security, service limits, and fault tolerance.

- The recommendations cover a wide range of best practices, such as underutilized EBS volumes, idle load balancers, highly utilized instances, unrestricted access, bucket permissions, and Direct Connect redundancy issues.

AWS Web Application Firewall (WAF)

- It is a service to protect Web applications against malicious HTTP requests.

- The service can monitor, rate limit, or, if needed, block HTTP requests based on certain conditions, including:

    - HTTP header and body details

    - Source IP address

    - The presence of SQL queries in the URL (high probability of SQL injection attack)

    - Traces of Cross Site Scripting (XSS) attack where your service can otherwise be used to inject and execute unauthorized JavaScript codes in the visitors' browsers.

    - Is fully integrated into CloudFront and Application Load Balancer (ALB).

        - CloudFront protection: The rules are applied globally in CloudFront locations as close to the end users as possible and far from the origin servers. This keeps the noise of DDoS attacks away from your valuable and expensive resources.

        - ALB protection: The rules are applied at the region level and protect resources behind internal and Internet-facing Load Balancers.

    - Rate limiting is useful when your architecture needs to curb the number of HTTP requests made by a client in a period of 5 minutes instead of indiscriminately blocking them all.

    - In addition to the default settings of the WAF service, if you need fine-grained policies to target specific requests, you can configure Web Access Control Lists (Web ACL) to match and decide between ALLOW and BLOCK:

        - The ACLs look for certain details in the requests including the source address of the traffic, country of origin (arguably) and size of different parts of the request. You can also use regexps to catch various types of matching requests.

        - You can define multiple ACLs and they are processed from the lowest number (similar to most traditional ACLs).

AWS Shield (Standard/Advanced)

- It is a service to provide protection against simple and complex Distributed Denial of Service (DDoS) attacks for your applications on AWS or even outside AWS on origin servers connected to CloudFront.

- AWS Shield Standard
  - Available to all AWS customers for free
  - Focused on the OSI Layer 3 and 4 attacks
  - Provides just enough protection against simple attacks such as SYN and UDP floods.
- AWS Shield Advanced
  - A paid service
  - Protection for the OSI Layer 7 (e.g., against HTTP and DNS floods) in addition to simple Layer 4 against common attacks
  - Monitoring and notifications via CloudWatch metrics. This mechanism can be up to a few minutes behind.
  - Ideal to stop larger and more complex DDoS attacks against CloudFront, Route 53 hosted zones, and Elastic Load Balancers
  - Customers with business or Enterprise support agreements can engage the AWS DDoS Response team, who can develop rules to mitigate the attacks for you.
  - If you fall victim to a DDoS attack and end up with extra AWS fees related to service scaling, you can request a refund in the form of credits.
  - The service can work hand in hand with the Web Application Firewall (WAF) service to apply custom mitigation rules defined via the WAF console.

AWS Network Firewall[7]

- Up until 2021 and before the release of AWS network firewall, if a customer wanted to deploy firewalls in their cloud environments, they would need to deploy third-party firewalls, including Palo Alto, Cisco ASA, or Fortinet Fortigate on EC2 instances. In addition to the licensing and EC2 fees, this would lead to complex architectures, especially in terms of routing, before or even after the advent of transit gateways. Furthermore, scaling such solutions could involve extensive design updates and potential downtimes.
- Although the deployment of next-generation third-party firewalls remains popular, the AWS network firewall is a new managed service that enables you to allow or deny sessions based on domain names or the key Layer 4 information: source and destination IP and port. The firewall can also allow or deny based upon rules compatible with the famous Suricata IPS rules.

---

7. The security configuration aspects of AWS network firewalls are beyond the scope of this book and here we will focus on the networking aspect of the architecture.

- The new network firewall uses stateful and stateless traffic inspection rule engines based on the firewall policies you create. These firewalls are scaled by AWS as needed.

- AWS network firewall revolves around the concept of firewall endpoints you drop in the Availability Zones you need to protect. A major design consideration is that the firewall cannot protect the subnets of its own endpoints (very similar to the design restrictions with the NAT gateways). Hence, designing and creating dedicated subnets for the firewall endpoints is essential.

- To push the interesting traffic through the managed firewalls, you need to update the route tables using the VPC Ingress routing feature and the endpoints you created.

For instance, suppose subnet A and B are both located in the same AZ. If you deploy a firewall endpoint in subnet A when a host in subnet B attempts to talk to the public Internet, based on the updated route table, it will send the traffic to the vpce-abc interface, which is the endpoint in subnet A. Then, the firewall engine is consulted, and if allowed, the session will go out through the IGW (and potentially NAT gateways) to the public Internet. The return traffic takes a similar path. It comes in from the Internet, and goes through the IGW (and NAT gateway) toward the endpoint, where it is again kicked over to the firewall. Once approved, it will be fed back to the originating host by the endpoint. [8]

- The main routes involved in the process mentioned above (and not all the routes) include:

  - Subnet A (hosts subnet): "0.0.0.0/0 to vpce-abc". This route acts as a default gateway for the subnet and sends anything beyond the subnet to the firewall endpoint located in Subnet B.

  - Subnet B (firewall endpoint subnet): "0.0.0.0/0 to IGW". This route is used by the endpoint to send the traffic processed by the firewall up to the IGW.

  - Finally, we create the "x.y.z.t/s to vpce-abc" route endpoint in the ingress route table for the IGW. This route uses the ingress routing feature and sends the traffic for subnet A back to the endpoint.

- As you might have noticed, the endpoint (vpce-abc) is brokering a 3-way conversation between the secured subnets (hosts), the managed firewall, and the IGW.

At a high level, the AWS Network Firewall firewalls (yes, that's right) are deployed in two different models:

- Distributed deployment model

  - Works without TGWs

  - Each VPC (or subnet within VPC) gets its own Network Firewall endpoint (effectively their own firewall).

---

8. The analogy I use in my classes is the way WAN optimizers or Squid proxy servers use the Web Cache Communication Protocol (WCCP) process on routers. Although, the context is different, but the flow is very similar.

- As mentioned above, each Network Firewall endpoint should be placed in a dedicated subnet.

- You can have different firewall policies and strategies for each VPC to secure them.

- Ideal for north-south (usually Internet-bound) traffic inspection.

- Works with a wide range of existing architectures implemented without transit gateways.

- Can protect multiple VPCs with dedicated IGWs or multiple subnets in the same VPC sharing the same IGW.

  - Regardless of the architecture, the routing strategy in distributed designs remains the same: the IGW uses VPC ingress routing to forward the traffic bound for the protected subnets to the endpoint. After processing using the off-path AWS firewall, the firewall endpoint forwards the traffic down to the protected hosts. And the protected hosts use a default route to send anything they have to the firewall endpoint and from there back to the IGW.

  - The protected subnet can be a simple subnet hosting the workload or something more complicated, including elastic load balancers.

- Centralized deployment model

  - Only works with Transit Gateways.

  - Builds a dedicated VPC to place the firewall endpoints and their subnets.

  - The endpoint uses the VPC attachment to reach the TGW and talk to the rest of the network through that.

    - Since this architecture uses TGWs, you would need a separate subnet for the ENI interface used for attachment. Once again, we do not use the endpoints subnet for anything else.

  - Although this model would require transit gateways, it offers more flexibility to support East-West (e.g., spoke VPCs) and North-South (e.g., Internet access or Extranet) architectures.

  - This model can preserve the IP address after processing the packet through the dedicated security VPC.

  - The costs of transit gateways need to be taken into account carefully. This becomes more important when inter-region routing is involved.

- Needless to say, if you have a strong use-case, you can always combine the two strategies of distributed and centralized.

Route 53 Resolver DNS Firewall

One of the major security concerns of any CISO relates to the spread of malware and other malicious codes throughout their environment. This risk astronomically increases when the hosts inside the network can freely make connections to the malicious resources, including the botnets, or the zombie hosts, in the wild.

In the public cloud, this could result in disastrous loss or exfiltration of potentially confidential data where the attackers manage to take data out of the VPCs, particularly when a resource inside the VPC is compromised.

With Route 53 Resolver DNS firewall, you can configure the VPC-level resolver DNS to inspect and filter outbound DNS queries. The firewall can reject, allow, allow/log if a match is found in its configured rules. For instance, you can have a rule to reject any DNS queries made for *.info domains, be more specific and reject outbound queries to test.info, or combine the two by configuring an allow statement for test.info and rejecting *.info. This configuration will exclude test.info from the blanket policy affecting all the .info domain names.

- In addition to the classic deny and allow actions, the firewall supports an alert action containing an implicit allow action. The logs can be found in the Route 53 Resolver logs.

- You can also configure the Route 53 Resolver DNS firewall to respond with a custom domain instead of the blocked domain when queried from within your VPC. For instance, when domain A is queried, the firewall intercepts the query and sends the custom response of domain B. This setting can be used for user redirection and is called overriding the query. You can also set a custom TTL for the response that will define how long the hosts in your VPC will be using the "redirected" name. For example, you can have your EC2 users see your company's internal "blocked content" warning website when certain websites are queried.

- You can have multiple rules as part of a rule group, and the order of those rules matters. The interface allows you to move the rules up and down the list.

- The DNS Firewall, by default, prefers Security over Availability. This means that if the firewall (for whatever reason) fails to respond to a query, the system will operate in Fail Closed mode and won't allow the queries through. The architect can change this behavior to Fail Open to prefer service Availability over Security – should the AWS DNS Firewall become unresponsive.

One of the main challenges in blocking malicious domain names has always been creating a reliable and up-to-date list of such addresses. While you could work with your security vendor to achieve and confirm such lists, AWS also provides the following two lists that can be readily used in your rules.

- AWSManagedDomainsMalwareDomainList: Domain names known to send or distribute malware.

- AWSManagedDomainsBotnetCommandandControl: Domain names known to command-and-control resources infected with malware/spamming.

Furthermore, keep in mind, with AWS, to protect their intellectual property and, for security reasons, to keep the lists away from their users. Hence, you cannot download or edit the two lists.

§*Exam Tip:* *Although I am satisfied with the number of details covered here on the DNS firewall, since it's a pretty simple feature, before taking the exam, I would set up a small lab and play around a bit. There are several different scenarios in the book on rejecting/accepting queries and how to handle fail open and closed use cases.*

Traffic Mirroring

For several years AWS Flow Logs was the only native feature in AWS that would provide users with session-level insights into their network conversations. For instance, you could test your network access policies by using the Flow Logs to determine the fate of each flow, ACCEPT or REJECT. Using Flow Logs, you could see key pieces of information about the flow, such as the protocol number and the source and destination IP addresses. While this turned out to be helpful in some scenarios, in many other cases, the network operators still had to use 3rd party tools such as Wireshark to gain deeper visibility into each session and packet, such as inspecting the payloads. AWS eventually made this possible by introducing a new feature called Traffic Mirroring.

In the most basic terms, now, if you own the source interface of its subnet, you can capture the traffic from one Elastic Network Interface (ENI) and use the VPC route tables to forward a copy of it to another ENI. To scale the solution better and provide higher levels of availability, you can also use a Network Load Balancer (NLB) with UDP listeners instead of a single ENI as the destination. Behind the load balancer, you can have a number of hosts to receive and analyze the incoming packets.

One important exception to the mirroring process is the packets that are dropped at the source by other AWS security mechanisms, including the security groups. Such packets will no longer be available for mirroring.

When architecting a solution with the Traffic Mirroring feature, the following points should be taken into account:

- Not permitting the VXLAN port (UDP 4789) on the destination can easily lead to time-consuming troubleshooting scenarios.

- Not every AWS compute instance supports traffic mirroring. This applies to both the source and destinations of the traffic. At this stage, the Nitro-based instances and some of the Xen instances support the feature. For the latest list of supported instances, check the AWS documentation.

- Similar to many other high-availability best practices with ELBs, it's recommended to enable cross-zone load balancing if you can place targets in different Availability Zones behind the load balancer.

- Some types of traffic are excluded by design from the traffic mirroring process. This list at the moment includes ARP, NTP, DHCP, and the instance metadata. Similar to AWS Flow Logs, you also cannot capture traffic related to Windows activation.

- Since AWS uses VXLAN encapsulation to tunnel the traffic from the source to the destination, it's the architect's responsibility to take into account the change in MTU sizes depending on where on the cloud the solution is deployed. In the absence of proper packet sizing, AWS will automatically truncate the new mirrored packets. There might not be a new checksum for the truncated packet.

- Although in a poor man's solution, you could run TCPdump to receive and observe the raw mirrored packets on the destination, tools such as Suricata or Zeek not only can unwrap the VXLAN capsulation but also help you analyze the captured data. There are also solutions out there, such as the one provided by Binovi technologies, to decrypt the packets.

Reference Architecture(s)

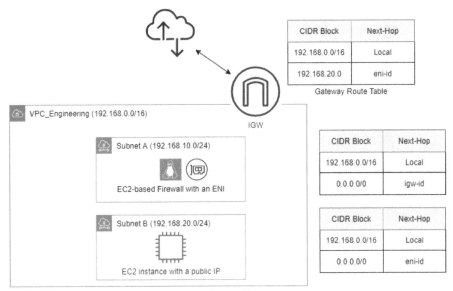

CIDR Block	Next-Hop
192.168.0.0/16	Local
192.168.20.0	eni-id

Gateway Route Table

VPC_Engineering (192.168.0.0/16)

IGW

Subnet A (192.168.10.0/24)

EC2-based Firewall with an ENI

CIDR Block	Next-Hop
192.168.0.0/16	Local
0.0.0.0/0	igw-id

Subnet B (192.168.20.0/24)

EC2 instance with a public IP

CIDR Block	Next-Hop
192.168.0.0/16	Local
0.0.0.0/0	eni-id

Figure 59

A reminder from earlier sections. VPC Ingress routing came out to resolve the issue of deploying third-party firewalls in AWS. The core component of this architecture is the gateway route table attached to the IGW (or, in some designs, VGW). If you recall, this route table determines how the ingress traffic will be handled.

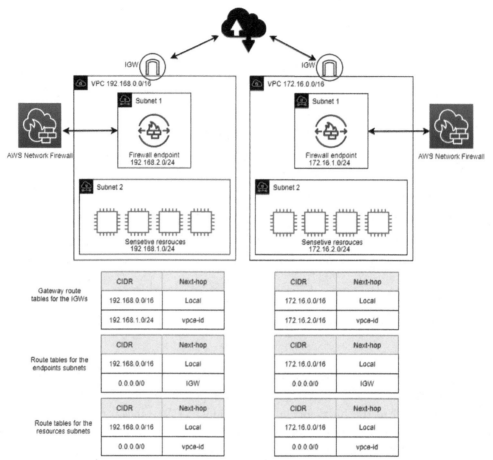

Figure 60

This architecture shows one of the possible distributed models to deploy an AWS network firewall. Here, each VPC gets its own endpoint. Notably, similar to NAT gateways, the endpoint cannot serve the nodes located in its own subnet, hence the dedicated subnet for the endpoints. This design provides inspection for the traffic between sensitive clients and the Internet. The architect needs to pay close attention to the routing details. The flow is very straightforward. By using VPC ingress routing on the IGWs, the traffic is fed to the endpoints. Once processed, it is sent to the sensitive subnets. On the way back, the hosts route the traffic to the endpoints, and again, once processed, it makes it back to the IGW and out to the Internet.

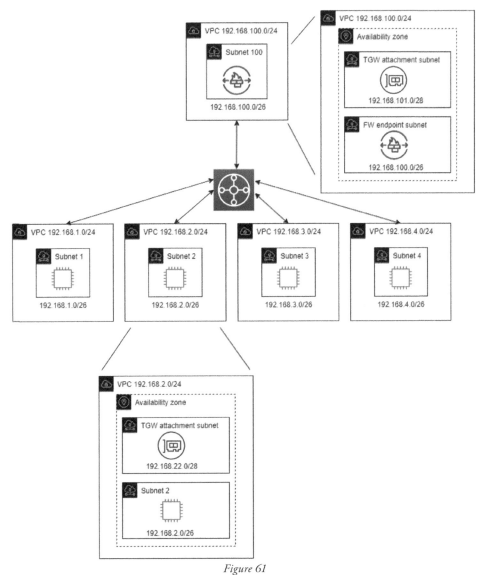

Figure 61

The detailed reference architecture for the central deployment model. In this architecture, the VPC hosting subnet 100 is acting as the security VPC by having the firewall endpoints in one of its subnets. This model can inspect inter-VPC traffic (east-west) and potentially north-south traffic (Internet-users) that does not exist here. Compared to the distributed model, the security VPC could be easier to add to the existing architectures and provide a great option if the customer is already using transit gateways. If the customer's network is still based on VGWs or transit VPCs, implementing this model by migrating to TGWs first can be costly and needs to be planned in multiple phases involving downtimes. As you notice, the endpoints and TGW attachments are placed in different subnets.

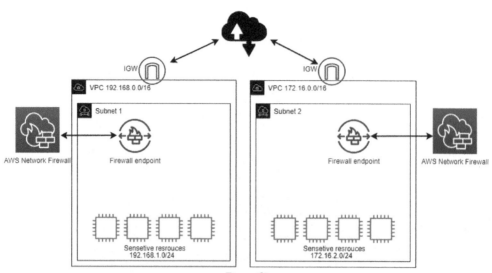

Figure 62

The diagram above shows an INVALID architecture.

The firewall endpoints cannot reside in the same subnet as the resources they are supposed to protect. The architect needs to revise the design with preferably dedicated subnets.

CHAPTER 17

Amazon CloudFront

In a traditional architecture, when you are hosting a Web site on your Web servers, the physical distance and latency between your users and the location of the Web server play a major role in their experience. For instance, users browsing a Web site hosted in India from the United States may experience long latencies of ~200ms. This number between the US east and west coasts is usually between 60 and 80ms. In many architectures, the speed of light introduces a hard limit that cannot be lifted.

Additionally, maintaining a single Web server or even a cluster of Web servers in a particular data center offers little help in case of Distributed Denial of Service (DDoS) attacks. Sooner or later, the attackers stand a good chance of saturating either the servers or links and circuits. Finally, physical redundancy has always been one of the top factors in achieving service reliability.

Content Delivery Networks (CDNs) are designed to bring a cached version of the content closer to the user for a predefined amount of time until either the content expires or is manually invalidated by the network operators.

- The content could be Web pages, images, or many objects that traditionally we could store on cache servers.

- When users browse a website using techniques such as DNS latency-based routing, they are served by the nearest copy of the content.

- If the content is not available on the edge servers or has expired, a fresh copy of it is pulled from a backend server called the Origin Server that hosts the original version of the content.

CloudFront is Amazon's multi-tier global CDN. At a very high-level, CloudFront works with the AWS global backbone, over a dozen Regional Edge Caches, and hundreds of Edge locations (also known as POPs) built to bring the content hosted on the Origin server closer to the users.

You have a few choices for the Origin server:

- S3 bucket
- Static Web site hosted on S3
- Your own Web server (which can be hosted in an external data center)

Amazon CloudFront works with the concept of Distributions as described below that are accessed by users.

A DNS domain name as part of the URL including random characters ending in cloudfront. net, such as https://a123xxxxx123.cloudfront.net/object.gif

For many network operators, the random Distribution name is not convenient if they are sharing it with their users.

- You can create a DNS CNAME or Alias record (Route 53 only) and use your own domain name as an alias pointing to the AWS-generated Distribution domain name.
  - Although this technique resolves the issue, it would add to the complexity of other CloudFront settings, such as enabling HTTPS.
- Some CloudFront customers still use the randomly generated DNS name especially if such names are used in the body of the codes such as HTML and not directly visible to the end users.

Secure communications in CloudFront

To secure communications in CloudFront, the customer needs to deploy HTTPS to both segments of the communication, between the users and CloudFront and between CloudFront and the Origin server.

- To enforce HTTPS between the users and CloudFront:
  - If you are using the default CloudFront-generated DNS domain name, you only need to update the Viewer Protocol Policy setting to require HTTPS.
  - If you are using a custom domain name, CloudFront needs to identify the distribution and know which SSL/TLS certificate to use for the domain name entered by the user. This can be done via:
    - Using Server Name Indication (SNI), which is an extension to the TLS that helps the client indicate which hostname it is connecting to by searching the request header for the domain name and mapping it to the right certificate. This is an extremely important enabler.
    - Having CloudFront assign a dedicated IP address to the custom domain in each edge location. Hence, when the request arrives, CloudFront can determine which Distribution and certificate to use.

- To enforce HTTPS between CloudFront and the Origin server for S3 buckets supporting HTTPS, although by default CloudFront matches the viewers' protocol, you can update the Viewer Protocol Policy to redirect HTTP to HTTPS or enforce only HTTPS.

  - The Website endpoints configured on Amazon S3 do not support HTTPS. Therefore, the communications between CloudFront and the Origin server (in this case, the bucket) cannot be done over HTTPS.

- To enforce HTTPS between CloudFront and your own Origin server (EC2 or on-premises), if you are using the CloudFront-generated DNS domain names, you need to update the Origin Protocol Policy, and of course, install the certificates on the Origin server.

Data Protection in CloudFront

- To secure data at rest, AWS uses different techniques at the POPs and regional edge cache locations:

  - Encrypted SSD storage at the Edge POPs

  - Encrypted Elastic Block Store volumes at the regional edge caches

- To restrict access to your content to a selected group of users, you can deploy:

  - A signed-URL architecture where individual files on CloudFront can be accessed only by the users who have the exact URL.

  - A signed cookie architecture where multiple files or an entire paid section of a Website can be accessed only by the users who can support and provide the signed cookies with the HTTP requests.

  - If you are using S3 to host your files, obviously, you need to make sure they cannot be directly and publicly browsed.

- To restrict access to your content to certain IP addresses (whitelist or blacklist), the Web Application Firewall (WAF) service can be used.

- To force users to go through CloudFront before hitting an Application Load Balancer to prevent situations such as DoS or DDoS-related outages:

  - Add a custom header to the incoming HTTP requests.

  - On the ALB listener, define a rule only to accept requests containing the header defined above.

CloudFront and serverless computing with Lambda@Edge

It is an extension of the AWS Lambda; a serverless computing feature. AWS Lambda functions can execute codes in languages including Python and Node.js on a certain schedule or in response to events such as incoming HTTP requests. They are called serverless because they do not need their own server (VM or bare-metal) to execute the code. The server and all the required maintenance are provided by AWS.

This feature was adopted by CloudFront as Lambda@Edge to customize the contents you are delivering to the users at the edge (in this case, CloudFront) instead of routing the traffic deep into AWS and performing the operation on resources such as EC2 instances.

The Lambda@Edge functions are linked to CloudFront Distributions and sit between the users and Origin server(s), watching the HTTP requests and responses and taking actions defined by the code if the conditions defined in the code are met. For instance:

- Inspect the header of incoming HTTP requests at the edge (CloudFront) and decide what content to deliver to the user depending on the parameters found in the HTTP header.

- During a maintenance event at the edge (CloudFront), generate and deliver a simple downtime HTML page to the users.

§*Exam Tip: Once again, I acknowledge the fact that operating CloudFront and dealing with all its details, including encryption and domain name management, is outside the comfort zone of many network engineers who are used to configuring OSPF, BGP, and RSTP but the reality is that in the cloud, we do not have the same clear-cut set of responsibilities as we did in traditional networks. In a cloud engineering environment (and, of course, on the exam), a network architect is expected to understand a fair amount of systems engineering (DNS, DHCP, etc.), security and content management as it relates to ELBs and CloudFront. I am confident that we have covered most if not all of that in the book.*

CHAPTER 18

The World of Container Networking with ECS and EKS

I know…I know…. But as far as the scope of the ANS-C01 exam goes, you need to know the basics of networking provided by the two AWS services for container management—Elastic Container Service (ECS) and Elastic Kubernetes Service (EKS), the Amazon proprietary way of managing containers and the de facto standard of managing containers at scale.

Having said that, the exam predictably leans toward ECS as an Amazon proprietary service, while the AWS Load Balancer Controller developed for EKS is explicitly called out as a service of interest by the exam guide.

Since the EKS is primarily a Kubernetes-based service, it's very light in terms of AWS documentation, and it can be best learned on the official Kubernetes Web site, although it is not the main focus of the exam.

§Exam Tip: *The ANS-C01 exam as it stands now and based on the latest blueprint, won't be heavily covering the containers. So, if anyone wants to leave this amazing chapter alone, I won't be yelling!*

Basics of containerization for network engineers

Let's go back to our sample customer and look at years of evolution in their physical data centers. The more experienced members of the servers team at Castlencia remember well when, back in the early 2000s, they had dedicated HP servers in the racks for each of their applications. In fact, they would put stickers on each of the physical DL servers to specify the application they were running on that piece of hardware. Some servers were underutilized, while others were always running hot and juggling torches. The system administrators would monitor resource consumption on each device and usually, during the week of Christmas, "right-size" them by moving the busier servers to more capable DL servers and pushing the lighter applications to less expensive DL servers. It might sound like a joke, but that's what many people would do back then.

The next generation came out several years later with the advent of virtualization. They could "pack" multiple applications on the same physical server in this iteration. Even though this tremendously helped them optimize the utilization of their resources, it didn't really address the issues with overhead. Now, each server was running a host (base) operating system, a hypervisor (usually licensed), and several guest operating systems that would have to be individually purchased and maintained. Bogdan, one of the older network engineers, vividly remembers when they started migrating from traditional server networking to virtual networking for each VM using Nexus 1000v in 2010. They are also very familiar with the cool features of their VMWare infrastructure, such as VMotion to move their VMs from the server to another with minimum impact. Today, they manage a fleet of thousands of VMs with their dedicated operating systems.

As usual, Bogdan worked across the IT organization to develop a wish list for how they want the next iteration of their servers and applications would look:

1. Currently, for each application, we have a heavy stack. There is the host operating system of the server, then the hypervisor, and then the VMs. Inside each VM, again, we have another operating system where the application sits. We need a lighter-weight stack to remove as much technical and management overhead as possible.

2. We need to keep our resource efficiency as high as possible

3. The new architecture must function not just in our physical data centers but also on the cloud as we migrate to a public cloud provider

Application containerization, if designed and implemented correctly, meets most of their requirements.

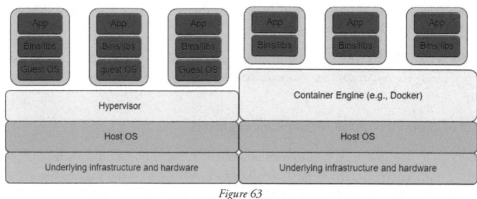

Figure 63

A traiditonal VM-based model vs a Containerizead model

Figure 64 shows a very high level view of the idea and why so many companies are moving to some containerized model. Think about this for a second, why would I need to run a full-blown guest operating system in each one of my VMs to run an application? How about running just the absolutely needed binaries and libarires instead of a multi-gig operating system?

A bit of general application containerization knowledge

Before diving into what AWS as a public cloud provider has to offer, let's cover a number of fundamental terms of application containerization. Most, if not all of them, are shared among all on-premises and cloud-based implementations:

- **Container**: "A container is a standard unit of software that packages up code and all its dependencies, so the application runs quickly and reliably from one computing environment to another". In other words, it's a contained environment defined on top of the host operating system to run your application. The containers you run on a server use the kernel of the host operating system for parts of their mission, but also carry a stripped-down version of some operating such as libraries to perform. The containers have become the standard form of packaging for microservices in modern environments. This packaging process is done with software development suits such as Docker. The first sentence of this paragraph was straight from Docker's documentation. Finally, containers are placed in pods. A pod is just like an eggshell. In most cases, it hosts one yolk (I mean container), but in exceptional cases, it might host more. A pod is barely an eggshell and does not affect how the containers function.

- **Orchestration**: Similar to the world of Virtual Machines (VM), the world of containers too has expanded exponentially. As a result, manually managing large fleets of containers is not technically feasible. In most environments, you need an orchestrator such as Kubernetes to perform critical actions like deploying applications, rolling out and rolling back updates, and scaling up and down the deployment. Deployment and all the management stuff. That being said, we all know someone who claims they can manage everything manually and eventually fail after burning a ton of resources! But in reality, you would need some form of orchestration if you were to go beyond a little test environment. Kubernetes (also known as K8s) is an open-source orchestration system for containerized environments.

- **Container image:** In the world of Docker, the images are stored in a safe place called a registry and can be downloaded to run containers. They are built based on recipes that you define in a text file called a Dockerfile. In the file, we specify the most basic information about the image, such as the ports we would like the container to expose and the dependencies within the container that we want to download and make available. Also, if we are compiling and installing any part of the application from its source, it is specified in the Dockerfile. After all, that's a complete recipe to show Docker how to build each image to eventually run its container. One of the favorite image bases for testing and production systems is Alpine Linux, with a staggeringly small size of just 5MB!

- **Tightly-coupled vs. Loosely-coupled containers:** Placing more than one container in a pod and having them share the resources as opposed to making each pod dedicated to only one container.

Amazon Elastic Container Service (ECS)

The Basics

- The Elastic Container Service (ECS) is Amazon's proprietary solution for container management

  - Its containers are built based on the well-known Docker container type. Although, Docker is not the only available container type. Docker is simply the most commonly used platform. Podman, LXD, Kaniko, and Containerd are some of the alternatives. But keep in mind, at this stage, ECS only supports Docker.

- Although it features a highly scalable and fairly easy to configure and maintain container management service, many large customers, especially the ones with existing Kubernetes infrastructure in their physical data centers, prefer EKS over ECS.

  - As a service fully developed by Amazon, based on Docker, ECS enjoys a complete set of documentation as well as full integration with most other Amazon critical services such as Identity and Access Management (IAM).

The ECS's terminology is different from that of native Kubernetes but let's check out this application's architecture before diving into the theories:

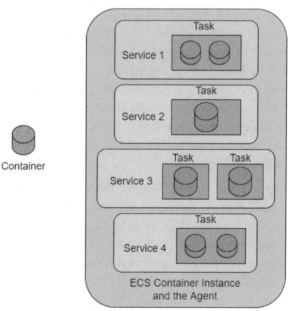

Figure 64

Here is an example of an ECS container instance running 4 different services. Each service has a number of tasks and the tasks have their own containers. As you can see we have flexibility in terms of the number of containers in the architecture but in most cases it is NOT the network engineer's call.

Now we are prepared to review some ECS-specific vocabulary in greater details:

- **Task Definition**: It's a JSON file (hence human readable) that acts as a blueprint for the application by defining up to 10 containers and their details in ECS.
  - The ECS create task definition wizard helps you to populate the fields that otherwise you would need to add/remove directly in a JSON file.
  - Some applications may have more than one task definition to define an array of containers for different functionalities of the application.
  - The task definition includes key pieces of information such as the information about resource assignment (e.g., memory and CPU units) and networking of the tasks created using each definition.
    - An important part of each task definition is the detailed blueprint you provide for the future containers, such as their individual resource management and network access to the outside world.

- **Task:** A task is an instance of a task definition. You can think of it as one pancake that you used your favorite recipe to make.
  - Tasks define a group of containers that are placed together
  - Tasks are run in a cluster by the scheduler service
  - The beauty of an orchestration system like the one offered by ECS is that if any of your tasks created by a task definition fail or stop, the ECS scheduler launches another instance of the same task using the same task definition as a blueprint.
    - This is an interesting core concept that most traditional network engineers are not used to. In our traditional world, we either had or didn't have redundancy. In the world of application containerization and orchestration, the logic has shifted to: If it's not working, use the same blueprint and launch another one to keep us up and running; no human intervention is needed.
    - That is what the scheduler service does!

- **ECS Container Agent:** Similar to any traditional "agent" in network and systems engineering, the ECS Container Agent is a software developed by Amazon that is installed on the ECS EC2 nodes to connect its containers to the cluster, receive instructions from ECS and manage them.
  - The agent comes in different flavors, including an installable RPM or pre-integrated in certain Amazon Machine Images (AMIs).

So far, what has been presented is based on EC2 instances as our ECS container instance.

But what if the customer described above becomes tired of EC2 instance provisioning, maintenance, and all the orchestration that goes with it?

Serverless operations using AWS Fargate

- AWS Fargate is a serverless compute engine that completely removes the need to provision and maintain EC2 instances
    - Perhaps the easiest and quickest way to run containers on AWS without having to deal with the host EC2 instances
- Fargate provisions the containers and enables your environment to automatically scale as needed, again without having to bring up and manage any EC2 instances
    - This is ideal in the case where you do not even have your own VPC and subnets
    - Using the wizard, you will get to choose the host operating system as some containers may need certain host operating systems to function properly
    - Currently, in 2022, Linux and the two flavors of Core and Full Windows Server 2019 are supported
- All the usual orchestration and management responsibilities such as scheduling the containers, planning load balancing, and worrying about strategies to achieve the highest availability are handled by Fargate.

Now that we have built an acceptable foundation around the basics of containers and ECS, let's dive into the networking part of the story:

Task networking within ECS

Regardless of where the tasks (and their containers) are hosted (EC2 or Fargate), the behavior of the networking service depends on how you set the Network Mode within the ECS Task Definition.

- Amazon ECS hosted on EC2
    - Three (actually four if you count "none") Network Modes are available; awsvpc, bridge, host, and "none" modes.
        - awsvpc mode
            - The AWS recommended mode
            - Each task receives its own Elastic Network Interface (only one) and a primary IPv4 address
                - The ENI is attached to the host EC2 instance
                - For dual-stack VPCs with IPv6 CIDR blocks, the ENI in Linux-based EC2 instances will also be assigned an IPv6 address
            - With a dedicated ENI, each task would enjoy (almost) the same networking functionalities as the EC2 instances so they can communicate with other resources such as other containers
                - Simple and straightforward architecture

- • Security groups would work.

- • Monitoring tools such as VPC Flow Logs would function

- • Inter-container communication within the same task is possible and done through the localhost interface

- • Easy communication flow with all the other resources in the VPC, similar to what is available to any ENA

- • Two major drawbacks of this mode:

  - • The tasks cannot have public IPv4 addresses; hence any outbound communication with the Internet is done from private subnets via NAT Gateways and inbound via Internet-facing load balancers. This is not much of a concern in Linux-based dual-stack environments with an egress-only NAT gateway. In such architectures, one-way communication out to the Internet is possible.

  - • If you choose the Fargate lunch type as opposed to EC2, the AWSVPC network mode would be the only possible option.

- • In larger-scale architectures where load balancing is required, when you create a service using the awspvc network mode for your tasks, you can only use Network and Application Load Balancers and not Classic Load Balancers.

  - • Even with an NLB or ALB, must still define your targets using their IP addresses, not their instance IDs.

- • And last but not least, with the AWSVPC network mode, you cannot configure a public IPv4 address on the ENI. As you will see later in this part of the book, this does not raise an unsurmountable issue.

- • Bridge mode

  - • Unlike awsvpc, there is no dedicated ENI for each task.

  - • It uses the clever idea of port mapping between the host ports and container ports.

    - • For example, port TCP 8080 on a container can be accessed from the outside world when it is mapped to port TCP 80 of the host

    - • The network operator can do this statically, but it won't be scalable as it creates a 1-to-1 mapping between the container and host ports. Such that, if container A is mapped to use the hosts port 80, no other containers can use the same port to expose their service

- The mappings can also be done dynamically by Docker
  - Less administrative overhead
  - Better port availability; now Docker maps the container ports to high-numbered random ports on the host side
  - Usually, a high numbered port such as those between 32768 and 61000 on the latest ECS-optimized images are selected (the ephemeral ports)
  - For example, 3 containers exposing their port TCP 8080 now can use the same ENI and primary IP address but using the random ports of 41358, 41671, and 55055.
  - Later in this section, when we cover scalability, I will show you could keep track of these random port numbers
- Host mode
  - Probably the most limiting of all the networking modes
  - Similar to the bridge mode, with direct but unchangeable 1-to-1 mapping between the host and container:
    - For example, port TCP 8080 of the container will be mapped to port TCP 8080 of the host without any possibility to remap statically or dynamically
    - Hence, only one container at a time can be accessed via the primary IP address and the port that the host and container are both using.
- None
  - The task will not have any external connectivity

Once the connectivity is established, the containers, just like any EC2 instance, can talk to each other and the rest of the world.

Architecting access to the rest of the AWS portfolio

In order to access various AWS services from your containerized application, you have two options:

- Routing through a NAT Gateway
  - If you recall, traditionally, this was one of the original methods to access services such as S3, and people didn't like it due to the cost and having to traverse the public Internet

- With a NAT Gateway, the traffic flow would be: From within the VPC, the container goes through the NAT Gateway and then via an Internet Gateway goes out to the Internet and hits the public side of S3

- Routing through VPC Endpoints

  - The preferred way; because of its lower overall cost and the fact that the traffic is kept within the AWS network; something that many organizations care about; especially the ones with strict regulatory concerns

  - I recommend you review the endpoints section of the book again on different strategies to limit access via the endpoints and secure them. There are also some interesting mini-scenarios on the topic in the book.

Architecting inbound/outbound access to the Internet

On its surface, if you treat each container as a lightweight application "server," it sounds straightforward that they can communicate easily with the Internet as long as there is an Internet Gateway and the routing for their subnet is properly set up; an assumption that is partially true. However, I strongly encourage you to take the following key point into account too:

- Obviously, in order to have bi-directional communication with the Internet, in addition to the private IPv4 addresses, you would need a public IP address on the ENI supporting your container(s). this can happen in a public subnet. Sounds easy, right?

- As you saw earlier, currently, it is not possible to configure public IPv4 addresses if the network type is set to AWSVPC.

  - For this networking mode, you need to configure a NAT Gateway. Think about cost and capacity planning. Read on; there are some alternate ideas in this chapter.

- If you have configured the Bridge and Host mode, you can assign public IPv4 addresses to your ENIs and directly communicate with the Internet.

  - Although from a security perspective, especially in large-scale microservices, it might not be a smart idea unless you have tightly configured firewalls and security groups

- Some organizations, especially the ones with strict compliance requirements, do not like the idea of placing their application servers or now their application containers in public subnets. They might also have no requirement for allowing the traffic initiated on the Internet to enter their environment (inbound traffic). In those architectures, keeping the containers in private subnets and connecting them to a NAT Gateway in a public subnet is the most viable solution.

  - The AWS NAT Gateway is a one-way cloud construct

  - Remember, if the cost of running AWS NAT Gateways exceeds your budget, there are always alternatives such as open-source firewalls (something as simple as Linux Iptables or as sophisticated as a Palo Alto or Forinet firewall). They all perform different forms of NAT, especially source NAT, as required in this scenario.

- This turns into the only viable architecture when the servers need to be accessed from the Internet. Currently, the AWS NAT Gateway does not support destination NAT or 1:1 NATting. In these architectures, you must use a 3rd party solution.

- Last but not least, ECS architectures based on Fargate are flexible when it comes to IP addressing and communicating with the public Internet. Depending on whether you launch them with or without a public IPv4 address, they can directly or indirectly (through a NAT Gateway) communicate with destinations on the Internet.

Architecting for scalability with ECS bridge network mode

Building applications and services in a microservices architecture using containers offers several key benefits, including scalability – meaning the service or application could scale up and down (or out and in) as needed without all the hassles we were used to in traditional environments. For example, losing 2 Web or database servers in a traditional cluster could lead to not only a long list of actions by human beings to remediate the situation but also losing capacity and deteriorating the end user's experience. Scaling up would not be much easier as new servers or VMs would have to be provisioned and properly added to the pool, an action that could have carried several availability risks.

When architecting scalable microservices with Amazon ECS, there are a number of techniques that the solution designer (especially a network engineer) needs to be aware of:

- Earlier in this section, I showed you that with dynamic port mapping, you could remove the limitations introduced by 1:1 port mappings between the container and host port numbers.

- When working with dynamic random port mapping in large-scale production environments, the network architects usually have several concerns:

  - How do we keep track of those ever-changing IP and port numbers, especially when they are linked as targets to load balancers?

    - Enhancements have been made to Elastic Load Balancers (ELB) in such a way that their target groups are automatically updated with the latest IP addresses and port numbers of the tasks that they are feeding as their targets.

  - How do we go about defining security policies when the port numbers are changing (hopping) so quickly? This actually reminds me of frequency hopping in electronic warfare and ELINT systems!

    - Although it would still be a security risk, you might want to consider opening up a wider range of high port numbers. In order to do so, it is strongly recommended that you have some firewall inspection (maybe even L7 inspection) in place to protect those ports.

- How about having a meaningful name for each service and maintaining their IP address and port numbers in DNS as they change by surfacing and disappearing tasks and their containers, each using their own port numbers?

  - Outside the world of Amazon ECS, distributed application architects for years deployed tools such as Zookeeper and etcd as a central location for providing critical functions such as naming, configuration information, and synchronization within large clusters. In 2018, Amazon came up with its version of the tool to cover at least parts of its functionalities.

  - Currently, Amazon ECS has a means called Service Discovery that works hand-in-hand with another fully managed Amazon service called Cloud Map to keep the DNS records of ECS tasks fresh and updated. These records include both the A record (for hostname to IP name resolution) and SRV records (for port numbers).

All in all, you do not have to worry about tasks and containers as they "pop up" in a self-healing microservices environment and change IP address and port number. The A and SRV records of the main service will be maintained as described above.

  - Food for thought: What if an A and SRV record is cached by a DNS client cache and the port number changes later, which, in turn, would change the SRV record?

Architecting for scalability with ECS AWSVPC network mode

When discussing the AWSVPC mode, one of the first questions that always comes up is about the number of Elastic Network Interfaces (ENI) in each instance. At the time of this writing, no AWS instance type can have more than 15 elastic interfaces. If you remember, in this mode, each ECS task gets its own ENI.

So, what does that mean in large-scale implementations, the number of tasks equals the number of elastic interfaces in that EC2 container instance?

Fortunately, the answer is no. By leveraging a technique called Elastic Network Interface (ENI) trunking, you can increase the number of ENIs attached to certain container instance types.

- First and foremost, ENI trunking strictly applies to EC2-based container hosts running the AWSVPC network mode

  - For instance, this conversation does not apply to EC2 instances running the Bridge mode or task running using Fargate

- This change can be made straight from the ECS console, under account settings.

- Always check the latest AWS documentation for the supported instance types and the maximum number of ENIs after increasing the limit. At the time of this writing, the feature was only available to certain Nitro instance types.

- Currently, ENI trunking is only available to Linux-based instances

- As you will see in the resource sharing section of the book, it is possible to share subnets. However, ENI trunking would not function in such subnets.

- Perhaps another benefit of Fargate; each task receives its own dedicated ENI, which makes the trunking feature unnecessary.

- Last but not least, my number one issue with the feature; if you enable the feature, it only applies to the instances that you launch going forward. The current instances, will still be limited by the default number of ENIs.

The challenge of Task Placement with different EC2 launch types

While Amazon takes care of spreading your tasks across different Availability Zones, as a network operator, you have the flexibility of defining placement strategies. While it's tempting to any network architect to define the policy based on what we believe is accurate, I strongly suggest everyone make this decision in partnership with the application and system owners.

The following strategies are available:

- AZ Balanced Spread: Spreads your tasks across Availability Zones and the instances prepared in those zones.

- AZ Balanced BinPack: Spreads tasks across Availability Zones and within the Availability Zones packs tasks by maximizing the memory usage of those instances

- BinPack: Packs tasks on the least number of instances by maximizing the usage of their memory.

- One Task Per Host: Perhaps the most obvious strategy. Ideal for heavy, unpredictable, and potentially unstable in-development tasks.

- Custom: A placement strategy defines how tasks are placed by spread, BinPack (based on both CPU and memory), or random. You can define multiple placement strategies under custom mode.

Load balancing for ECS in large scale environments

All the principles of Elastic Load Balancers apply with the difference that this time instead of target groups made of servers, we have tasks (and eventually containers) as the targets. Having said that, there are certain nuances specific to deploying ELBs for ECS that you need to be aware of:

- Although depending on the architecture requirements, you could choose Network, Application, or Classic Load Balancers. If you are using Fargate instead of EC2, Classic Load Balancers cannot be used.

- In most architectures, especially when you have Web services, as usual, the Application Load Balancers, with their ability to define a wide range of host and path-based routing, is a better choice.

- With Network Load Balancers, if you are using the AWSVPC network mode, the targets have to be registered using their IP addresses and not the instance IDs. This would further lead to all the details we discussed for the NLBs when registered by using their IP addresses, such as how you could preserve the source IP address.
  - Consequently, since the only available mode to Fargate is AWSVPC, if you are using Fargate and not EC2, the entire target registration process must be done using IP addresses
- If you recall, from the Elastic Load Balancers section of the book, the ALBs support Security Groups configured directly on them in addition to the Security Groups that you could have on the backend instances. The same principle exists here, too; that offers two layers of protection; one at the ALB and the other one right at the container instance.

Auto Scaling for ECS

As you can imagine, in large environments, the application and network architect would want to keep deployments adaptive to the changes in demand. The services created in ECS are no exception, and you should be able to update the number of running tasks in response to changes in certain CloudWatch metrics. For example, depending on CPU and memory utilization, you might want to scale out (increase the number of tasks) or scale in (decrease the number of tasks).

Although in the Associate Solutions Architect exam, you might've learned several AWS Auto Scaling strategies, Amazon ECS only supports two main types of automatic scaling:

- Target Tracking Scaling
  - Also called the Cruise Control scaling type, it is the recommended type by AWS. If your car is equipped with cruise control and you have a long trip in front of you, you can simply set a target speed and let the internal computer handle the rest as the road condition changes.
  - In this mode, Auto Scaling automatically creates and monitors the required CloudWatch alarms. ECS Scaling then calculates the adjustment by adding or removing tasks needed to get the monitored metric as close as possible to the target value.
    - Do not manually modify or delete the alarms
  - Three available metric types are available to track:
    - CPU utilization
    - Memory utilization
    - ALB request count per target
  - For each metric type, you can define a target, and Auto Scaling will try to keep your metric at or near the specified target by adding or removing tasks.

- Undeliberated and hurriedly scale-in and scale-out actions in response to changes in the metrics by any service can be harmful. You might end up over-provisioning or severely impacting the availability of a service. Hence, this type supports two cooldown periods:
  - Scale-in cooldown period: The amount of time the algorithm holds off on removing any more tasks after the last scale-in action (default 300 seconds)
  - Scale-out cooldown period: The amount of time the algorithm holds off on adding any more tasks after the last scale-out action (default 300 seconds)
- You also have an option to disable scaling altogether. If set, your environment will only grow automatically, and Auto Scaling will not tear down any tasks.
- Food for thought: What if you define more than one target tracking scaling policy for a particular ECS service?
  - Later in the book, we have some interesting scenarios on this!
- Step Scaling
  - You can create your own set of alarms in CloudWatch and
  - Only use it if the target tracking method and its automatically created metrics are not sufficient for your specific needs
  - In response to your alarms, you can define simple scaling actions such as:
    - If CPU utilization is greater than 85%, then add 10 more tasks
    - If CPU utilization is less than 35%, then remove 10 more tasks
    - If CPU utilization is greater than 85%, then increase the number of tasks by 20%. If defined by percentage as opposed to the number of tasks, you can also define the minimum increments of the number of tasks by which you are scaling in or out
      - Ideal for custom responses to certain threshold breaches
    - If CPU utilization is greater than 50%, then set the number of tasks to 7
      - You can define multiple actions with different thresholds

Also supports a cooldown period, as described in the previous section

The last scaling-related concept to cover is the Capacity Provider feature introduced in December 2019. Thus far, you might have noticed that building the underlying infrastructure, especially if your ECS environment involves EC2 instances, needs to be done before running the tasks or scaling them out. This is not a trivial undertaking in a large-scale environment and could shift your focus away from the application to the infrastructure.

It would be absolutely helpful to the application owners to offload the responsibility of monitoring and scaling the infrastructure to AWS and let them focus on the applications. The capacity providers are introduced to attach to a cluster and become part of its capacity-providing strategy to manage the underlying infrastructure.

- For EC2-based launch types; this is done by attaching the EC2 Auto Scaling Groups to capacity providers
  - The EC2 Auto Scaling Groups define several key pieces of information for the underlying infrastructure of the cluster, including:
    - The maximum, minimum, and desired number of instances
    - A launch template that defines the instance types and their network and operating system
- For Fargate-based launch types, this is done by placing the new tasks on a predefined infrastructure of Fargate or Fargate Spot.
  - Similar to the EC2 spot service, Fargate Spot provides deeply discounted capacity (up to 70%) only if AWS has such capacity to spare.
- For each cluster, the capacity providers become part of a capacity provider strategy and form how the underlying infrastructure is automatically scaled.
  - With more than one capacity provider assigned to the cluster's capacity strategy, you can define the two values of base and weight.
    - Base: The minimum number of tasks to use a particular capacity provider
    - Weight: How the tasks are split across multiple capacity providers. For example, for two providers with the weight of 1 and 10, you will have 10 times more tasks handled by the second provider as it scales the environment.

Hence, putting everything together, now you have two scaling settings. On the task level, you can create policies and control when and how new tasks are launched, and on the infrastructure front, you can use the EC2 Auto Scaling Groups in your Capacity providers to determine when the underlying infrastructure of container instances is expanded or shrunk.

AWS Kubernetes EKS

I hope you have a solid understanding of networking for containerized environments in the cloud by now. Essentially, what we covered in the ECS section had one core message; the containerized environment has very similar connectivity needs. Additionally, containerized environments at scale would need some sort of orchestration, which, again, as we described, is a system responsible for deploying and managing the containers.

As you saw, ECS was a fully managed proprietary service by AWS. It's fairly easy to launch and build highly scalable containerized applications. Furthermore, in the mini-scenarios, you will see how the containers talk to each other and get access to the outside world beyond their own task or host.

But there is a catch. The catch here is the word "proprietary." In the simplest terms, an ECS environment is and remains limited to the AWS deployments. Recently, AWS has made efforts to expand the use cases of ECS to on-premises by introducing services such as ECS Anywhere, but ECS remains largely an AWS service with its own orchestration in a black box.

On the other side of the ring is the ECS's heavyweight competitor, Elastic Kubernetes Service (EKS), powered by Kubernetes. In this service, instead of the ECS's proprietary orchestration system, the open-source Kubernetes (K8s) with thousands (if not millions) of successful and large-scale deployments worldwide takes care of automating deployment, scaling, and managing containers.

In the context of the ANS-C01 exam and AWS depth of documentation, quite predictably, the greater weight is given to ECS, and many EKS documents are only available on third party Web sites such as the official Kubernetes Web site (Kubernetes.io). However, certain topics, such as the AWS Load Balancer Controller for Kubernetes clusters, are specifically called out by the exam guide, and you are expected to know the network engineering side of them.

Consequently, the EKS part of this book targets the areas a network engineer would need to succeed at the ANS-C01 exam and those required to build a solid foundation to understand the much broader concept of Kubernetes.

All that aside, you might be surprised by the number of details exposed as part of EKS here and ECS masks.

But what is stopping me from building my own Kubernetes cluster on a set of EC2 instances?

Nothing. In contrast to what some beginners think, it is absolutely possible to design and run your own control plane using Kubernetes on EC2 instances the same way you would on your physical servers in a traditional data center. It won't be quick and easy for a network engineer, but 100% doable.

Amazon EKS offers a fully managed service, so the control plane, although made of Kubernetes, is managed and scaled as needed by AWS. As a result, if any of the control plane's components fail, AWS will detect the unhealthy situation and replace them. Additionally, as a managed version of Kubernetes, the patching and updating process is fully owned by AWS. The service inherently has complete integration with other key AWS services such as IAM, VPC networking, and Elastic Load Balancers.

We have already covered the basics of containerization, such as the definition of containers and orchestration systems. Let's take a look at a few extra terms as they pertain to the concept of Kubernetes:

Container pods, nodes, and clusters:

Similar to ECS and as the name implies, a node is a virtual or physical machine that hosts and runs a number of containers. In the world of Kubernetes, the containers run in a construct called a pod.

Containers can share pods if the application dictates such a requirement. If they do, they also share resources such as storage, memory, and network stack.

Eventually, a group of pods forms a cluster.

So, one container per pod or more? In real-world scenarios, your application architects should have very good reasons to collocate the containers in the same pod and start sharing resources such as memory and CPU. By the same token, as the environment scales up, new containers in new pods are launched. We don't overload the pods unless there are really compelling reasons to collocate containers and have them share resources in the same pod.

- These decisions, as they relate to how microservices are architected, can best be made by the application or enterprise architects, not the network engineering teams.

The high-level architecture of EKS

At a very high-level your EKS environment consists of two VPCs:

- A Kubernetes control plane VPC fully managed by Amazon, where the main brain of the system is located.

- A worker nodes VPC managed by you; where your containers and other AWS constructs are located.

What's in the managed Control Plane?

Just a reminder that the key difference between a self-managed Kubernetes cluster running on a bunch of EC2 instances or physical servers in a data center and what EKS has to offer is that the control plane of the Kubernetes cluster in EKS is built and fully managed by Amazon. That is where most of the heavy-lifting of a Kubernetes environment lies.

- The control plane of EKS is a single tenant, so it cannot be accessed by other accounts and is built inside an AWS-managed VPC that spans multiple Availability Zones to ensure the highest level of redundancy and availability.

- In each Availability Zone, the EKS service also places a Network Load Balancer with auto scaling groups and a NAT Gateway to ensure the components of the control plane scale as needed and would have one-way connectivity to the Internet.

But what are the main components of the EKS control plane that a network engineer needs to be aware of?

In distributed systems such as containerized environments orchestrated by Kubernetes, you need a system to manage the configuration and state data and, if needed, the certificates and tokens. Etcd is a highly available open-source distributed key-value store designed for such sensitive missions to hold critical information. In EKS, etcd is built and managed by Amazon as part of the control plane.

- In fact, its role in an EKS cluster is so crucial that by default AWS creates three etcd instances in three different Availability Zones

- Predictably, all the data stored here is encrypted by AWS KMS

The other vital part of the managed control plane in EKS is the doors of the control plane to the outside world or the Kubernetes API servers. EKS, by default, places them in two Availability Zones.

The API servers' functionality includes:

- Finding the best nodes for the new pods; also known as the process of scheduling.

Receiving and processing API calls not just from the users, as we will see below, but also from the other components of EKS.

All the components above are automatically deployed by EKS in private subnets. And since they are fully managed by Amazon, you don't need to worry about deploying, scaling, or managing the components.

Finally, EKS drops Amazon-managed ENIs (as private endpoints) in each Availability Zone of the customer-managed VPC to establish communication between the control plane and the worker nodes in your cluster that are running the containers.

This communication can be two-way:

- For the nodes to talk to the EKS control plane to register themselves. This allows them to receive "orders" from the control plane to run the applications in their containers.

- For the API server part of the EKS control plane to talk to the nodes and communicate the commands issued by the cluster admins, such as those entered via the kubectl command.

What is the buzz about the "kubectl" command?

One of the beauties of Kubernetes is that it allows you to use an API-based command line tool to communicate with its clusters' control plane and run almost any action against the clusters. In fact, I know someone who was attracted to Kubernetes only after poking around the tool! Kubectl supports a wide range of operations from deploying applications to viewing configurations and managing nodes – almost everything you can imagine within a Kubernetes environment. The overall operation of the tool on AWS (EKS) is very similar to how the tool is used in traditional Kubernetes environments. Having said that, working with the tool and mastering its details is beyond the scope of this book and the ANS-C01 exam.

How about managing EKS clusters and their specific details?

In addition to Kubectl, AWS provides another tool called eksctl exactly the purpose of managing the EKS clusters. The tool can be used for common EKS-related functions such as creating clusters, nodes, and automating certain actions. Again, working with the command line and details of Kubernetes clusters is not part of the scope of this book and the Advanced Networking exam.

I understood the control plane, but what goes on the worker nodes?

The architecture of the worker nodes in EKS is somewhat different from that of native Kubernetes, say on Linux clusters, but as far as a network engineer is concerned, once a new node joins the cluster by its admin and boots up, a component of Kubernetes called Kubelet comes to life on the node. It works with another component called Container Runtime to set up the containers on the node. The worker node also immediately reaches out to the API server in the Amazon-managed VPC to register itself and report its available CPU, memory, and storage.

In AWS EKS, this communication channel can be done either through the private endpoint (ENI) described earlier or via the public IP address of the API server, depending on the cluster's settings.

Either way, the constant communication between the nodes and the control plane goes on during the entire life of the node. That is how the node keeps the control plane appraised of its situation, and that is how the control plane knows exactly where it can place the next workload without needing you to tell Kubernetes where the capacity exists.

So, once everything is deployed, you have a number of worker nodes (say EC2) running our pods with the containers inside. This is all good in terms of high-level architectures.

Let's turn the tables for a second and imagine you are asked to come up with an idea to make sure the pods/containers could talk to each other, the rest of the environment, and the Internet; how would you plan that?

Think about it for a second.

The ideal case would have the ability to perform native VPC networking and treat each one of the pods just like an EC2 instance and its own fully routable IP address. This would have several key benefits, including simple routing and having access to all the observability tools in AWS, such as VPC FlowLogs.

And that is how exactly it is implemented in AWS through an open-source project:

- Amazon EKS supports native VPC networking using the Amazon open-source VPC Container Network Interface (CNI) plugin for Kubernetes.
    - This project's details are available on GitHub.
- The Amazon CNI plugin designed for Kubernetes assigns a private IPv4 or IPv6 address from the VPC to each pod.
    - The IP address comes from the secondary IP addresses assigned to the elastic network interfaces of each instance

What the last statement means is simple: Each Amazon EC2 instance type supports a limited number of ENIs, and each ENI, in addition to its primary IP address, can have a certain number of secondary IP addresses.

- So as the pods are scheduled (and launched), the secondary IP addresses of the ENAs of the node are grabbed and assigned to them.
    - Needless to say, the secondary IP addresses of the ENAs are fully routable within the VPC. Hence, this trick makes it possible to have smooth and end-to-end communication between the pods and the other resources in the same VPC
- Although this trick resolves the seamless connectivity issue for the pods, it introduces another issue.
    - The number of ENAs per instance and the number of IP addresses per ENA are both finite (and well documented in EC2 documents). Hence, there is always a

theoretical limit on the number of pods you can launch on a given EC2 worker node.

- For example, while a t1.micro can only run 4 pods, in theory, you can have up to 737 pods on a r6g.16xlarge. Just to reiterate, when the AWS CNI is in use, these pods will have the secondary IP addresses of the ENIs and can communicate with all the other resources, as though they are regular EC2 nodes sittings in the same VPC. This sentence is worth repeating...

- In case you are curious, the CNI plugin itself also runs in a pod!

Within VPC and inter-VPC traffic flows in EKS

Up to this point, you have learned that with Amazon CNI, each pod receives an IP address from the secondary ENI of the node. This IP address is fully routable, and this architecture hugely simplifies the overall connectivity between the pods *within the same VPC*. Also, you might have noticed that several times in the previous chapters I highlighted the fact that this is all within the same VPC. There is a good reason for that:

- By default, Amazon EKS performs Source Network Address Translation (SNAT) for the IPv4 pod traffic bound for destinations outside the VPC.

  - Hence within the same VPC, the pods freely use their own IP addresses to communicate, but to get out of the VPC, EKS instructs the hosting worker node to perform SNAT.

  - The pod traffic is source NAT'ed to the primary IP address of the primary ENI of the worker node.

    - Hence, outside the VPC, the pod's traffic is seen as it's generated by the hosting EC2 node itself.

    - This is ideal when the EC2 node has a public IP address

  - If your nodes are located in private subnets, you have the option to use the kubectl command as shown below to disable this behavior and move the responsibility of source NATing the traffic to an external NAT construct such as the AWS NAT Gateway.

    - Kubectl set env daemonset -n kube-system aws-node AWS_VPC_K8S_ CNI_EXTERNALSNAT=true

    - By setting the EXTERNALSNAT flag to TRUE, you request EKS to cease any in-node SNAT, as your external NAT construct will later take care of the operation.

    - As pointed out many times in this book, the AWS NAT Gateway is not the most economical cloud construct and could easily drive your consumption bills up if deployed recklessly.

Increasing pod density beyond adding ENAs

An effective IP addressing scalability technique in EKS was introduced in the summer of 2021 for the pods running on EC2 Nitro instances. In those cases, instead of an individual IPv4 address, you can assign a /28 prefix to the ENI, replacing the previously single address with a range of 16 addresses available to the interface.

For example, if an instance had 4 ENIs and you enabled Custom Networking, eliminating the primary ENI from pod placement as mandated by Custom Networking would leave you with 3 ENIs. Previously you were limited by the number of unique IP addresses you could assign to those ENIs; say 14 per ENIs, so 42 pods. After enabling the prefix assignment now, you can have 16 addresses in place of each individual IP address that you could have assigned to each ENI. Hence, if your ENI #1, ENI #2, and ENI #3, could carry 15 (effectively 14) IP addresses each, now they could have 14x16 IP addresses each for pod addressing. That is a much larger pool of addresses to use to schedule pods.

Although on the surface this sounds really exciting, as usual, it comes with catches. AWS has developed a script called *max-pod-calculator.sh* that could do the math for you taking into account all the other scalability concerns and recommendations. The final number would be lower than what your math would yield but still much higher than if you went with individual IP addresses for each ENI.

You can use the following command to enable prefix assignment mode:

```
kubectl set env daemonset aws-node -n kube-system ENABLE_PREFIX_DELEGA-
TION=true
```

EKS and pod security

One of the key takeaways up to this point is that although EKS has a Kubernetes-based service, some certain features and architectures are unique to cloud networking, specifically AWS. One of them is pod security and implementing fine-grained security groups for each pod.

- Prior to the product updates in September 2020, the application architects had to partner with security and network engineers to implement Kubernetes affinity and taint properties to attract and repel pods to nodes. This would help get by node-level security groups.
  - Each node had certain inbound and outbound policies, and the architects would make sure pods would land on the right nodes
  - This model was complex and would not scale well.
- Now it's possible to define security groups at the pod level. Although this feature comes with several key considerations:
  - Available to both EC2-based and Fargate implementations
  - Currently unavailable to Microsoft Windows nodes

- Effectively disables the SNAT feature discussed earlier. So, to access the Internet, you must implement your own external source NAT solution.

- For any IPv6 use case, check the latest documents to ensure your idea/architecture is supported. This is an ever-changing space.

CHAPTER 19

Billing

- Site-to-site IPSec VPN
  - Has the two billing components of connection per hour and outbound data transfer (out of AWS)
- Direct Connect
  - Has the two billing components of port per hour and outbound data transfer (out of AWS)
  - Since the Direct Connect link between AWS and the customer is a private link, the data transfer costs are much lower than those of IPSec tunnels over the public Internet, although in both cases, the customer is only charged for the outbound traffic.
- Internet Gateway
  - No cost for the construct itself, however; you will be charged for outbound data transfer.
- NAT Gateway
  - Has three billing components of hourly rates for the gateway, data processing charges for each gigabyte that passes through the gateway, and the data transfer charges when the gateway sends traffic out to the Internet.
    - This warrants careful design considerations to ensure the architecture indeed requires a NAT Gateway. For instance, in some scenarios, you might be able to replace NAT Gateways with Internet Gateways hardened through NCALs or Security Groups. In some other scenarios where the AWS public services such as S3 are accessed through a NAT Gateway, the gateways can be replaced with VPC endpoints that do not have this complex charging model. This is commonly seen as an opportunity in legacy architectures if you as an architect are trying to reduce your OPEX.

- Gateway VPC endpoints (to access AWS public services such as S3 and Glacier)
  - They are free of hourly or data transfer charges. That is why to improve your architecture, you might be able to replace your NAT Gateways with Gateway VPC endpoints.
- PrivateLink (Interface endpoints and Gateway Load Balancer endpoints)
  - Has the two billing components of endpoint per hour and data processing rates for each gigabyte traversed through the endpoint.
- Elastic Load Balancers
  - In addition to the regular hourly fees, AWS added a second component to the ELB charges by using the Load Balancer Capacity Units (LCU), Network Load Balancer Capacity Units (NLCU), Gateway Load Balancer Unit (GLBU) parameters for Application, Network, and Gateway Load Balancers respectively.
    - In Application Load Balancers, four dimensions are monitored and the customer is only charged for the one that stands out (has the highest value):
      - New Connections (per second)
      - Active Connections (per minute)
      - Bandwidth (Mbps)
      - Rule evaluations (per second)
    - In Network Load Balancers, three dimensions are monitored and the customer is only charged for the one that stands out:
      - New Connections (per second)
      - Active Connections (per minute)
      - Bandwidth (Mbps)
    - In Gateway Load Balancers, three dimensions are monitored and the customer is charged for the one that stands out:
      - New Connections (per second)
      - Active Connections (per minute)
      - Number of processed bytes (GB)
    - Also, since Gateway Load Balancers work with their own endpoints (built based on PrivateLink) in addition to the GLBU value calculated above, the customer is charged for the hourly and GB data transfer rates of the endpoints.
  - With Classic Load Balancers, the customer is simply billed for hourly usage and bandwidth.

- Route 53
  - AWS charges the customers on a per-million-query basis (name resolution request).
    - Latency-based routing is more expensive than standard routing, and geo location and proximity-based routings are more expensive than both
    - AWS doesn't charge the customers for Alias A records targeting resources such as ELB, S3 website buckets, and CloudFront distributions.
  - When you register a public domain with AWS or transfer an existing domain to AWS, you pay an annual fee.
  - AWS also charges the customers for each Hosted Zone on a monthly basis.
    - Do not leave unused Hosted Zones in your Route 53 settings.
  - AWS charges the customers for health checks configured for AWS and non-AWS endpoints.
    - The health checks for non-AWS resources are more expensive.
  - AWS charges the customers for using the Route 53 resolver DNS firewall. The billing process will be based on the number of domains used by the rule groups and the number of queries made from within the VPC with firewall group association.
- Data transfers
  - In addition to the costs covered above, AWS may also charge the customer for data transfer in each direction.
    - Same region – Same Availability Zone
      - Private IP addressing: No charge for data transfers
      - Public and Elastic IP addressing: The customer is charged for the data transfers.
    - Same region – Different Availability Zones
      - The customer is charged for data transfers regardless of the IP addressing.
      - This is something to watch closely if you are designing multi-AZ solutions
    - Different regions
      - The customer is charged for data transfers regardless of the IP addressing.
- VPC peering
  - The customer is always charged for data transfers in each direction. In 2021, AWS stopped charging customers for data transfers over VPC peering within one AZ.

You still need to be mindful of data transfer charges in inter-region architectures involving VPC peering sessions.

- Elastic IP addressing

  - The customer is not charged for the first Elastic IP address on the EC2 instance. However, adding more Elastic IP addresses will be charged.

  - Parking an Elastic IP address unused and not attaching it to an instance also results in charges.

- CloudFront

  - Amazon offers a free tier that includes 2,000,000 requests per month and 50 GB of data transfer credit across all the customer's edge locations.

  - The customer can only invalidate up to 1000 paths for free per month.

  - The customer will be charged if CloudFront real-time logs are requested.

  - The customer will not be charged for any data transfer from the S3 and ALB if designated as the Origin servers to the CloudFront edge locations. Otherwise, there will be a fee.

  - Lambda@Edge functions on CloudFront have two fee components. The customer is charged for the number of requests and resources (memory and duration spent to execute the code each time).

- Transit Gateway

  - They have two or potentially three fee components.

    - The customer will be charged for the number of hours that the gateway is attached to the VPC as well as the data processing on a per GB basis.

    - The customer will also be charged as usual for data transfer if the traffic, for example, is inter-region.

- AWS Network Firewall

  - They have two fee components

    - The customer will be charged for the number of hours that the Firewall endpoint exists.

    - The customer will also be charged for the traffic processed by the firewall on a per GB basis.

      - Since the Network Firewall relies on the NAT gateways for address translation, if your architecture has both, the hourly and data processing charges of the AWS NAT gateways are waived if each has a corresponding firewall. You will not be double-charged.

CHAPTER 20

Automation

AWS uses CloudFormation as the cornerstone of its Infrastructure as a Code (IaaC) approach. The service is used to automate the deployment of various types of resources in the cloud. This is particularly helpful if the customer needs to follow specific procedures and templates to create such resources. Compared to manual deployments, this process can be done more quickly and is less prone to human mistakes, although there are still manual steps involved.

CloudFormation uses text file templates created in Yet Another Markup Language (YAML) or JavaScript Object Notation (JSON) formats to clearly and accurately define all the resources and their properties that the customer needs to have in their AWS stack.

§ **Exam Tip:** *Learning YAML is always a good idea, especially for less experienced engineers. It gives you a great foundation not just in cloud automation (the exam and production) but also in the area of systems engineering, especially if you are looking to take the RHCE exam for Linux.*

While JSON appears to have a stricter structure with all the commas and brackets, with YMAL, too, you need to follow detailed indentation, or the template will fail. In the real world, eventually, it comes down to the organization's standards to choose YAML or JSON. Such decisions can also be made based on what has been done in the past and how. For instance, if an organization has extensive coding experience with Ansible and YAML to automate their Linux servers or data center routing and switching solutions, they would probably prefer to keep the number of standards and languages as low as possible.

To use CloudFormation in an IaaC environment at a very high level, the customer needs to take two steps:

- Create the template in YAML or JSON format. The template defines all the resources required for the deployment, including VPC details, EC2 instances, databases, Security Groups, NACLs, and NAT Gateways or Internet Gateways. The code also defines the specific properties of each resource, such as the CidrBlock, where VPC is the resource with the resource type of AWS::EC2::VPC.

- Create the stack using the AWS CloudFormation Console by feeding the template.

When creating AWS resources or defining their properties, the order of actions is critical. For example, although it might sound obvious in detailed template coding, you cannot attach an Internet Gateway to a VPC unless both the VPC and the Gateway have already been created. Similarly, you cannot create a route table with the 0.0.0.0/0 route for the Gateway until the attachment is created.

To implement dependencies when creating resources, the templates support an attribute called DependsOn that allows you to specify the order of actions to create resources in a template. Furthermore, to implement dependencies when defining properties of resources, the templates support the target property of !Ref that allows you to determine whether the property is dependent on the creation of certain other resources. For example, consider the following code:

```
MyIGW:
    Type: AWS::EC2::InternetGateway
    DependsOn: MyVPC
AttachGateway:
    Type: AWS::EC2::VPCGatewayAttachment
    Properties:
    VpcId: !Ref MyVPC
    InternetGatewayId: !Ref MyIGW
```

Here a resource called MyIGW is created after another resource called MyVPC. The new resource has the two properties of VpcId and InternetGatewayId that. Both are dependent on the two main resources.

§*Exam Tip:* *As you see above (and I have more scenarios in the book), in any form of automation and scripting, the order of actions matters a lot; you cannot install the roof before the walls are built.*

The majority of AWS resources and their details can be configured using CloudFormation. Generally speaking, all you need to do to create and configure your AWS stack is to find the right resource type for the resource and its child properties.

Some customers still need to configure non-AWS resources and need to keep everything under one umbrella, in this case, CloudFormation. For instance, a customer might want to configure Linux servers or Cisco virtual routers in their VPC or even on-premises. By default, there are no typical resource types for such external non-AWS resources. AWS has set aside a special resource type called AWS::CloudFormation::CustomResource (or Custom::String) to define such resources. Using this special resource type, the network operator can either execute a Lambda function (such as Python codes to configure the routers or servers) or simply send a notification to an SNS topic.

CloudFormation service additionally has a manual workflow where the customer can review, approve, maybe test, and then deploy the code. The service works well in partnership with another AWS service called CodePipeline. By leveraging both, the customer can minimize the risk of human mistakes and implement the DevOps concept of Continuous Delivery. CodePipeline creates a workflow that describes two or more stages that a software change goes through. It also defines the actions taken on it from the beginning until the point of releasing to production.

PART 2

ANS-C01
MOCK EXAM

CHAPTER 21

ANS-C01 MOCK EXAM 1

1. You are architecting an SD-WAN in the cloud solution for a large enterprise with 750 global offices. Part of the design requires you to deploy two SD-WAN appliances in the eu-west-1 region to connect the AWS footprint in the UK region to the rest of the enterprise. Which of the following statements is accurate about the correct architecture? (Choose TWO)

   ✓A. The SD-WAN appliances need to be placed in a dedicated VPC
   B. The SD-WAN appliances need to be placed in the same VPC as the other virtual appliances, such as firewalls
   C. Both SD-WAN appliances need to be placed in the same subnet
   ✓D. Each SD-WAN appliance needs to be placed in a separate subnet

2. As a Solutions Architect, you are assisting a small customer in extending their SD-WAN solution to the cloud. Currently, due to licensing concerns, they are planning on keeping their SD-WAN appliances in their physical data center in Virginia, U.S.A. Their goal is to add their AWS footprint in the us-east-1 region to their global WAN. The customer has 2 site-to-site IPSec VPN tunnels to their Transit Gateway in us-east-1 and can achieve up to 2.5Gbps throughput by leveraging ECMP over the VPN tunnels. Which one of the following options would be your main concern when architecting the solution for the customer?

   ✓A. Lack of Direct Connect of any capacity
   B. Lack of Direct Connect of at least 10Gbps
   C. Lack of enough number of tunnels. The customer would need at least 4 in the ECMP bundle. All to the same Transit Gateway.
   D. Lack of enough number of tunnels. The customer would need at least 4 in the ECMP bundle. Two on separate Transit Gateways.

3. You are working for a cloud integrator and have been involved in a major WAN migration project for an Australia-based customer. The customer's network engineering team is currently deploying a Cisco SD-WAN appliance in their physical data center.

This device is to have a GRE tunnel over a Connect attachment via a Direct Connect transport link to their only Transit Gateway located in the ap-southeast-2 region. You receive a call from a network engineer who needs help configuring the GRE tunnel on the Cisco device. He is not sure what IP address to use for the destination of the tunnel. Which of the following options presents the best answer to his question?

A. It would be the WAN IP address of the Cisco vEdge device
B. It would be one of the IP addresses configured on their Transit Gateway as its CIDR block
C. It would be the IP address assigned to the Direct Connect attachment of the Transit Gateway
D. The interface needs to be configured as "ip unnumbered"

4. You are architecting an AWS edge solution for an IoT customer with millions of devices sold in 58 countries. The units are designed to talk UDP over port 9977 back to a number of servers they will set up in the us-east-1 and eu-central-1 region. The devices have only 256K of memory and are extremely sensitive to latency or jitter. The solution must offer high availability. Which of the following options best meets this customer's requirements?

A. Use CloudFront with signed URLs
B. Use CloudFront and make all the objects cacheable at the edge
C. Use Standard Global Accelerators
D. Use Custom Global Accelerators

5. As a freelance chief cloud architect, you are contacted by an AWS customer. They have installed over 51,000 IoT devices at partner Gas Stations across Europe for years and managed them centrally out of their data center in Berlin, Germany. All the units have two identical hardcoded server IP addresses that cannot be changed unless through a local firmware upgrade. Now they are considering getting out of their physical data centers and moving to the cloud. You are evaluating AWS Global Accelerator as the most viable option. Which of the following options, if insisted on, could make the architecture fail?

A. To maintain the same hardcoded server IP addresses on the IoT devices
B. To expand the regions from one to two by adding London as a second region
C. To move the region from Germany to England, which will impact the origin of the public IP addresses owned by the company
D. To advertise the same two IP addresses to AWS via Direct Connect

6. As a chief architect, you get pulled into a design discussion around a customer migration case to AWS. The customer currently has 40 Web servers offering a popular application to users in Europe. They have successfully migrated 10 of them from behind an on-premises Citrix NetScaler load balancer to AWS EC2 instances, while the rest are still in their physical data center in Italy. You have completed the deployment of the backend database servers, so the EC2-based Web servers have access to the same data as the

Web servers in the data center. The design goal is to provide the application to the users in the next 6 months while the migration project is being completed seamlessly with no compromise in performance. Choose the most viable architecture that offers deterministic latency.

A. Create an ALB and make the 10 EC2 instances its targets. Leverage Route53 and Geoproximity information to spread the load between AWS and the data center.

B. Create an NLB and use the IP addresses of the servers to make all the 40 servers its targets. Create a Global Accelerator and define the ALB as an endpoint. Shut down the NetScaler.

C. Create an ALB and use the IP addresses of the servers to make all the 40 servers its targets. Create a Global Accelerator and define the ALB as an endpoint. Shut down the NetScaler.

Key word

7. As a cloud technical support engineer, you receive a case where a Global Accelerator (Standard mode) customer is complaining about traffic not reaching their backend EC2 servers. They have deployed 5 servers running an ICMP-based experimental academic tool that runs out of the us-east-2 region. The servers are behind an Application Load Balancer and should be reachable via the hostname of app01.xyz.com . The app01 is an alias record created in Route53 for the original name suggested by AWS. The IT team deemed the original name too long and hard to memorize. Which of the following options describes the potential root cause?

A. The AWS Global Load Balancer does not support ICMP-based endpoints
B. The name should be created using CNAME records and not alias records
C. The ALB load balancers cannot be deployed for ICMP traffic
D. The IT team needs to enable stickiness for the target group of the 5 servers

8. You are being consulted by a team of enterprise architects who are working on an idea to offer an external version of their highly successful internal tool to the general public. In order to accomplish the goal, they are planning on deploying 10 servers on EC2 instances evenly spread between us-west-1 and us-east-1 regions. It's essential for the application and the homegrown security tools to capture the original IP addresses of the visiting clients at the two Elastic Load Balancers in both regions. Which of the following options describes a viable solution to complete the high-level design?

A. The company can deploy one Network Load Balancers natively in each region to front their servers
B. The company can deploy one Application Load Balancers natively in each region to front their servers
C. The company can deploy one Classic Load Balancers natively in each region to front their servers
D. All the three types of CLB, NLB, and ALB can natively preserve the source IP address

9. A cloud engineer enables DNSSEC for their public domain on Route 53. Which of the following options describes the benefits of the service?

    A. Protection against DoS and certain DDoS attacks
    B. Data integrity for DNS responses
    C. Data origin authentication and data integrity for DNS responses
    D. All the above

10. An RFP for a customer under FedRAMP is calling for DNSSEC support. Which of the following statements is accurate about the service?

    A. It protects DNS messages by encrypting them
    B. The private key part of ZSK is used to sign the A records
    C. The maintenance of the Zone Signing Key (ZSK) is the customer's responsibility
    D. The private and public key parts of the ZSK are placed in DNSKEY records

11. A junior cloud engineer is preparing for a promotion interview with a chief architect. She is currently studying the DNS delegation process and how it works in the cloud. She has fully grasped the concept of the NS records but is not entirely sure how the trust model works when DNSSEC is enabled. Which of the following options is NOT accurate about the DS record in this context?

    A. The DS (delegation signer) is used in DNSSEC to transfer trust from a parent zone to a child zone
    B. The DS record contains the hashed DNSKEY record
    C. The DS record contains the public KSK
    D. The DS record is placed in the child zone

12. As a presales Enterprise Cloud Architect (ECA), you are talking to a large bank headquartered in Germany. They are currently evaluating the new Route 53 DNS query logging feature (RQL). The feature itself looks appealing to them, but they are not sure about where they will be sending and storing the logs. Which of the following statements would be accurate and can be added to the workshop you are preparing for them? (CHOOSE THREE)

    A. Use S3 if you are trying to simply check the box of logging the queries as part of an EU compliance requirement
    B. Use CloudWatch Logs to leverage the same familiar environment as many other logs to search and store
    C. Use CloudWatch Events (EventBridge) to leverage a high-capacity bus and storage
    D. Use Kinesis Firehose to receive and process in real time; also to integrate with their Splunk infrastructure.

13. The SRE team of a large enterprise would like to monitor the status of the NAT Gateways that the cloud implementation team has deployed in 25 VPCs of their AWS footprint. Recently the developers have installed two applications known for making tens of thousands of outbound connections to the Internet at a very high rate per second. The actual climbing rate is not documented. More than anything else, they are interested

in the total number of active connections and failed attempts on each NAT Gateway. Which of the following tools would offer the best view into the counters?

A. CloudWatch metrics
B. Kinesis Firehose
C. CloudWatch Logs
D. Send the logs straight to S3 but analyze using Athena and its standard SQL queries

14. As part of cost analysis practice, the SRE team of a large enterprise would like to monitor the top talkers of the NAT Gateways that the cloud implementation team has deployed in 5 VPCs of their AWS footprint. The company has recently gone through a merger and a few less-known applications have been deployed to their VPCs. Which of the following two tools would offer the best choices to have access to such logs and look up entries as needed? (CHOOSE TWO) – *Hint: Try not to mix up with the previous question!*

A. CloudWatch metrics
B. Kinesis Firehose
C. CloudWatch Logs
D. S3 and Athena as it supports standard SQL queries

15. Before moving to the cloud, a cloud design engineer is testing exterior routing between two private Autonomous Systems (AS) called EU-LAB-01 (AS#65515) and EU-LAB-02 (AS#65516) in a lab environment. There are two fiber connections between a pair of routers in each AS, and there is an active iBGP session between the two BGP speakers in each AS. Which of the following options can potentially be a correct method to influence traffic leaving EU-LAB-01 to EU-LAB-02 to prefer the path via its primary router R1 over its secondary router called R2?

A. Increase Local Preference by 500 for all the traffic received from EU-LAB-02 via R1.
B. Increase Local Preference by 500 for all the routes received from EU-LAB-02 via R1.
C. Decrease Local Preference by 50 for all the traffic received from EU-LAB-02 via R1.
D. Decrease Local Preference by 50 for all the routes received from EU-LAB-02 via R1.

16. A cloud engineer is examining various BGP features and attributes between two private Autonomous Systems (AS) called EU-LAB-01 (65520) and EU-LAB-02 (65522) in a lab environment prior to moving anything to the cloud. There are two fiber connections between a pair of routers in each AS, and there is an active iBGP session between the two BGP speakers in each AS. Which of the following two options can potentially show the correct methods to influence traffic leaving EU-LAB-01 to EU-LAB-02 to prefer the path via its primary router R1 over its secondary router called R2? (Choose TWO)

A. Decrease Local Preference by 50 for all the routes received from EU-LAB-02 via R2.

B. Increase Local Preference by 500 for all the routes received from EU-LAB-02 via R1.

C. Increase the AS_PATH for the AS 65520 routes leaving this AS by prepending 4 instances of the AS number on R1.

D. Increase the AS_PATH for the AS 65520 routes leaving this AS by prepending 3 instances of the AS number on R2.

17. As part of a design retrofit project, you are optimizing a two-tier AWS architecture built a few years ago. The Web frontend is used to receive thousands of request messages per second. The messages are forwarded to the backend servers, where they are processed in the order they arrive. Over time the number of messages increased from a few messages to thousands of messages per second. You are planning on using SQS (FIFO) to decouple the two tiers for better scalability and prepare them for an imminent migration to a more scalable design. Which of the following design options provide an acceptable solution to access Amazon SQS from the VPC while minimize any security risks?

A. Assign public IP addresses to the components that need to access SQS.
B. Create a NAT Gateway for the VPC.
C. Create an AWS PrivateLink for SQS in the VPC.
D. No action is required. SQS will be available via private IP address from within the VPC.

18. You are paged into an AWS VPN troubleshooting case where the customer's IPSec tunnel won't establish. The initial conversation with the customer reveals that they have placed the VPN headend behind a Next Gen Firewall, which is also performing NAT. Which of the following options indicates a possible solution to the customer's problem?

A. Permit IKE UDP 500. Permit ESP IP Protocol 50.
B. Permit IKE UDP 500. Permit ESP IP Protocol 50. Permit AH IP Protocol 51.
C. Configure NAT-T on the VPN headend. At least permit UDP 4500.
D. Configure NAT-T on the Next Gen Firewall. At least permit UDP 4500.

19. After a major outage caused by a SYN flood attack against a fleet of on-prem servers of a banking company, their Cloud Security team is now investigating tools and methods to thwart similar attacks against the AWS deployments in the future. Which of the following tools or methods can provide such a level of protection on AWS at no extra cost?

A. AWS Shield Standard
B. AWS Shield Advanced
C. AWS Inspector
D. AWS GuardDuty

20. After a sophisticated Application Layer Distributed Denial of Service (DDoS) attack against a group of Apache Web servers on AWS, the security team of a state lottery organization is evaluating AWS Shield Advanced and WAF in the us-west-2 region to

protect their infrastructure; especially twice a week when the results come out. Which of the following statements is NOT accurate about these tools and must NOT be presented to regularity auditors?

A. They can be used to foil both Denial of Service Attacks (DoS) and Distributed Denial of Service (DDoS) attacks
B. Conditions can be defined based on the country of origin of the offending traffic using Web ACLs
C. They can drop traffic if a script that is likely to be malicious is detected
D. To protect your application against the most recent threads (documented CVEs) AWS GuardDuty needs to be added to the list of tools.

21. While analyzing your Web farm's access logs, you come across a large number of URLs attempted against your Web servers in your main VPC. They contain keywords similar to those of SQL queries, such as the following:

http://aussiecert.com/wordpress/wp-content/intranet/endpoint.php?user=-1+union+select+1,2,3 ,4,5,6,7,8,9,(SELECT+user_password+FROM+users+WHERE+ID=1)

Which of the following tools can provide some protection to your Web servers even if they are unpatched and vulnerable to such malicious attempts?

A. AWS WAF
B. VPC NACLs
C. EC2 Security Groups
D. AWS Shield Standard

22. As a chief architect, you need to approve a design proposal. After a successful brute force attack against the SSH service on one of the Linux servers of a small food chain in AWS, a network engineer is trying to implement a solution as soon as possible to get notified if any of his 25 Linux servers in a VPC rejects more than 10 SSH login attempts in 5 minutes. Choose the THREE actions that the engineer needs to take to complete the task. (Choose THREE)

A. Install the CloudWatch Logs agent on the EC2 instances running the Linux servers.
B. Choose one of the AMI Linux servers shipped with the CloudWatch agent.
C. Ensure that each server sends its SSH logs to a log stream tagged with its instance ID, and the log streams are aggregated into group logs.
D. Ensure that each subnet of Linux servers sends its SSH logs to a log stream tagged with its subnet ID. The log streams are aggregated into group logs for the entire VPC.
E. In CloudWatch, create metric filters for each log group and if certain keywords related to the failed SSH attempt are found more than 10 times within 5 minutes, trigger a CloudWatch alarm.
F. In CloudWatch, create metric filters for each log group and if certain keywords related to the failed SSH attempt are found more than 10 times within 5 minutes, create a new SNS topic. Subscribe the administrator's account to the topic.

23. A cloud engineer is reviewing the documents handed off to them by a Professional Services (PS) firm that has designed their new cloud environment. Which of the following statements is correct about the load balancer defined below?

Name: LB-Prod02
Scheme : internet-facing
Listeners: Port:80
Protocol: HTTP
IP address type: ipv4

Targets: Instances:
i-04c9330000000001 (www12):80
i-04c9330000000001 (www12):8080
i-04c9330000000001 (www12):8081
i-04c9330000000001 (www12):8082

   A. LB-Prod02 can be an Application Load Balancer. It is listening for HTTP sessions and forwarding traffic to multiple ports on the same AWS instance, in this case, www12.
   B. LB-Prod02 can be a Network Load Balancer. It is listening on TCP 80 and forwarding traffic to multiple ports on the same on-prem server, in this case, www12.
   C. LB-Prod02 can only be a Classic Load Balancer. It is listening on TCP 80 and forwarding traffic to multiple ports on an AWS instance, in this case, www12.
   D. There is a mistake in the configuration developed by the PS firm. AWS Elastic and 3rd party load balancers cannot forward traffic to multiple ports on the exact same server.

24. A senior architect is reviewing a cloud-based Web application that needs to guarantee end-to-end encryption for user data to pass regulatory audits. Below is the configuration review of the Application Load Balancer prepared by the team. Which of the following statements is correct about this configuration file?

Load balancer

Name   LB-Prod-East-Wing-134

Scheme: internet-facing

Listeners:

Port:443 - Protocol:HTTPS

IP address type   ipv4

VPC   vpc-06a111111110 (VPC-HIPAA)

Subnets

subnet-07cdcd23213a4 (Sub-003), subnet-07cdcd23213d3 (Sub-002)

Routing

Target group   New target group

Target group name   tg1010

Port   443

Target type   instance

Protocol HTTPS

Health check protocol   HTTP

Path   /

Health check port   traffic port

Healthy threshold   5

Unhealthy threshold   2

Timeout 5

Interval 30

Success codes   200

Targets

Instancesi-04c222222e3e1 (Forth):4433

A. The ALB configuration won't pass the audit as the health checks between the users, and the EC2 instance are not encrypted.
B. The ALB configuration won't pass the audit because the listener, by default, will also listen to TCP 80 (HTTP), and it is explicitly disabled for the path /.
C. The ALB configuration will pass the audit as long as the server port on the instance is changed to 443, the default port for HTTPS.
D. The ALB configuration will pass the audit as it stands now without any changes.

25. To further troubleshoot an application beyond the Flow Logs you are planning to use Traffic Mirroring. The load will be limited to one client talking to one server at 0.75Mbps. Which of the following options better describes your findings at the destination where you are running TCPdump?

A. You will receive every packet fully regardless of its size. Although the packets will have the VXLAN header.
B. You will receive every packet fully regardless of its size. The packets will not have the VXLAN header as it will be stripped by the destination ENI.
C. AWS will automatically truncate some packets depending on the MTU. The packets will have the VXLAN header.
D. You will have the option to truncate some packets depending on the MTU. The packets will have the VXLAN header.

26. As a Cloud Solutions Architect, you are preparing a Proof of Concept (PoC) for a customer to try Traffic Mirroring. The tests will be done in two different stages in terms of the load and scale, where stage 1 will cover lower B/s traffic, and stage 2 will cover much larger amounts of Web traffic to be redirected to the destination. Which of the following statements is accurate about the two stages of the PoC?

   A. For stage 1 the customer can use an ENI on an EC2 instance to receive the traffic, while stage 2 might require an ALB
   B. For stage 1 the customer can use an ENI on an EC2 instance to receive the traffic, while stage 2 might require an NLB with TCP listeners
   C. For stage 1 the customer can use an ENI on an EC2 instance to receive the traffic, while stage 2 might require an NLB with UDP listeners
   D. All the options presented here could be valid depending on the details not presented in the scenario

27. Since the data center in which you have a large cage is not an AWS Direct Connect location, you are evaluating various options to get to one of the DX locations across the city. Which of the following types of connectivity options can connect your facilities to the DX location?

   A. VPLS
   B. EoMPLS
   C. Q-in-Q
   D. All of the above

28. A regional retailer in Europe currently has a special VPC running core services required by the other VPCs, including monitoring, security, Active Directory, and logging. The core services VPC is connected to the data center using a 10G Direct Connect link for management purposes. Recently they completed the migration of their database servers from their physical data centers to the databases VPC. As a senior architect, you need to ensure the databases are available not just to the systems in the core services VPC but also to the on-prem front-end systems, while the migration teams are moving them to the cloud. Which of the following solutions provides an efficient and cost-effective architecture?

   A. Add a 1G Direct Connect link to the architecture. Create a private VIF to connect the database's VPC to the data center.
   B. Use the existing Direct Connect link and run an IPSec tunnel from the data center to the Virtual Gateway of the databases VPC.
   C. Use the existing Direct Connect link and create separate private VIFs for the databases VPC
   D. You can safely use the current architecture to communicate with the database servers in every VPC as long as two-way name resolution, either using proxies or inbound/outbound resolvers, is in place.

29. To provide a dedicated connection with lower data transfer rates to your VPCs, you just ordered a 10G Direct Connect. Which of the following statements is NOT accurate about the process of creating a private Virtual Interface?

    A. The customer is given the option of choosing the Gateway type between a Virtual Private Gateway and Direct Connect Gateway
    B. The customer is given the option of choosing "Another AWS account," which will also become responsible for the billing of the VIF separate from the owner of the Direct Connect link
    C. The customer is given the option of choosing the VLAN ID
    D. The customer is given the option of choosing the MD5 password value to authenticate the BGP session

30. You recently added a pair of AWS NAT Gateway to your arhcitecture. One of your SRE team members raises cncerns about monitoring those gateways. She believes their capacity can easily be maxed out with the new applications they are deploying and users might increase the bills unreasonably by pushing too much traffic through them. Which of the following statements are accurate about monitoring and accounting for AWS NAT Gateways?(Choose TWO)

    A. You could use CloudWatch to monitor key metric for the NAT Gateways such as the total number of active connections, attempts, transferred bytes, and packets
    B. You could use CloudWatch to monitor key metric for the NAT Gateways such as the total number of active connections but to closely monitor the transferred bytes, and packets you would need a 3rd party tool
    C. To identify the top talkers to avoid excessive costs VPC Flow Logs should be used. The logs can be sent to either S3 or CloudWatch Logs
    D. To identify the top talkers to avoid excessive costs VPC Flow Logs should be used. The logs can only be sent to S3 and then digested by Athena

31. You are creating a Public Virtual Interface over a 10G Direct Connect to the US East 1 region. Which of the following statements is correct about connectivity options using this session?

    A. You will have access to the AWS public services within the US East 1 region
    B. You will have access to the AWS public services and VPCs within the US
    C. You will have access to the AWS public services within the US
    D. You will have access to the AWS public services globally unless restricted by AWS

32. To meet the new security requirements outlined by the Information Security department, a cloud engineer is developing plans to span certain sessions from some of her EC2 instances in 5 of their VPCs located in the US West region to an AI/ML-based traffic experimental traffic analyzer. She has the option to deploy one instance of the traffic analyzer on-prem or anywhere in their AWS deployment in the US West. If she decides to keep the service on-prem the company is willing to fund a 1G Direct Connect link to provide a reliable connection. Which of the following options would lead to lower AWS fees and still meet the connectivity requirements?

A. Deploy the tool in one of the VPCs and enable VPC peering to the originating VPCs

B. Create a new VPC. Deploy the tool in the new VPC. Enable VPC peering to a hub VPC and from there to the VPC hosting the analyzer tool

C. Establish a Direct Connect link between the two networks with a public VIF. Enable MTU 9001. Deploy the tool in the existing data center.

D. Establish a Direct Connect link between the two networks with a private VIF. Enable MTU 9001. Deploy the tool in the existing data center.

33. A medical research company has S3 buckets in US East (Ohio), US Each (Virginia), and US West (Oregon). These buckets are accessed by a large number of medical facilities across the US to share medical images anonymously for research purposes. To provide their staff with more reliable access, the headquarters in Seattle has just ordered a 10G Direct Connect link in one of the US West locations into AWS with access to the S3 buckets. They are currently using VGWs with some vague plans to upgrade to TGWs. How should the cloud design engineer modify their architecture to be able to access the S3 buckets in all the US regions via Direct Connect?

A. They need 3 DX links each in one region

B. They need 2 DC links, one in one of the US East and the other one in one of the US East regions

C. They need to move the DX from US West to US East (Ohio)

D. The existing architecture allows access to all the three regions

34. You are architecting a multi-region AWS network for a multinational pharmaceutical corporation headquartered in New Jersey, located on the east coast of the United States but with offices across NA, APAC, MENA, and EU regions. As the first phase of the work, you created 35 VPCs in different regions. The regional offices use VPN connections to get access to their local VPCs. To have a more reliable connection to the VPCs across AWS for the headquarters, you ordered 4x10G AWS Direct Connect links at the us-east-1 region. Which of the following statements would be accurate about this architecture after full implementation without using Direct Connect Gateways or public VIFs?

A. Users in HQ can only use the DX to access VPCs in the us-east-1.

B. Users in HQ can only use the DX to access VPCs on the Americas continent

C. Users in HQ can use the DX to access VPCs anywhere in the US as well as AWS public services anywhere in the world

D. Users in HQ can use the DX to access VPCs and AWS public services anywhere in the world

35. You are planning on adding a 1G Direct Connect link to your network in the us-west-1 region to have a more reliable and cost-effective connection to S3. Which of the following statements is NOT correct about AWS public VIFs?

A. AWS performs inbound packet filtering to validate the source of the traffic originated from the network, and you must own those prefixes.
B. AWS may advertise all local and remote AWS Region prefixes to your router
C. AWS may advertise the public address of non-region CloudFront POPs to your router
D. AWS strips all BGP communities before advertising a prefix to your router

36. You are including a single 10G Direct Connect link in your design proposal for your customer to have a more reliable connection to AWS with a more predictable throughput to S3. Which of the following statements is accurate about AWS public VIFs?

A. AWS public VIFs can be used to access both customer VPCs and public resources such as S3
B. AWS public VIFs can be used with AWS Direct Connect Gateway
C. AWS public VIFs can be created using private AS numbers
D. When creating a public VIF, if the customer does not own a private AS, they can request AWS to assign one, but it only to be used between the customer and AWS cage in the Direct Connect location

37. You are investigating an unpredicted traffic pattern from AWS into your network via your new 10G public VIF in the us-east-2 region. This link was configured by the cloud engineering team less than a week ago and was the 13th Direct Connect link globally owned by your company. You notice that some of the prefixes you are advertising to AWS have the BGP community of 7224:9300, while the others have no BGP communities set. Given these settings and the existing architecture, how do your routes get propagated within AWS?

A. All of the prefixes will be advertised to all the AWS public regions
B. All of the prefixes will only be advertised to the us-east-2 region
C. The prefixes tagged with the BGP community of 7224:9300 will be propagated globally, while the rest will be filtered out and discarded
D. The prefixes tagged with the BGP community of 7224:9300 will remain in the us-east-2 region while the rest will be propagated to all AWS public regions

38. As an interim solution, you have deployed a pair of Layer 3 switches as your BGP router, sending and receiving routers to/from AWS Direct Connect via your 1G connection to your AWS resources in the EU Central region. Now you are trying to address some concerning reports regarding resource exhaustion on your low-end border routers. Also, you need to ensure your prefixes advertised to AWS do not leave the eu-central-1 region. Which of the following combinations would meet the design requirements? (Choose TWO)

A. Configure an outbound BGP policy on the border routers to advertise your prefixes with the BGP community of 7224:9100
B. Configure an outbound BGP policy on the border routers to advertise your prefixes with the BGP community of 7224:9200

C. No need to configure any inbound BGP policy. By default, AWS only advertises the routes from the same region to each customer

D. Configure an inbound BGP policy on the border routers to only accept prefixes with the BGP community of 7224:8100 from AWS

E. Configure an inbound BGP filter on the border routers to only accept prefixes with the BGP community of 7224:8200 from AWS

F. No need to configure any inbound BGP policy. By default, AWS only advertises the routes within the same region to each customer

39. You have your first AWS Direct Connect set up in US West. This connection is to be used to access AWS public services, including your S3 buckets and SQS. You hear from your AWS account team that prefixes advertised by AWS over the public VIF must not be advertised beyond your network. How do you ensure this design requirement is met?

A. Configure a BGP filter and tag all the prefixes received from AWS with the well-known LOCAL-AS community

B. Configure a BGP filter and tag all the prefixes received from AWS with the well-known NO_EXPORT community

C. Configure BGP filters on your border routers connecting your AS to your neighboring ASs, match all the AWS prefixes and prevent them from leaving the network.

D. All public prefixes are advertised from AWS with the well-known BGP community of NO_EXPORT. No further actions are required.

40. As a cloud Enterprise Architect, you are presenting a solution to the customer. Since the customer operates 3 different AWS accounts, the solution involves creating a large shared subnet for 150 EC2 instances that will be launched into it. Each department will own a number of instances. Which of the following statements is accurate about the process of sharing the subnet? (Choose TWO)

A. Subnets can only be shared by the owner account

B. Once a subnet is shared with account A, account A can, in turn, share the subnet with account B

C. Only the two permissions of ec2:DescribeSubnets and ec2:DescribeVpcs are required

D. To be successful, all the three permission of ec2:DescribeSubnets, ec2:DescribeVpcs, and ram:CreateResourceShare will be required

41. Your AWS account creates a Transit Gateway that will act as the central point of contact for the 5 VPCs owned by your company. You only own one of those VPCs and all the other ones are owned and operated by other AWS accounts in your organization. Which of the following statements is accurate about the architecture in which the Transit Gateway is shared with the other accounts? (Choose TWO)

A. Once the TGW is shared with account A, the owner of that would be able to connect their VPCs to the TGW and not their on-premises networks

B. Once the TGW is shared with account A, the owner of that would be able to connect their VPCs and all of their on-premises networks to the TGW

C. To successfully complete the operation, you need to have ec2:DescribeTransitGateway and ram:CreateResourceShare permissions

D. Each account you share the TGW with will be placed in an isolated segment similar to traditional VLANs. They can communicate with each other but not with other accounts connected to the same TGW

42. You are using Route 53 geolocation routing policy to route users to the right resources based on their location in 8 different geographical regions. For Europe last year, you created a record that still directs your users to the English pages and contents. After expanding your customer base in France, the marketing department now needs to offer French-speaking content as soon as possible. The plan is to offer French users an option to choose their preferred language. How would you achieve this design goal using AWS Route 53?

A. Create a dedicated record for France. Since priority goes to the smallest geographic region, the traffic can be routed to the servers hosting dual English/French pages.
B. Create a separate record for Europe. Route the England, Scotland, and Ireland traffic to the English pages.
C. Change the routing policy from geolocation to latency-based and let the traffic be routed to the resources closest to each user.
D. Change the routing policy from geolocation to failover and define the resources serving France as the primary destination while keeping the English resources as the secondary destination.

43. As a support lead, you are paged into an incident where the customer is complaining about a lack of connectivity from the outside to his fleet of 25 Web servers. The EC2 instances running the HTTP service reside behind an Application Load Balancer. Your initial investigations reveal that the FQDN advertised to the public is not resolving to the IP address of the ALB and fails. The customer insists that they have not made any change since they successfully stress-tested the environment with a number of clients and thousands of sessions. Which of the following options indicates a solution that could have prevented this situation?

A. Create a Lambda function to react to the change and update the A record accordingly
B. Use an ALIAS record for the ALB instead of the A record
C. Use PRT record for the ALB in addition to the A record
D. Use a Network Load Balancer instead of an Application Load Balancer and recreate the A record pointing to the new IP address of the ELB

44. The Systems Administrator of a small company is planning to install a new agent on a group of 10 EC2 instances. Currently, she does not have access to the AWS console or the AWS CLI managed by the cloud engineering team. How should this administrator obtain information on the exact instance type of each server running on EC2?

A. Run curl http://169.254.169.254/latest/meta-data/instance-type from the CLI within each EC2 instance
B. Run curl http://169.254.169.253/latest/meta-data/instance-type from the CLI within each EC2 instance

C. Run curl https://169.254.169.123/latest/meta-data/instance-type from the CLI within each EC2 instance

D. Run curl https://169.254.169.1/latest/meta-data/instance-type from the CLI within each EC2 instance

45. A member of a Red Team staging a reconnaissance initiative against an online accounting company has tricked the Blue team and gained access to the shell of one of their Linux servers in AWS. She currently does not have access to the AWS CLI or console. Which of the following approaches can help her gather intelligence on the AWS Availability Zone and Region the host is located in?

A. Run curl http://169.254.169.253/latest/meta-data/availability-zone

B. Run curl http://169.254.169.254/latest/meta-data/placement/availability-zone ✓

C. TCPdump and capture traffic to/from 169.254.169.254 and set the search keyword to "availability zone".

D. She can bring up an instance in an arbitrary VPC, permit inbound ICMP and, based on the ping latency, identify the region. Once the region is identified, he can spin up another instance in the same region and again, based on round trip times, determine the exact Availability Zone

46. To limit access to some confidential data, a junior cloud engineer has created and applied the following bucket policy to an S3 bucket. He would like to restrict access to the S3 bucket only to connections made through a certain VPC endpoint located in the Payroll VPC. However, the initial reports indicate that all the users, including the legitimate data consumers of the bucket have lost access to it. Which of the following options indicates a potential root cause of the issue preventing legitimate users from having READ/WRITE access to the bucket?

```
{
  "Version": "2020-1-1",
  "Id": "NewS3Policy",
  "Statement": [
    {
      "Sid": "limit_to_payroll_ep13",
      "Principal": "*",
      "Action": "s3:*",
      "Effect": "Deny",
      "Resource": ["arn:aws:s3:::Payrollbkt13",
              "arn:aws:s3::: Payrollbkt13/*"],
      "Condition": {
        "StringNotEquals": {
          "aws:SourceVpce": "vpce-13abc"
        }
      }
    }
  ]
}
```

A. The Effect statement needs to be changed to "Allow"
B. The Principal statement needs to be changed to "Any"
C. The Action statement is missing. It needs to be created and set to "PutObject"
D. The SourceVpce might be pointing to the wrong VPC Endpoint ID

47. After completion of their multi-year cloud migration project, an international hotel chain is optimizing its configuration details. In the original design, they applied the following bucket policy as a template to the S3 buckets that they needed to restrict access to them to certain endpoints within each VPC. Now, after the final consolidation phase, they have removed all the VPC endpoints that were scattered all over the place and created one trusted VPC instead. The goal is to update the policy to be able to manage all the VPC endpoints using a unified policy. How would you update the existing below policy in the Low Level Design document?

```
{
    "Version": "2020-1-1",
    "Id": "Consolidated-PL01358",
    "Statement": [
        {
            "Sid": "limit_to_trusted_vpc_shield",
            "Principal": "*",
            "Action": "s3:*",
            "Effect": "Deny",
            "Resource": ["arn:aws:s3:::customers_pci_data",
                    "arn:aws:s3::: customers_pci_data/*"],
            "Condition": {
                "StringNotEquals": {
                    "aws:SourceVpce": "vpce-1358abc"
                }
            }
        }
    ]
}
```

A. Use the same aws:SourceVpce statement and include all the VPC Endpoints in the trusted VPC
B. Create new aws:SourceVpce lines and add one VPC Endpoint per line
C. Replace the aws:SourceVpce with aws:SourceVpc and identify the VPC using its ARN
D. Replace the aws:SourceVpce with aws:SourceVpc and identify the VPC using its VPC ID

48. In preparation for an upcoming change window on two new VPCs owned by the finance department, you have received a CloudFormation YAML file from your development team. The script contains the following section. Which of the following choices is NOT accurate about the excerpt?

Step113:
Type: 'AWS::EC2::VPCPeeringConnection'
Properties:
VpcId: !Ref fin-01
PeerVpcId: !Ref fin-02

A. A-After successful execution a VPC peering session will form between the fin-01 and fin-02.
B. B-Step113 will not be executed until fin-01 and fin-02 are created.
C. C-The VPCs fin-01 and fi-02 can be in two different AWS accounts.
D. D-If fin-01 and fin-02 have any overlapping CIDR blocks the operation will fail.

49. As a cloud architect, you are working for a satellite imaging company that only uses S3 to store and access very high-resolution image files. Also, from time to time, the researchers might need to share the images with external customers. Your current project is to provide a dedicated 10G Direct Connect link into AWS to provide greater and more consistent throughput. You are also planning on advertising your public IP prefixes to AWS and only accept the routes directly related to the S3 service in your region. Which of the following statements is true about the upcoming Direct Connect data transfer charges?

A. Any outbound data transfer from S3 over the public VIF to the prefixes owned by the customer will be charged at Direct Connect data transfer rates. All the other data will be transferred at higher Internet rates to the external parties.
B. Any outbound data transfer from S3 over the public VIF to the prefixes owned by the customer will be charged at Direct Connect data transfer rates. All the other data will also be transferred to the external parties at the Direct Connect rate only if the Direct Connect and VIF are under the same AWS account.
C. All the data will also be transferred at the Internet data transfer rate but only for the outbound direction.
D. All the data will also be transferred at the Internet data transfer rate but only for the inbound direction.

50. You are presenting your most recent design to an AWS customer. Their goal is to have 4x10G Direct Connect links bundled up as a single LAG as their primary access channel to their AWS deployment in the ap-east-1 region (Hong Kong). Currently, they have a fleet of AWS EC2 instances in a number of VPCs as well as a large group of S3 buckets. To implement the architecture, your design includes a number of private and public VIFs. Also, to guarantee a minimum acceptable service, you suggest they set the minimum number of active links value to 2. Which of the following statements is accurate about the traffic routing pattern after a Direct Connect LAG failure is detected?

A. All VPC-related traffic will begin to ride the VPN tunnels, but the S3-related traffic will be dropped until the DX is restored
B. All VPC-related and S3-related traffic will begin to ride the VPN tunnels
C. All VPC-related traffic will begin riding the VPN tunnels, but the S3-related traffic will take the path via the public Internet

D. All VPC-related and S3-related traffic will begin to ride the VPN tunnels, but the VPC-related traffic will take precedence if there is not enough tunnel bandwidth

51. Your network includes 5 VPCs in AWS that communicate with each other and your physical data center over a VPN connection using a central VPC called Transit_VPC_01. Your cloud architects are evaluating the option of upgrading the architecture to use transit gateways. Which of the following options is NOT a valid benefit of using transit gateways in this particular design?

Only 8500

A. Transit gateways support MTU sizes of a maximum of 9001
B. By default, a transit gateway's attachment is associated to its default route table
C. Each VPC will be considered an attachment and can only be associated to one route table
D. Each transit gateway's route table can still exist without having any attachments

52. As a solution architect, you are working with a greenfield customer. In the first wave of their migration from on-premises to the cloud, they will have 8 VPCs. You are also planning to use a 1G Direct Connect as the primary connection and IPSec VPN as the secondary path. All the VPCs should be able to communicate with each other and with the data center via a transit gateway. Which of the following statements is accurate about the minimum number of route tables to implement this architecture?

A. You would need 10 route tables. One for each VPC, one for the VPN attachment, and another one for the Direct Connect attachment
B. You would need 3 route tables. One for all the VPCs, one for the VPN attachment, and another one for the Direct Connect attachment
C. You would need 2 route tables. One for all the VPCs and another one for the Direct Connect and VPN attachments
D. You would need only 1 route table to associate all the attachments.

53. You are architecting a transit gateway solution for a greenfield customer with 12 VPCs. You decide to assign the IP subnets of 10.1.0.0/16, 10.2.0.0/16,10.3.0.0/16 through 10.12.0.0/16 to their VPCs. All the VPCs will be connected to one transit gateway, and the customer needs to make sure all the VPCs can communicate with each other. Which of the following options describes the correct routing solution?

A. Associate all the VPCs with the default route table and make sure their routes are propagated.
B. Associate all the VPCs with the default route table and make sure their routes are propagated. On the VPC side, manually create a static route to send 10.0.0.0/8 to the transit gateway.
C. Associate all the VPCs with the default route table and make sure their routes are propagated. On the VPC side, manually create a static route to send 10.x.0.0/8, where x is the subnet address of the VPC to the transit gateway.
D. Associate all the VPCs with the default route table and make sure their routes are propagated. On the VPC side, manually create a static route to send 10.0.0.0/8 to the IP address of the transit gateway.

54. As a solutions architect, you are assisting a customer new to AWS. In their current design, they have 16 VPCs connected to one transit gateway, where they also have their VPN connection attached. In their architecture, every VPC should be able to communicate with other VPCs as well as the on-premises networks. Their networks are all from the 10.10.0.0/16 subnet. One of their VPCs is called VPC_WSUS_YUM_NA and has an Internet Gateway attached to it as the only VPC with direct access to the Internet. Which of the following options shows how the route table of VPC_WSUS_YUM_NA should be configured?

   A. The route table will only have a default route pointing to the transit gateway.
   B. The route table will have a default route pointing to the Internet Gateway and another default route pointing to the transit gateway.
   C. The route table will have a default route pointing to the transit gateway and another route for the destination of 10.10.0.0/16 pointing to the transit gateway.
   D. The route table will have a default route pointing to the Internet Gateway, a route for the local subnet pointing to the value of local, and another route for the destination of 10.10.0.0/16 pointing to the transit gateway.

55. You are architecting a transit gateway solution for a higher education institute with 24 VPCs, each representing one of their schools. The school VPCs are not supposed to communicate with each other for security reasons, but they need to communicate with the VPN solution created between AWS and their on-premises firewalls. You decide to assign the IP subnets of 10.10.0.0/16, 10.11.0.0/16,10.12.0.0/16 through 10.33.0.0/16 to each school VPC. All the VPCs will be connected to one transit gateway. You started by creating two route tables, one for the VPCs and another one for the VPN. Which of the following TWO options describe the route tables correctly? (Choose TWO)

   A. The VPCs route table will have 24 routes, one for each VPC pointing to the TGW
   B. The VPCs route table will have 24 routes, one for each VPC pointing to the VPN connection
   C. The VPCs route table will have only one default route pointing to the VPN connection
   D. The VPN route table will have only one default route pointing to the on-premises firewalls
   E. The VPN route table will have 24 routes, one for each VPC pointing to the respective VPC attachment
   F. The VPN route table will have 24 routes, one for each VPC pointing to the TGW

56. After a security breach in which four of your EC2 instances were compromised, you are revising your AWS architecture. Currently, you have 6 VPCs, all in the us-west-1 region and connected to a transit gateway where you also have your VPN connection to the data center attached. You also have a route for the 10.0.0.0/8 network pointing to the VPN connection in the VPCs route table. Each VPC also has a dedicated Internet Gateway, and each EC2 instance is tightly protected by Security Groups. The postmortem security assessment indicates that the Security Groups, predictably, were unable to block the malicious codes. Your goal is to ensure all the sessions to/from the

Internet go through a pair of next generation firewalls similar to the architecture you have in your data center. However, in this fiscal year, you have no budget to purchase licenses and subscriptions for the virtual next generation firewalls to be deployed in the cloud. Hence you are trying to leverage the on-premises firewalls. Which of the following options can help this customer?

A. Replace 10.0.0.0/8 with a default route pointing to the VPN connection
B. Add 10.0.0.0/8 pointing to each one of the VPCs to the VPN route table
C. Add a default route pointing to the VPCs to the VPN route table
D. Add 6 routes to the VPN route table pointing to each one of the VPCs

57. As a cloud support engineer, you are on a troubleshooting call with a new transit gateway customer. The customer has 16 VPCs, all connected to the same transit gateway, where they also have their VPN connection attached. The issue is that VPC3 cannot communicate with VPC12. Each VPC is associated to a different route table. You log into one of the EC2 instances in VPC3 and run the ping command to another Linux server in VPC12. Although the ping command fails, the TCPdump session on the destination server indicates that the ICMP packets you generated from VPC3 were received at VPC12. Which of the following solutions can resolve the issue with no adverse impact on the other parts of the network?

A. Disassociate VPC12 from the current route table and associate it to the same route table that VPC3 is associated to
B. Disassociate VPC3 from the current route table and associate it to the same route table that VPC12 is associated to
C. Propagate the VPC3 attachment to the route table that VPC12 is associated to
D. Propagate the VPC12 attachment to the route table that VPC3 is associated to

58. You are working as a cloud engineer with an architect to expand your current AWS footprint. Currently, you have 6 VPCs called VPC_B, VPC_C, VPC_D, VPC_E, and VPC_F. They are all connected to the same transit gateway and are associated to three route tables as shown below, and propagation to their respective route tables has been enabled:

VPC name	Route Table
VPC_B	RT2
VPC_C	RT2
VPC_D	RT3
VPC_E	RT3
VPC_F	RT4
VPC_G	RT4

As part of the expansion plan, you are introducing a new VPC called VPC_A to host several major shared services such as AAA. The number of consumer VPCs is expected to grow in the near future. The architect has provisioned a new route table called RT1 to associate the new VPC to. How would you set up the routing with minimum effort to ensure all the other VPCs can communicate with the shared services VPC while preserving the current segmentation strategy?

A. Associate all the VPCs to RT1 and deploy NACLs to replicate the current segmentation layout. This would minimize the maintenance efforts by reducing the number of route tables.

B. Associate all the VPCs to RT1 and deploy Security Groups to replicate the current segmentation layout. Propagate VPC_A attachment to RT2, RT3, and RT4 in addition to RT1 for the return traffic.

C. Propagate VPC_A attachment to all the route tables. Propagate all the VPCs attachments to RT1.

D. Associate VPC_A attachment to RT2, RT3, and RT4 in addition to RT1. Associate all the other VPCs to RT1 in addition to their respective route tables.

59. The SRE team of a large bank is designing a solution to monitor the status of two main events that have been very annoying in recent weeks. They would like to trigger actions when they happen in their AWS footprint and with its Transit Gateways. First of all, they would like to monitor the BGP sessions, then the up/down status of the IPSec tunnels. The events should trigger a Python code that makes certain API calls to their paging application and it pages the on-call engineer into an active incident. Which of the following options proposes a valid solution?

A. Use TGW Network Manager to monitor the TGWs. Set rules to trigger the Python code when the incidents happen. The details can be logged in CloudWatch.

B. Use TGW Network Manager to monitor the TGWs and the events of interest. The events can be sent to EventBridge and EventBridge would execute the Python code for either incident.

C. Use TGW Network Manager to monitor the TGWs and the events of interest. The events can be sent to EventBridge and EventBridge would execute the Python code for the IPSec events but the BGP events need to be sent to Lambda.

D. Use TGW Network Manager to monitor the TGWs and the events of interest. The events can be sent to EventBridge and EventBridge would engage Lambda to run the Python code for either incident.

60. You are architecting a secure connectivity solution for an insurance company with 6 VPCs in us-west-1. The customer has previously created all the Security Groups they required in one of their VPCs and would like to be able to reference those in other VPCs. The exact direction of traffic among the VPCs is still to be determined. Which of the following connectivity options provides an architecture that can satisfy the requirements of this customer?

A. AWS PrivateLink
B. Transit gateway with tight NACLs at the subnet level
C. VPC peering
D. Transit gateway

61. As a solution architect, you are assisting a customer in evaluating different connectivity options to implement a shared services VPC in AWS. This VPC will be accessed by internal users around the world from hundreds of other VPCs owned by the same company. The marketing team is also looking to turn the services in the shared VPC into a paid service in the future and offer them to external customers at scale. Which of the following connectivity options can better meet this customer's requirements to connect the shared VPC to spoke/client VPCs?

    A. Transit gateway
    B. PrivateLink
    C. VPC peering
    D. Transit VPC

62. As a Cloud support engineer, you are on a troubleshooting call with a customer who has just migrated their AWS architecture from using Virtual Gateways/Transit VPC to Transit Gateway. This is an SMB account, the customer has 10 VPCs, and they use VPN to reach their on-premises network where they're running site-to-site IPSec VPN on a single firewall as the customer gateway. The customer, after reading about transit gateways features, has created 4 VPN tunnels and is expecting to reach close to 5Gbps between their environment and AWS, but evidently, they cannot achieve more than 2.5Gbps. Which of the following options can be TWO root causes of the issue? (Choose TWO)

    A. The on-premises firewall only supports 2-way ECMP
    B. The transit gateway only supports 2-way ECMP
    C. The customer is trying to use ECMP with static routing pointing to a loop back interface
    D. The customer is trying to use ECMP with BGP multi-path

63. As a solutions architect, you are assisting a customer in making the right decisions as to their connectivity options to AWS. They currently have 15 VPCs in eu-south-1 and use a transit gateway to connect them all. They also use VPN tunnels connected to the same transit gateway to manage their VPCs. They also use the public Internet to access Amazon storage. In the wake of a new project with heavy use of S3 and Glacier in the eu-west-1 and eu-south-1 regions, they are inquiring about their Direct Connect choices to improve the connectivity to those services and avoid traversing a large number of hops until they hit S3 and Glacier via the public Internet. Which of the following architectures can meet this customer's requirements?

    A. Order a 10G Direct Connect and use a Direct Connect Gateway in the same region to connect to the transit gateway. Create a public VIF on the Direct Connect.
    B. Order a 10G Direct Connect and use a Direct Connect Gateway in the same region to connect to the transit gateway. Create a private VIF on the Direct Connect.
    C. Order a 10G Direct Connect independent of the transit gateway and configure it with a private VIF.

D. Order a 10G Direct Connect independent of the transit gateway and configure it with a public VIF.

64. You are working as a newly hired chief cloud architect for an international bank with hundreds of branches and offices across North America, Europe, Asia Pacific, and Africa. Your first project is to revise the connectivity architecture in their AWS deployment, which was done back in 2016 using the concept of transit VPC. Back then, the total number of VPCs was 25 globally. Hence, the transit VPC architecture using 3rd party virtual routers made sense for a while. Soon after multiple waves of cloud migrations, the bank will have close to 900 VPCs in multiple regions that are accessed by their headquarters in London, UK, via 4 10G Direct Connect links. Your initial high-level idea is to use transit gateways in each region to build a global network of VPCs. Which of the following options should be studied carefully as a potentially serious design constraint? (Choose TWO)

A. The number of VPC attachments
B. The number of regions
C. The number of Direct Connect links and their concentration in one region
D. The number of routes advertised from on-premises to AWS over the Direct Connect links
E. The number of routes advertised from AWS to on-premises over the Direct Connect links

65. As a cloud architect working for an IoT chip designer, you are developing a solution for your employer to best integrate a new 1G Direct Connect link into your existing architecture. The Direct Connect cross-connect was ordered last month to enable the engineering teams to smoothly and quickly upload sizable CAD drawings from the main office to the EC2 instances in one of the 5 engineering VPCs. This operation is done as soon as the design engineers complete an iteration of their design and need to continue the work on EC2. Currently, you have one transit gateway in the us-west-2 region and have all the VPCs attached to it. You also have 2 VPN tunnels terminated at the transit gateway. Which of the following architectures provides the connectivity required by this customer while minimizing the data transfer fees?

A. Attach the 1G Direct Connect to the transit gateway via a Direct Connect Gateway and create a transit virtual gateway. Run BGP.
B. Attach the 1G Direct Connect to the transit gateway directly. Run BGP.
C. Attach the 1G Direct Connect to the VPCs independent from the transit gateway. Create Public Virtual Interfaces for each VPC.
D. Attach the 1G Direct Connect to the VPCs independent from the transit gateway. Create Private Virtual Interfaces for each VPC.

MOCK EXAM 1 - Detailed Answers

1.   (A)(D) As described here, it is possible to have more than one SD-WAN appliance (usually for redundancy). The appliances are required to be placed in a dedicated VPC (usually called Connect VPC) and in separate subnets.

2.   (A) If the customer wants to maintain their SD-WAN appliances on-prem, they would have to deploy Direct Connect between their data center and their AWS footprint. Currently, VPN attachments are not supported as transport for SD-WAN connect attachments. Please note, this limitation does not have anything to do with throughput.

3.   (B) When creating or modifying the Transit Gateway settings, you have an opportunity to configure what is called a Transit Gateway CIDR block. These are the addresses used by the TGW itself. Later, when you are creating the Connect peer as part of your SD-WAN architecture, you can specify an IP address from that range in the Transit Gateway GRE address text box. This is the address used as the outer address and used by your peer device (in this case, the Cisco SD-WAN appliance) to connect to and build the GRE tunnel.

4.   (C) The protocol used (UDP) and the requirements can only be satisfied by Global Accelerator. Please note this is non-HTTP traffic. We can also safely rule out (D) as it would pin certain devices to an endpoint which would serve no purpose here.

5.   (D) All the options except D are safe. You can bring Your Own IP to AWS and let AWS advertise that prefix for you. In this case, two IP addresses can be used to maintain the same server IP address after moving the workload to the cloud. Adding a new region would be a great (although costly) idea. What you must not do is advertise the routes back to AWS, as it would result in complex (and potentially) asymmetric routing scenarios. Generally speaking, if your decision is to do BYOIP, let AWS handle everything about the prefix. One of the common mistakes is to keep on advertising the same prefix that you decided to allow AWS to use for your services out to the Internet. Once again, let them handle everything about the prefix for you.

6.   (B) You can achieve more deterministic latency (and jitter) by using the Global Accelerator service, as the request will be injected into the Amazon network sooner than later. This could save your traffic quite a few hops on the public and potentially lossy or

congested Internet. Only NLBs can spread the load in the form suggested here between AWS and on-premises. This topic was extensively discussed in the ELB section. After the configuration is done, you won't need the NetScaler as the NLB will be directly feeding the servers; on-prem or in your VPCs. As food for thought you can imagine a scenario where someone would want to keep the NetScaler between the on-prem servers and the NLB; what were the ramifications? Any benefits?

7. (A) The Global Accelerator service only supports TCP, UDP, and TCP_UDP services.

8. (B) When Global Accelerators are combined with Load Balancers, the choice of ALB helps you preserve the source IP address. While this provides you with the IP address of the visiting clients, it brings some complexities to your architecture, including new security configurations to make sure the Security Groups, NACLs, and potentially firewalls all permit the incoming packets with their original source IP address.

9. (C) DNSSEC ensures the messages are from the right origin and untampered.

10. (B) The public key part of ZSK is placed in the DNSKEY record and shared with external DNS resolvers as they reach out, while the private key part of it, expectedly, is used to sign the records, including A and AAAA.

11. (D) The DS record is a special type of record and lives in the parent zone and shows the querying resolver that the child also supports DNSSEC.

12. (A)(B)(D) All the options except EventBridge are valid methods, especially the last choice (Kinesis) for large implementations and where you prefer to use Splunk to consume the data in the back.

13. (A) CloudWatch metrics can offer the level of details about the status of the Gateway itself. Do not let the other options, especially (D), throw you off. The question is NOT about logging the details of translations (which you could use S3+Athena). This question is strictly about the status and health metrics of your NAT Gateways.

14. (C)(D) For a reason, we placed this question right after the previous one. Many students mix them up! You should not. While the previous question was about the health metrics of the NAT Gateways, this question is about the translation tables. CloudWatch Logs or S3 are the best tools for the purpose. Also, as mentioned in the question, Athena would allow you to run standard SQL queries against those tables. CloudWatch log also offers what is known as filters. Two choices with similar outcomes but different means.

15. (B) There are multiple ways to influence the path certain traffic takes to leave a network using BGP. One of the most straightforward solutions using built-in BGP knobs is to tweak the Local Preference value. When you have iBGP between your BGP speakers in an AS and modify the Local Preference for a set of routes on one of the speakers, all the other BGP speakers learn about it, and that BGP speaker will be used as the primary exit

point. This architecture will also create a classic active-passive setup where you can later use between your network and AWS or two ASs within your environment.

16.   (A)(B) This is another active-passive setup. Here you have two options to prefer the path via R1 over R2. You can either increase the Local Preference value on the exit point of choice (R1) as indicated in option B or decrease the Local Preference value on the less preferred exit point as shown in option A. Regarding Options C and D, generally speaking, the process of AS_PATH prepending is one of the valid ways to influence inbound traffic (into an AS) and not outbound. This question is specifically about outbound traffic (the traffic leaving an AS).

17.   (C) AWS Simple Queuing Service (SQS) is a managed and distributed queueing service offered by AWS. Being one of the early services offered by AWS (2004), it is extensively used in microservices architectures, especially when the system designers intend to decouple their application's components for better scalability (think of it as piping). SQS automatically scales as you need to accommodate billions of requests per day. From an AWS networking perspective, however, SQS is also one of the services primarily available via the public Internet. Later on, AWS introduced VPC endpoints for SQS, which made it possible for the service to be reached from within VPCs without having to use public addresses, perform NAT or traverse the public Internet that to many organizations meant taking security risks. This goal was achieved through AWS PrivateLinks or, in AWS terminology, powered by PrivateLink. Please note that AWS PrivateLink can be used to connect to AWS-owned services (such as this scenario or connecting to S3 buckets from within AWS) or to reach your partners or SaaS provider VPC securely.

18.   (C) For an IPSec tunnel to be successfully established, at a minimum, two "holes" are needed in the firewall. You need to permit the Internet Key Exchange (IKE) protocol which is used to set up the Security Associations (AS) over port UDP 500. You also need to permit the IP Protocol number 50 to support Encapsulation Security Payload (ESP). This is the minimum you would need to bring up the IPSec tunnel, but in this question, we are also dealing with another twist: the Network Address Translation (NAT) between the two IPSec endpoints. NAT, as you know, updates the source and destination address fields in the header of the packets and this "manipulation" is not something that sits well with IPSec. The most common solution to the issue presented here is to encapsulate packets at the source using UDP (port 4500) and let the NAT gateway touch the new header and not the original one which IPSec at the destination would watch carefully. On the outside, to the NAT gateway, the new session appears to be a UDP stream (Port 4500) whose header can be safely manipulated, but on the inside, you are maintaining the original packet protected by IPSec. This technique is called NAT Traversal or NAT-T for short.

19.   (A) SYN and UDP floods, as well as Reflection attacks and many other Layer 3 and 4 malicious attempts, can be foiled by AWS Shield Standard, which by default comes with all AWS accounts at no additional cost. The customer does not have to subscribe

to the Advanced service, which might be costly and is an extra service to purchase. In more sophisticated attacks, you might want to consider the AWS Shield Advanced service, which offers you 24x7 access to the DDoS Response Team (DRT) and can compensate your account and protect you from auto-scaling traps where the attackers make your infrastructure scale out and charge more in response to their traffic. They are not required here. Regarding the other options, AWS inspector is an automatic security posture assessment tool while GuardDuty is a threat detection service; both paid services with benefits unrelated to this scenario.

20. (D) In a basic Denial of Service (DoS) attack, the service becomes unavailable to other users due to the threat of a malicious actor from certain and specific sources. You can think of this attack as repeatedly calling someone's landline with no call waiting to prevent them from attending to other callers. This attack can be rather easily thwarted by blocking the offending source (in our example, the malicious calling number). The attacker can take this to the next level by calling from random numbers or hiring a group of people to call from all sorts of random numbers. This attack would be much harder to foil and is called a Distributed Denial of Service (DDoS) attack. In an even worse scenario, the attackers can turn random and innocent phones into their agents (bots) to call the victim at random times from random locations. This would take the damage and risks to a whole new level. AWS can detect many DoS and DDoS attacks using the Shield service. You can define IP ranges and even countries that you feel the illegitimate traffic is coming from. You can also use the Web Application Firewall (WAF) to protect your Web applications against a wide range of threads, including Cross-Site scripting or SQL injection attacks. This can be quite helpful if your IIS, NGINX, or Apache server is missing a critical patch and is waiting to receive an update as soon as time permits. You can also inspect the requested URLs (or HTTP body or headers) for any unusual patterns. None of these services would need the AWS GuardDuty to operate, which continuously analyzes the meta-data and logs found on other AWS components such as CloudWatch.

21. (A) The sample log entry clearly indicates SQL queries being injected into the regular Web URLs. In this type of threat, the attacker tries to run a SQL query against your database server to read more data than they are permitted or take other malicious actions. The WAF service can inspect the incoming URLs and foil the attack if any sign of SQL injection is found in the HTTP packets. For instance, on a vulnerable server, a student might be able to see the scores of other students in addition to his score by injecting a well-crafted SQL query in his normal URLs. This could lead to a disaster if, for instance, the leaked information is protected by regulatory laws or contains sensitive personal data or passwords.

22. (A)(C)(E) This is one of the classic use cases of CloudWatch logs or metrics agents (now collectively known as a unified agent). The agent, as described above, sends the logs for the service in the form of log streams identified by the instance-id. They are then aggregated into log groups which can be processed by metric filters. Finally, if the filters detect a

matching pattern with the frequency defined within the time window frame you specify, they can trigger a CloudWatch alarm. This feature especially comes in handy when you are running services such as SSH, Apache, or Microsoft IIS.

23. (A) With the most recent updates, all the AWS load balancer can load balance to multiple ports on the same server or instance except Classic load balancers. In this case, as the text clearly shows, the LB is forwarding to an "instance" and not an external or on-prem IP address.

24. (D) The health check protocol of HTTP (TCP80) works just fine between the ALB and backend servers, in this case, the instance. Please note the instance, as you see here, can be listening to a different port than the listeners for the actual traffic.

25. (C) AWS truncates larger packets, and since VXLAN is used to carry the packets over, you will see the (annoying) headers as you are looking at your application-generated packets!

26. (C) The only available architecture to have a scalable backend destination is to deploy an NLB with UDP listeners. Keep in mind, the traffic will be tunneled over with VXLAN headers, a UDP-based protocol.

27. (D) You can use a wide range of Layer 2/3 connectivity options such as Q-in-Q (802.1ad – double VLAN tagging), MetroE, VPLS, or MPLS L3 VPN to connect your remote data center to an AWS Direct Connect location. This form of connectivity is usually provided by a 3rd party carrier that receives your route on one end and hands them off on the other end of the circuit, which can be the Direct Connect location (customer owns the CE or customer equipment). Alternatively, they can be owned and fully operated by the AWS customer as part of their global network (customer owns CE, PE, and P routes).

   In real life, if you have no presence in the same Direct Connect location, most WAN solutions can provide you with such a level of access from your facility. This is not to be confused with AWS Hosted Connections that are provided by an AWS Partner (APN). A possible analogy is that with Hosted Connections the partner owns the dedicated connection and provisions slices of it to the customers present in that location, while with third party WAN access, the customer owns the dedicated connection and the third party, similar to any other WAN provider, only connects the customer buildings to the Direct Connect location. Final piece of advice; if you are preparing for a job interview and do not have a clear understanding of the technologies mentioned here, go back and review them. It would probably take a few hours to learn how each backbone technology works, at least at a high level. It's not fun to be a network engineer and have no idea what VPLS means.

28. (C) While it does not make sense to order a new Direct Connect link just for the databases VPC you can still use the existing Direct Connect with a new private VIF dedicatedly created for the databases VPC.

As a tip, remember you cannot extend the peering relationship between two VPCs to VPN or Direct Connect users. For instance, if VPC A and VPC B have peering between them, you cannot use the Direct Connect to VPC A to get to VPC B. This limitation, almost entirely, became obsolete when the complex peering solutions were replaced by TGW hub and spoke architectures.

29.   (D) While all the other options are accurate, using MD5 to enforce BGP peer authentication in Direct Connect is mandatory. You have to choose a password or accept the randomly selected one.

30.   (A)(C) The health metrics of the NAT Gateways can be monitored using CloudWatch. You could track the top talkers by digesting the VPC Flow Logs using either S3/Athena or CloudWatch Logs. Athena offers a SQL-like query language

31.   (D) Upon creation of a public VIF, AWS advertises a large number of prefixes (in the order of thousands) to the customer. These routes are used to reach various AWS public services in different regions. AWS, by default, applies 3 communities of 7224:8100, 7224:8200, and none to its advertised routes for the routes originated in the same region as the Direct Connect, in the same continent as the Direct Connect and Global. The customer can configure their BGP policies to accept or simply filter out what is and is not needed on their end.

32.   (A) In the US, the Direct Connect and Peering pricing is at 1c per GB. However, with Direct Connect, you are only charged for the outbound traffic transfer (sending traffic out of AWS), while with peering, you are charged for both directions. Depending on the type of traffic, direction of traffic, and the region (outside the US), your best choice might vary. In this case, we are spanning the traffic, which will result in strictly one-way traffic from 5 VPCs to the AI/ML analyzer host. So far, both options look similar until we apply the tie-breaker. AWS Direct Connect fees, in addition to the regular data transfer fees, also charge the customer for "port hour," which varies based on the connection types. Finally, as always, keep in mind you cannot have transitive routing over VPC peering sessions.

In real life, Japan has slightly higher port-hour fees compared to the other regions. For data rates, always check the latest details for various regions on the AWS Web site.

33.   (D) The customer currently must have a public VIF on their Direct Connect, which gives them access to their S3 buckets in their region. Once connected, AWS sends thousands of public prefixes to enable the customer to access AWS public services in various regions. The customer later has the choice to filter out some of the prefixes and only keep the ones for their interest. For instance, in this case, the customer can only accept prefixes with the BGP community of 7224:8200 (i.e., the same continent as the Direct Connect location).

In real life, be careful if you're using older AWS documentation. In general, connectivity across AWS over time has gone through multiple iterations, and it's best to always check the latest updates.

34. (A) By default, the company will have access to the VPCs in their local region (us-east-1) using private VIFs. With public VIFs, they could establish VPN connections to other remote regions, and even better, with AWS Direct Connect Gateways, they could natively reach the other regions using private VIFs– currently, both are prohibited by the scenario.

35. (D) While all the other options clearly describe the behavior of AWS public VIFs, AWS, in fact, uses BGP communities to signal the origin of the routes they are advertising to the customer. Specifically, 7224:8100 is assigned to the routes belonging to the same region as the Direct Connect location. 7224:8200 is allocated to the routes from the same continents, while none (no communities assigned) indicates the global (other regions) origin of the route. This helps the customer receive only what they need or care about. For example, if you only have S3 buckets in your region, you probably don't want to receive thousands of other prefixes from AWS for S3, SQS, and CloudFront POPs from all around the world.

36. (C) The public VIFs can only be used to reach AWS public services such as S3. By design, AWS public services in almost all regions become available to you as soon as you bring up the public VIF. Hence, unlike private VIFs, you will not need an extra construct (i.e. Direct Connect Gateway) to help you reach the remote regions. You can always use public or private 2 or 4-Byte AS numbers, although using private AS numbers currently would take away your ability to use the AS_PATH attribute to influence routing if you have multiple connections – which is not the case in this scenario.

37. (A) When advertising your prefixes to AWS, you have the option to signal AWS how far you want them to travel within the AWS network. For instance, whether you want your prefixes to be contained within the same region as the Direct Connect location or you want them to be propagated globally (i.e., available to Direct Connect locations in other regions). AWS expects to see the BGP community of 7224:9100 if you want them to keep your prefix in the same region, 7224:9200 if you only want your prefix to be propagated to all AWS regions for your continent, and 7224:9300 to share them with all the regions globally. If you don't apply any BGP communities, the routes will, by default, be sent to all the regions (global propagation). In this case, the customer's routes are being advertised to every single region which might have been used outside the pre-defined architecture.

38. (A)(D) The routes advertised by AWS with the BGP community of 7224:8100 belong to your local region and advertising your routes with the BGP community of 7224:9100 will keep them local to your region. This combination will help you minimize the number of routes you are exchanging with AWS.

39.   (D) AWS always tags their prefixes with the BGP community of NO_EXPORT before advertising them to you. So, if you do not intentionally strip the tagging (which is not a good idea), your BGP peers will not announce them outside your AS.

40.   (A)(D) Sharing a subnet would allow other AWS accounts to launch resources such as EC2 instances in it. In order to do that, the permissions described in option D must exist.

41.   (B)(C) Sharing a transit gateway would allow AWS accounts to connect their VPCs and on-prem networks and have full connectivity and routing between them and other connections. The permissions need to exist as described by option C.

42.   (A) With the Geolocation routing policies, you can define a more specific but overlapping region and it would take precedence over the general policy for the overarching geographical region. For instance, in this case, defining a dedicated record for France would allow you to direct its users to the servers with bilingual (or, if needed, French only) content while still maintaining the primary content for the rest of Europe in English. Later on, for example, if you need to add content in German, all you need to do is define another overlapping but more specific record for Germany pointing to the servers hosting your German pages.

43.   (B) To maintain the elasticity of its load balancer, AWS uses a changing set of IP addresses behind the DNS names that they assign to Elastic Load Balancers after you create them. Later on, when the load balancer is facing a large and growing number of sessions, AWS uses different IP addresses to respond to the clients. This behavior cannot be observed by a limited number of clients or sessions. Also, the main advantage of alias records over traditional A records, as seen in this scenario, is that any change in the IP address of the resource is automatically detected by Route 53. For example, if the DNS name of lb-1.us-east-1.elb.amazonaws.com is assigned to your load balancer by AWS and the IP address of it changes in response to patterns of traffic; Route 53 recognizes the change and starts responding using the new IP address for lb-1.us-east-1.elb.amazonaws.com. There are other techniques to architect such solutions that we will see later in the book.

44.   (A) The IP address of 169.254.169.254 is reserved by AWS to provide the underlying information (i.e., metadata) about EC2 instances through the Metadata Service running on each instance. This address is link local and can only be accessed from within the instance. As an exam and interview tip, you can extract several other key pieces of information through the Metadata Service, such as the region, CPU architecture, and account ID.

45.   (B) If browsed, the URL mentioned here returns the metadata related to the Availability Zone and Region of the instance. Please remember the address of the Metadata Service at 169.254.169.254 is link local and has to be browsed from within the instance.

46.   (D) The parts of the policy that define the type and level of access are flawless. However, this policy is defining an exception to a sweeping deny policy. The exception is defined through the condition and the StringNotEqual statement, where the string has to match the string vpce-13abc. This simply means if you get the string wrong, the exception won't apply, and no one would have access.

47.   (D) The original policy, as shown, limits access to just one VPC endpoint called vpce-1358abc. You can replace the endpoint with the actual VPC to expand access to all the endpoints in that VPC, which in this case, is a trusted VPC.

48.   (A) The resource type AWS::EC2::VPCPeeringConnection, when executed successfully, "requests" a VPC peering session between two VPCs which has to be accepted by the peer which can be in another AWS account. The !Ref defines the dependency, and all the well-known VPC peering limitations (including CIDR blocks separation) apply to this peering as well.

49.   (A) Regardless of the owner of the VIF and port, AWS will charge the customer at the regular (and lower) Direct Connect transfer rates if the outbound traffic is sent from S3 to the public prefixes owned by them and actively advertised to AWS through the Direct Connect public VIF. All the other charges will be made at the Internet data transfer rate, which is usually significantly higher (sometimes more than 4 times).

50.   (C) It is a common low-cost practice to use VPN tunnels as a backup channel for Direct Connect links. In such scenarios, when the Direct Connect (LAG or single link) goes down, AWS automatically initiates the failover of the VPC-related traffic to the VPN tunnels (i.e., the private VIFs). Now, what happens to the public VIFs? For instance, traffic between your facility and AWS public resources such as S3. This traffic will automatically be routed through the public Internet, which may result in taking paths with a higher number of hops and latency.

51.   (A) As of 2020, AWS transit gateways support the MTU size of up to 8500 Bytes between all the different types of attachments, excluding site-to-site IPSec VPN tunnels. In other words, in one packet, you can carry up to 8500 bytes if it travels between Direct Connect, VPC, transit gateway Connect, or peering attachments.

52.   (D) Since it is a flat architecture, you can get away with only one route table where all the attachments, including the VPCs, VPN, and DX, are associated to. Once implemented, the default (main) route table will have the routes for all the attached networks. This could raise security questions, but at least in this scenario, that would not be a concern.

53.   (B) This is a typical flat architecture where all you need to do is to associate your attachments, in this case, the VPCs, to the default route table. You also need to make sure the VPCs know how to get out and communicate with other VPCs. This is done by adding a static route for the outside world (again, in this case, the other VPCs) to the route table of each VPC. In this simple scenario, although you have the option of

ling a default route pointing to the transit gateway to each VPC, a more granular ign would be to add a static route with the destination of 10.0.0.0/8 and the next hop of the tgw-xxx to the route table of each VPC. Needless to say, AWS constructs such as NAT gateways, Internet Gateways, and Transit Gateways are not addressed by their IP address but are simply referred to by their names.

54. (D) In order to have connectivity to the other VPCs, the Internet, and the internal resources within VPC_WSUS_YUM_NA you would need at least 3 routes. In addition to the local route for internal connectivity, you would have one path out of the VPC to the other VPCs at 10.10.0.0/16 via the transit gateway and a default route for anything that doesn't match the other routes (i.e., destinations located outside of the company's range) to the Internet via the Internet Gateway.

55. (C)(E) To create the isolated architecture described in this scenario, at a minimum, you would need 2 route tables. The route table that the VPN connection is associated to will contain routes for each one of the VPCs. This route table will be consulted when a packet arrives from the on-premises network, so the TGW can determine where to send the packet next (i.e., toward which VPC?). The TGW will also have another route table associated to the VPCs. It would need only one default route pointing to the VPN connection. This route table will be consulted when a packet arrives from one of the VPCs. As you can imagine, the route table must not include any route from other VPCs to stay compliant with the security requirement but should have one route (which can be the wide default route) to send all the traffic down to the on-premises firewalls. This architecture can serve several key purposes, including using the already-purchased and licensed on-premises firewalls for inter-VPC traffic inspection or if the company has strict requirements for an Internet egress stack. They can build such a stack in their physical data center and send all Internet-bound traffic down to on-premises to push through the stack before sending it out to the Internet. This would be a valid architecture, although in the real world, depending on other requirements, you might want to consider Direct Connect instead of the VPN connection.

56. (A) This option provides a solution to route the Internet-bound traffic down to the on-premises network via the VPN connection. When a packet arrives from one of the VPCs at the transit gateway and hits the VPCs table, it will match the default route and be sent down to the data center. From there, similar to any on-premises traffic, you can route it to your Internet egress stack. In the real world, while this solution works, you need to be mindful of the latency it would add to every session, especially if your data center is not near the AWS region and all the data transfer fees.

57. (D) The issue here evidently is that the ICMP echo request packets can make their way to VPC12, but the ICMP echo reply packets cannot reach VPC3. In scenarios like this, when two VPCs are associated to two different route tables in the same transit gateway, and the goal is to have connectivity between the two, you need to make sure each VPC propagates its routes to both route tables and not just the one that it's associated to. If

only one VPC propagates its routes to both route tables, the one-way communication issue that you observe here will surface.

58.   (C) To answer this question, you need to remember while route table can be associated to multiple VPCs, a VPC at any point in time can be associated to only one route table. With this restriction in mind, our only powerful tool to provide connectivity between VPC_A and other VPCs is via mutual route propagation. We can also safely rule out option A as it would lead to massive administrative overhead not just to configure the current design but also to accommodate future changes. Finally, our solution will preserve the current segmentation strategy where only the pairs of (B,C), (D,E), and (F,G) can talk to each other without any cross-pair communications.

59.   (D) The chain of events need to start from Network Manager, to EventBridge and then to Lambda to execute the Python function. The TGW Network Manager is a central monitoring tool for TGWs and their attachments. The tool can monitor and report several key factors including BGP sessions, VPN connections and IP route table modifications. The events are sent via the EventBridge to Lambda to trigger the Python piece of code.

60.   (C) Currently, in AWS, you cannot reference Security Group in other VPCs connected to the same transit gateway. Also, the use of AWS PrivateLink won't be a valid option as Privatelinks are ideal for one-to-many scenarios where one VPC is acting as the service provider or shared services hosting location, which is not the case here with their unknown traffic patterns.

61.   (B) Here, the customer has two requirements; scale and security. The solution needs to scale to hundreds and potentially (after onboarding external customers) to thousands of client VPCs. Furthermore, although security might not be the number one concern with internal VPCs, it eventually will turn into a priority after adding the external customers to the architecture. You can easily eliminate VPC peering as it would fail you on both fronts. Transit VPC also doesn't look like a great idea as it won't scale easily and cannot be secured without extensive efforts (keep in mind you are working with a combination of external routers from other vendors and AWS security mechanisms for each and every customer). Although transit gateways can meet your scale requirements, securing such a high degree of connectivity freedom between the shared services and external customers could quickly turn into a challenge. AWS PrivateLink provides a scalable solution, able to accommodate thousands of users and integrate them into a load balancer while limiting their level of access to exactly the service you intend to expose.

62.   (A)(C) Each VPN tunnel, even with transit gateways, still supports up to 1.25Gbps. However, now with transit gateways, you can have multiple tunnels and perform equal cost load balancing (ECMP) across them (up to 50Gbps). In this case, the customer apparently is not using more than 2 of their tunnels at the same time. Needless to say, the customer gateway (e.g., firewall or router) needs to fully support the ECMP using

BGP multi-path as well. At first glance, this might seem trivial, but many firewalls, especially those running older versions of code, have issues running BGP or performing ECMP with BGP multi-path.

63. (D) In order for the customer to receive the AWS public routes and use them to connect to AWS public services such as S3, DynamoDB, and Glacier, all they need to do is to order a new Direct Connect link and configure it with a public VIF. As soon as the session is up, the customer will receive thousands of routes from AWS and will have access to all the AWS public resources across all the regions.

64. (B)(E) This is a classic example of architecting in AWS while dealing with ambiguity. As mentioned in the question itself, the idea of using transit gateways by this customer is still in its infancy and is a high-level proposal that may or may not work. On the other hand, it might work but require drastic changes to the other parts of the network, which would have to be studied carefully. In this scenario, we know the bank will be using Direct Connect links in one region (eu-west-1). Given the number of links and the fact that in one region, there are multiple Direct Connect locations, it should not pose a serious risk to the architecture. You can rather easily achieve a very high degree of redundancy by using different locations or port grouping/channeling technologies. However, we also know the bank has a presence in at least 4 AWS/geographical regions. This could become a challenge when you consider the fact that the Direct Connect in London will use an AWS Direct Connect Gateway (a global construct) to reach the transit gateways of each region, and currently, the maximum number of transit gateways per Direct Connect Gateway is 3. You can get around this limitation by creating "batches" of transit gateways and connecting the representatives of each batch to the Direct Connect Gateway instead of attaching them individually. For instance, you can provision transit gateways in the eu-west-1, eu-east-1, eu-north-1, and eu-south-1 regions and peer them all to the transit gateway in, say, eu-north-1 using the inter-region peering capability (effectively forming a batch). Then instead of connecting multiple transit gateways to the Direct Connect Gateway individually and burning the hard limit of 3 gateways, you can connect only the one in eu-north-1 to the Direct Connect Gateway. Finally, while you can aggregate and send up to 100 prefixes from on-premises to AWS, each transit gateway can only send 20 routes back to the Direct Connect Gateway. This can pose another serious design challenge when you consider the number of VPCs, which will be close to 900.

65. (D) In order to integrate a Direct Connect link into an existing architecture where you also have transit gateways, you have two general options. First, you can use a Direct Connect Gateway and the transit gateway. While this solution would work, in cases similar to this particular customer where heavy file uploading (data transfers into AWS) is an objective, you will be incurring significant costs for pushing data through the transit gateway. Second, you can also take the traditional path and build a parallel network and attach the Direct Connect link to your VPCs by assigning them VLAN

numbers and using Private Virtual Interfaces. In the traditional model, the customer won't be charged for inbound data transfers (uploads to AWS).

CHAPTER 22

ANS-C01 MOCK EXAM 2

1. You are working on a troubleshooting case where an AWS customer is having issues with the two SD-WAN appliances they are trying to deploy in the eu-west-2 region. Their plan is to implement an active/passive strategy and use one of the appliances at a time. To implement the solution, they have deployed the two SD-WAN appliances in a VPC called Connect VPC. Each appliance is placed in separate subnets and has its own GRE tunnel up and active to the same Transit Gateway. They are using BGP with the AS number of 63999 between the TGW and their SD-WAN appliances. Their main complaint is that AS_PATH prepending is not influencing the paths between the appliances and Transit Gateway as expected. Which of the following options is the most probable root cause of the issue?

   A. The customer needs to move the SD-WAN appliances to the same subnet
   B. The customer needs to use static routing for one path and BGP for another. The path with static will be preferred until the next hop is reachable
   C. They need to use private AS numbers above 64512
   D. They need to use different AS numbers for the TGW and their appliances

2. You are architecting an SD-WAN solution for a large customer. They have 2 SD-WAN virtual appliances installed in a separate VPC and are now planning the proper overlay to connect them to their Transit Gateway. The solution needs to support up to 15Gbps over the Connect attachment. Which of the following options indicates a valid overlay design with minimum administrative overhead?   1 x GRE Tunnel = 5 Gbps

   A. They need to run 3 GRE tunnels over the Connect attachment
   B. They need to run 1 GRE tunnel over the connect attachment
   C. Due to the throughput requirements, this must be done using Layer 2 tunneling technologies such as 802.1q
   D. Due to the throughput limitations of the underlying VPC attachment, they would need to use two separate Transit Gateways. No overlay (tunneling) is required.

3. You are connecting your AWS footprint in Tokyo to the rest of your global WAN through an SD-WAN solution. To implement the architecture and due to budget constraints, you have installed only one large SD-WAN appliance in a dedicated VPC called Connect VPC. Which of the following statements is accurate about the design of the Connect VPC? (Choose TWO)

A. You must have Direct Connect between your data center and Connect VPC
B. The connect VPC has an Internet Gateway with a default route in its routing table
C. The connect VPC has a route for the GRE peer address to the Transit Gateway in a different VPC
D. The connect VPC has a route for the BGP peer address to the Transit Gateway in a different VPC

4. You are asked by a curious junior cloud engineer about various use cases of the MP-BGP setting when configuring a Connect attachment for SD-WAN in AWS. Which one of the following options accurately demonstrates such use cases of the option?

A. Customers with both Ipv4 and Ipv6 routes
B. Customers with Ipv4 routes but different AS numbers on the SD-WAN appliances and their Transit Gateway
C. Customers with Ipv4 routes who also want to extend their MPLS networks into the cloud via the vpnv4 address family
D. Customers with Ipv4 and Ipv6 routes, who also want to have IPv4 or IPv6 multicast routing enabled between on-premises and their VPCs

5. You have configured a subnet of IPv4 addresses to host 15 EC2 instances acting as servers for your experimental video game. Your gamers will be coming from at least 32 countries, and you decided to use AWS Global Accelerator (Custom mode) to provide them with the best gaming experience. Which of the following options suggests an idea that most likely will be approved by your InfoSec team?

A. When creating the endpoints leave all the traffic control settings as AWS default
B. When creating the endpoints set the traffic control knob to permit all and configure the Security Groups
C. When creating the endpoints set the traffic control knob to deny all and configure the Security Groups
D. When creating the endpoints individually, specify the IP addresses and ports of each endpoint

6. After using a Custom Global Accelerator solution for about six months, a customer is complaining about poor user experience. Your investigations reveal that one of their backend servers is swarmed by very intensive UDP sessions, and choosing larger instance shapes is no longer an option. Which of the following ideas might be a viable solution to spread the load?

A. Deploy an Application Load Balancer and change the endpoint from the EC2 instance to the ALB

B. Deploy a Network Load Balancer and change the endpoint from the EC2 instance to the NLB

C. Increase the number of available UDP ports on the server by at least 150 to increase the number of mappings at the Global Accelerator level.

D. None of the above would provide a viable solution

7. As a solutions architect, you are presenting Custom Global Accelerator to one of your customers. Their main objective is to use the service to roll out a new online education platform during and after the Pandemic. The platform will be using both TCP and UDP sessions for a variety of services, including voice, video, file transfer, and chat. Which of the following statements is NOT accurate about the service?

A. Custom Global Accelerators only support UDP for health checks

B. Custom Global Accelerator do not have any native health check mechanism for the backend servers, and the platform needs to implement that and some failover mechanism

C. With Custom Global Accelerator can be guaranteed that the users are homed to the closest servers with the best performance unless there is a failure with the backend servers

D. With Custom Global Accelerator, you can have Application Load Balancers as a valid endpoint

8. As a senior member of the network engineering team of a large partner you are approached by a junior cloud engineer. She has a question about the Internet Gateway that you added to the three VPCs used by Global Accelerator. Those VPCs have internal Application Load Balancers (ALBs) with private subnets. She would like to know how a private subnet behind an ALB can receive traffic from the public Internet via Global Accelerator. Which of the following options indicates a correct explanation?

A. The ALB type needs to be changed from internal to Internet-facing

B. The ALB needs to be replaced by an NLB if we are going to keep the Internet Gateway

C. The Internet Gateway is necessary, but no default route is needed

D. The Internet Gateway is NOT necessary

9. As a cloud consultant, you are working with a large warehouse business where they store millions of auto parts and ship them across the US as the orders come in. They have 30 warehouses in different states. The system that controls the pick-up robots is controlled by an application that is ultra-sensitive to latency, and that is why for years, the company used local SANs in each warehouse. Previously, they tried a few different data center consolidation strategies, and they all failed as the latency slightly exceeded the on-premises numbers. Which one of the following migration strategies could help the customer plan a potential migration to the cloud and still include the robotic control system as well?

A. Use AWS Local Zones and S3 in each metro area

B. Use AWS Local Zones and S3 in each region

C. Use AWS Outposts and S3 on Outposts
D. Keep the application in local data centers but move the data storage to the cloud. In this case S3 in each region.

10. As a chief architect for an integrator, you are preparing a response package to a large cloud migration RFP. This is for a power plant with a gradual road map to migrate some of their services to the cloud. The document clearly mentions that availability always takes precedence over security. A quick study of their environment where they are still using industrial systems from the 90s confirms the accuracy of the statement. No system must ever go down until it fails (for the most part). As part of the proposal, you suggest the native DNS Firewall on AWS, but you also know that the service does not have an uptime of 100%. Which of the following options best describes the safest architecture?

A. Configure the service as fail open
B. Configure the service as fail closed
C. Deploy a 3rd party DNS firewall
D. Do not configure the service and highlight it as a risk

11. An AWS-based SaaS company is rolling out a new service that includes communicating some financially critical information with their customers. Several customers contact their account teams and raise serious concerns about the current architecture, which requires them to use the public Internet to access the service. Which of the following architectures would address the issues?

A. Place all the new application's server instances behind at least one Elastic Load Balancer and provide the customers with the public IP address of the service.
B. Place all new application server instances behind at least one Elastic Load Balancer and provide the customers with the private IP address of the service. After verifying the customer's information, establish VPC peering between the provider and consumer VPCs.
C. Use AWS Gateway VPC endpoints.
D. Use AWS PrivateLink technology.

12. You are working for a SaaS-based startup. After the initial product rollout in the us-west-1 region (N. California), which was limited to customers in the same region using the local software stack, your marketing teams are now looking to expand their offerings to several large customers on the East Coast (us-east-1 and us-east-2) as soon as possible and with the minimum initial cost. Which of the following options better satisfies the requirements outlined by the marketing team?

A. Create two new VPCs in the us-east-1 and us-east-2 regions. Peer them with the current VPC in the us-west-1 region. Create two Elastic Load Balancers in each new region pointing to the existing software stacks and instruct the new customer to create VPC endpoints in their VPCs to those regions.
B. Create two new VPCs in the us-east-1 and us-east-2 regions. Create two Elastic Load Balancers in each new region pointing to the existing software stacks and

instruct the new customer to create VPC endpoints in their VPCs to those regions.

C. Create two new VPCs in the us-east-1 and us-east-2 regions and build two new software stacks. Create two Elastic Load Balancers and instruct the new customer to create endpoints pointing to the new load balancers.

D. No changes are required. Given the cross-region capabilities of PrivateLinks, the new users should be able to create endpoints pointing to the load balancers in the us-west-1 region.

13. A Seattle-based insurance company is acquired by another larger business. They both have significant AWS presence, both use the 172.16.0.0/12 for their AWS deployments, and both are under the same security teams with no great concern about data confidentiality. Which of the following architectures would enable the smaller business to consume an application hosted in one of the VPCs owned by the acquiring company?

A. Create VPC peering between the two VPCs and make sure the routing policies only route traffic related to non-overlapping subnets

B. Create VPC peering between the two VPCs and use a NAT gateway between the two VPCs

C. Create a VPC endpoint using AWS PrivateLink to connect to the load balancer in the destination VPC.

D. The smaller company can consume services hosted by the larger business, but they first need to re-IP their AWS deployment.

14. The Cloud Engineering team of an international bank is expanding its AWS presence to ap-southeast-2 in Sydney. Currently, they have a large footprint in ap-southeast-1 with 265 VPCs in Singapore. In ap-southeast-1 the IT team offers ERP services via Privatelink into a special VPC called VPC-ITS-ERP-01. The team has just finished creating the initial 175 VPCs in ap-southeast-2 and needs to provide 165 of them with access to the same ERP services in ap-southeast-2. This traffic should never traverse the public Internet. Which of the following architectures would be a viable option? (Choose TWO)

A. Create the full stack of the ERP services in ap-southeast-2 and call it VPC-ITS-ERP-02. Use PrivateLink endpoints in each VPC in the region to connect to an Elastic Load Balancer in VPC-ITS-ERP-02.

B. Create the full stack of the ERP services in ap-southeast-2 and call it VPC-ITS-ERP-02. Use PrivateLink endpoints in each VPC in the region to connect to the servers in VPC-ITS-ERP-02. Make sure the new ERP instances have Elastic Network Interfaces.

C. Create a new VPC in ap-southeast-2 and call it VPC-ITS-ERP-02. Place a new Elastic Load Balancer in the new VPC. Establish VPC peering to VPC-ITS-ERP-01. Define the original ERP stack in ap-southeast-1 as its targets. Establish PrivateLink between the other VPCs in ap-southeast-2 and the load balancer in VPC-ITS-ERP-02.

D. Establish VPC peering between the VPCs in ap-southeast-2 and VPC-ITS-ERP-01.

15.   The Computer Science school of higher education institute has recently given a group of 350 students access to individual Windows and Linux EC2 instances. The instances are all placed in one VPC. The SecOps team of the University receives reports of data breaches and unauthorized access to several EC2 instances. As the first step, they need to be alerted as soon as a port scan attempt is underway. Which of the following options offers the most efficient solution?

A.   Enable Flow Logs at the VPC level with a filter configured to ALL. Send the logs to an S3 bucket. Download the files on a monitoring EC2 instance. Schedule a shell script with the "egrep" keyword to catch any statement logged with the REJECTED keyword against the same IP address within a short period of time. Email the root user if a matching pattern is found.

B.   Enable Flow Logs at the VPC level with a filter configured to REJECTED. Send the logs to CloudWatch. Under the Log group, create an alarm to notify the network administrator of the matching pattern of REJECTED within a short period of time.

C.   Enable Flow Logs at the interface level of the management server with a filter configured to REJECTED. Email the root user as soon as a matching pattern is found.

D.   Enable Flow Logs at the interface level of each EC2 instance with a filter configured to ALL. Send the logs to CloudWatch. Under the Log group, create an alarm to notify the network administrator of a matching pattern of REJECTED within a short period of time.

16.   After failing the initial assessment related to a major regulatory audit, the auditor has given an online shopping business 3 days to meet their requirements. First and foremost, going forward, you need to track changes made to your AWS resources at the API level (CLI or Console) and send the logs to a dedicated S3 bucket. You also need to be able to analyze millions of such API call logs, which indicates what changes were made to your cloud setup. Which of the following options describes the best course of action?

A.   Use AWS Config to have a history of API calls for your account and send the logs to an S3 bucket. Use S3 for the other types of logs requested. Enable Inspector to analyze the logs.

B.   Use AWS CloudTrail to have a history of API calls for your account and send the logs to an S3 bucket. Use S3 for the other types of logs requested. Enable GuardDuty to analyze the logs.

C.   Use AWS Config to have a history of API calls for your account and send the logs to an S3 bucket. Use S3 for the other types of logs requested. Enable CloudWatch Logs to analyze the logs.

D.   Use AWS CloudTrail to have a history of API calls for your account and send the logs to an S3 bucket. Use S3 for the other types of logs requested. Enable AWS Inspector to analyze the logs.

17.   A cloud engineer is setting up a new Elastic Load Balancer in AWS for his externally exposed 2-tier Web application. The Web front will be available through an HTTPS address with TLS 1.3 and the load balancer will offload encryption before forwarding

the traffic to the backend servers. Which of the following TWO statements are c
about this setup?

A. Make sure in addition to the default HTTP listener, the Load Balancer also has an
HTTPS (TCP 443) listener.
B. Create only one listener and configure it to support only HTTPS (TCP 443)
C. Two subnets in 2 different Availability Zones must be selected. Create a target group
with Web instances listening to HTTP
D. Since there is one Load Balancer, the architecture can be built using one subnet in
one Availability Zone. Create a target group with Web instances using HTTP
E. Since encryption will terminate at the Load Balance, no certificate is needed on it.
F. Choose a certificate from AWS Certificate Manager to deploy on the Load Balancer

18. A junior cloud engineer is designing a small Web load balancing solution in AWS.
Although his users are internal corporate customers, they will be visiting the Web site
from remote offices using the public Internet, Furthermore, for security reasons, he
needs to fully encrypt the users' traffic as far as possible from their personal devices into
AWS with authentication on his backend servers. He has 2 Apache Web server instances
listening to TCP 443 (HTTPS) behind the load balancer. Which of the following
options provides an architecture that meets the design requirements?

A. Choose AWS Application Load Balancer and use AWS Certificate Manager (ACM)
to deploy a certificate on the load balancer with HTTPS listeners. Perform SSL/
TLS offloading on the Load Balancer.
B. Choose AWS Application Load Balancer and deploy a certificate to the load balancer
with HTTPS listeners. The load balancer will process the sessions at Layer 4 and
pass them on to the backend servers.
C. Choose AWS Network Load Balancer and deploy a certificate to the load balancer
with HTTPS listeners. Perform SSL/TLS offloading on the Load Balancer.
D. Choose AWS Network Load Balancer. Enable HTTP support on the back-end
instances.

19. As a cloud networking architect, you are working with a large customer to design and
implement a hybrid name resolution solution between their physical data centers and
AWS. Currently, they have 8 BIND servers on Linux in their two data centers. They also
extensively use the Route 53 resolver service for their 10 VPCs. Ultimately, they would
like to have full name resolution between the two environments over Direct Connect.
However, your current task is to propose a solution to enable the on-premises hosts to
resolve the hostnames of resources in their VPCs. Which of the following options helps
them implement such a solution?

A. Deploy an outbound endpoint in one of the VPCs and configure conditional
forwarding on the BIND servers.
B. Deploy an inbound endpoint in one of the VPCs and configure conditional
forwarding on the BIND servers.
C. Deploy 10 outbound endpoints in each one of the VPCs and configure conditional
forwarding on the BIND servers.

D. Deploy 10 inbound endpoints in each one of the VPCs and configure conditional forwarding on the BIND servers.

20. As a senior cloud engineer, you are tasked to enable the on-premises hosts to resolve the hostnames of your AWS-based resources. There is a redundant VPN channel between the two locations. On your side, you are using Cisco ASA firewalls as the VPN headend. You also remember that the architect who designed the project mentioned all the Windows DNS servers should be able to leverage "the CIDR+2" of AWS VPCs for name resolution when the AWS-based resources are queried. How do you evaluate this ask?

A. This cannot be done over VPN but would have a native solution over Direct Connect
B. This cannot be done over VPN if Cisco ASA firewalls are in use. It would have a solution if the VPN were built on a router with permit access lists for UDP 53
C. This can be done as it stands directly between the Windows servers and the CIDR+2 address
D. This can be done as it stands but not directly between the Windows servers and the CIDR+2 address

21. As a chief architect, you are reviewing a hybrid name resolution solution for a customer. Their goal is to leverage the AWS inbound and outbound endpoints for Route 53 and simplify their architecture. They currently have a fleet of Linux BIND servers configured in their physical data center and on AWS. They have a pair of 100G Direct Connect links between their data center and AWS. Pick the TWO options that together would provide an acceptable solution. (Choose TWO)

A. Deploy inbound endpoints in each VPC and configure conditional forwarding on the on-prem BIND devices. This will take care of name resolution for AWS-based resources from their physical data center.
B. Deploy outbound endpoints in each VPC and configure conditional forwarding on the on-prem BIND devices. This will take care of name resolution for AWS-based resources from their physical data center.
C. Deploy inbound endpoints in each VPC. This will take care of name resolution for on-prem resources from AWS.
D. Deploy outbound endpoints in each VPC and outbound rules. This will take care of name resolution for on-prem resources from AWS.

22. A gaming company is planning to use CloudFront for their Web content in North and South America. After they created their distribution point, AWS automatically assigned them the following name: https://a1234xyz.cloudfront.net./. This random name worked for some time as they were using the URL in the body of another HTML file, and no one really complained. But now, after making changes to their Web architecture, they would like to use their own domain name and possibly instruct their users to access that URL, so it must be user-friendly. Replacing that name with their custom domain name has resulted in some domain name-related SSL/TLS warnings. Which of the following high-level solutions could resolve the issue? (Choose TWO)

A. Request a public or private certificate from AWS Certificate Manager (ACM).
B. Request a public certificate from AWS Certificate Manager (ACM).
C. Import certificates into AWS Certificate Manager (ACM) in any region.
D. Import certificates into AWS Certificate Manager (ACM) in US East (North Virginia) only.

23. A network engineer is designing a load balancing solution in AWS to receive HTTP traffic from thousands of external users and distribute them across a group of 4 Linux Web servers. Two of the Web servers are EC2 instances, and the other 2 are on-prem servers in their local data center to be migrated to AWS at a later date. There is a 10G Direct Connect link between the data center and AWS. Regardless of the location of the server, the development team needs to ensure the HTTP requests of one session only go to the same Web server throughout the entire session. Which of the following options meets the requirements of this scenario?

A. Use Network Load Balancer. Create a target group and register the instances and external servers as targets. Ensure a Connection Draining feature is enabled.
B. Use Application Load Balancer. Create a target group and register the instances and external servers as targets. Ensure a Sticky sessions feature is enabled.
C. Use Classic Load Balancer. Create a target group and register the instances and external servers as targets. Ensure a Sticky sessions feature is enabled.
D. To make it a supported architecture, move the two on-prem servers to two EC2 Amazon Linux instances. Use any type of AWS Load Balancer. Create a target group and register the instances and external servers as targets.

24. To cut costs related to AWS data transfer, your company has decided not to replace the more modern interface endpoint for S3 with regular gateway endpoints. This took away their ability to perform transitive routing and access S3 over Direct Connect. Which of the following architectures describes a correct course of action to build an acceptable alternative? (Choose TWO)

A. Access S3 via the public Internet
B. Setup an ELB and a fleet of proxy servers behind it. Access S3 over Direct Connect through the proxy servers.
C. Build an IPSec VPN tunnel and make sure the S3 traffic takes the path via the tunnel
D. Use AWS Outposts service and run S3 on Outposts

25. The cloud engineering team of a large enterprise would like to forward the HTTP requests for /projectx/ and all its subdirectories to a new target group called ProjectX with minimum costs. Which of the following solutions better meets the requirements?

A. Create an Application Load Balancer and inspect the URLs in the HTTP request messages. Route the traffic to the desired target group if the pattern matches / projectx using host-based routing.

B. Create a Network Load Balancer and inspect the URLs in the HTTP request messages. Route the traffic to the desired target group if the pattern matches / projectx/* using host-based routing.

C. Create an Application Load Balancer and inspect the URLs in the HTTP request messages. Route the traffic to the desired target group if the pattern matches / projectx/* using path-based routing

D. Create an Application Load Balancer and inspect the URLs in the HTTP request messages. Route the traffic to the desired target group if the pattern matches / projectx using path-based routing and then add the sub-directories to the same rule.

26. The SRE team of a video service provider is studying the amount of load received by each one of the EC2 instances behind two Application Load Balancers to better size the instance types for potential spikes of traffic. The load balancers receive an equal amount of traffic forwarded by route 53. Currently, they have 100 EC2 instances; twenty are located in AZ 1 behind ALB01, while the rest are placed in AZ 2 behind ALB02. Which of the following statements is true about the load on each instance when it's analyzed by the SRE team?

A. Each instance always roughly receives 1% of the total load

B. Each instance in AZ 1 receives 2.5% of the total load, while instances in AZ 2 receive only 0.625% of the total load

C. Each instance in AZ 1 receives 5% of the total load, while the instances in AZ 2 receive no load unless both instances in AZ 1 fail.

D. Each instance in AZ 2 receives 1.25% of the total load, while the instances in AZ 1 receive no load unless both instances in AZ 1 fail.

27. You are about to embark on a 24-month Go-to-Cloud migration journey. As part of the first phase, you are targeting 150 servers offering a TCP-based application from behind a virtual on-prem load balancer that serves millions of users. You are planning to use AWS Elastic Load Balancers and move the servers in batches of 10 servers per weekend from your on-prem facilities to AWS. Which of the following options offers a viable and smooth migration plan?

A. Create a Network Load Balancer with 2 target groups, one pointing to your VPC and the other one to the on-prem facilities. Use the IP address of the servers and register all the 150 servers in the on-prem target group. During each maintenance window, register 10 servers in the cloud-based target group and deregister them from the on-prem target group.

B. Create an Application Load Balancer with 2 target groups, one pointing to your VPC and the other one to the on-prem facilities. Use the IP address of the servers and register all the 150 servers in the on-prem target group. During each maintenance window, register 10 servers in the cloud-based target group using their instance-IDs and deregister them from the on-prem target group. Use Host-based routing during the migration.

C. Create an Application Load Balancer with 2 target groups, one pointing to your VPC and the other one to the on-prem facilities. Use the IP address of the servers and register all the 150 servers in the on-prem target group. During each maintenance window, register 10 servers in the cloud-based target group using their IP addresses and deregister them from the on-prem target group. Use path-based routing during the migration.

D. After deploying a Network Load Balancer, you can safely and smoothly move all the servers to EC2 instances during one maintenance window.

28. After failing to fulfill some requests from the users on the Internet, you are urgently expanding a fleet of Web servers. In your current target group attached to a Network Load Balancer, you have 35 servers hosted in your traditional data centers located in two locations in Virginia called IAD510 and IAD520 and 15 EC2 instances. The emergency plan now is to expand the fleet to use 25 other servers in a peered VPC in the same region. You need to ensure all the servers, if healthy, are still available to the customers. There is a 10G Direct Connect link between your headquarters and AWS. Which of the following options describe the best approach?

A. Create a new target group and register all the servers in the group by their IP addresses regardless of their location.

B. Create a new target group and register the new EC2 instances in the peered VPC using their IP addresses.

C. Register the new EC2 instances in the peered VPC using their IP addresses in the existing target group.

D. Network Load Balancers cannot send traffic to targets outside their VPC.

29. The platform architecture of a SaaS company has gone through multiple iterations over the years. They started with bare-metal servers in data centers, then virtual machines, and containers in data centers, and then EC2 instances in AWS. Which of the following options offers a serverless approach to offering their Python3 Online Survey application to end users?

A. Use AWS Elastic Container Service (ECS) behind an Application Load Balancer. Ensure the ALB forwards traffic to different ports associated with different containers.

B. Use AWS Elastic Container Service (ECS) behind a Network Load Balancer. Ensure the ALB forwards traffic to different IP addresses associated with different containers.

C. Use one AWS Lambda function as the target for a target group linked to an Application Load Balancer.

D. Use multiple AWS Lambda functions as needed as the targets for a target group linked to an Application Load Balancer.

30. As a cloud architect, you are helping the QA team of a software development company to test the latest version of their flagship application. The new application has been deployed on 4 EC2 instances and usually over 150 instances servers as production Web servers. Your goal is to limit the traffic headed toward the 4 servers to the sessions originating from the QA department and only if the users are browsing using Mozilla Firefox. All the other sessions should, as usual, be routed to the fleet of production servers.

What architecture will satisfy the requirements of this customer using Application Load Balancers?

A. Define a new rule with two IF statements to match the source IP address and the host header field of the HTTP requests. Define a THEN statement and forward the matching traffic to the dedicated target group containing the 4 QA servers.

B. Define a new rule with two IF statements to match the source IP address and the user agent field of the HTTP requests. Define a THEN statement and forward the matching traffic to the dedicated target group containing the 4 QA servers.

C. Define two new rules with one IF statement in each. One statement to match the source IP address and the other statement to match the host header field of the HTTP requests. Define a THEN statement and forward the matching traffic to the dedicated target group containing the 4 QA servers.

D. Define two new rules with one IF statement in each. One statement to match the source IP address and the other statement to match the user agent field of the HTTP requests. Define a THEN statement and forward the matching traffic to the dedicated target group containing the 4 QA servers.

31. As a member of the NRE team of an online job search service running a hybrid architecture, in the middle of the night, you are paged into an incident involving multiple BGP session-down/reset events between one of your physical datacenters and AWS. Initial investigations reveal that a change window earlier that night has added 14 more subnets to the internal routing table of the company. This has resulted in 104 BGP routes on the border router being advertised to AWS via the site-to-site VPN session. Which of the following statements offers a viable solution?

A. Filter out 4 prefixes and reduce the number of to-be-advertised prefixes to the VGW to 100

B. Use BGP aggregate-address command and summarize the routes to 100 or fewer

C. Use BGP and only advertise a default route from the data center to the VGW

D. Open a case with AWS technical support and increase the quota to 120 prefixes for the impacted route table

32. To better access a group of VPCs, you are architecting a Highly Available Direct Connect solution with two cross-connects at the same location for a fast-growing cryptocurrency trading business. You use both of their edge routers (R1 and R2) and create two BGP sessions to AWS. You also configure iBGP between the two edge routers. Assuming the outgoing path is preferred to be through router R1, how would you prevent asymmetric routing in this scenario? (Choose THREE different ways)

A. Advertise the routes with a higher MED out of R2

B. Advertise the routes with a lower MED out of R2

C. Advertise the routes with a longer AS_PATH out of R2

D. Advertise the routes with a longer AS_PATH out of R1

E. Apply the community tag of 7224:7300 to the routes leaving R1

F. Apply the community tag of 7224:7100 to the routes leaving R1

33. The network engineering team of a US-based insurance company with a single 1G Direct Connect link in the us-east-1 region is rearchitecting their border network to improve access reliability at a lower cost. The plan is to add a 10G Direct Connect link in the US East region (North Virginia) but in a different Direct Connect location. The two links are connected to separate BGP speakers on your side, and there is an iBGP between them. As the first phase of design, you would like to make sure as long as the 10G link is up, it is used by AWS to route traffic toward your network and not the 1G link. How would you achieve this design goal?

   A. Configure inbound BGP policy on your data center border router connected to the 10G link and increase the AS_PATH length for the routes received from AWS
   B. Configure an inbound BGP policy on your data center border router connected to the 1G link and increase the AS_PATH length for the routes received from AWS
   C. Configure an outbound BGP policy on your data center border router connected to the 10G link and increase the AS_PATH length for the routes announced to AWS.
   D. Configure an outbound BGP policy on your data center border router connected to the 1G link and increase the AS_PATH length for the routes received from AWS

34. You are paged into an AWS Direct Connect troubleshooting incident where the customer's engineering team is complaining about the wrong path their traffic is taking to leave their data center routers into AWS. They have a primary 10G and a backup 1G Direct Connect link terminated on two border routers in two Direct Connect locations in the same region. The setup was working properly until this issue was detected. The team states that they have set a higher Local Preference value for the prefixes received from AWS via an inbound BGP policy on the router with the 10G link, yet they are still seeing some significant amount of outbound traffic on the 1G backup link which at times leads to packet drops due to link saturation. The 1G link is supposed to be utilized ONLY if the 10G link is down, and that's the only case where the performance degradation for some low-priority applications is accepted as a known risk. Which of the following options could be the root cause of the issue?

   A. They might be sending more specific routes out of the 1G link to AWS
   B. The iBGP session between the two customer routers might have gone down
   C. Instead of Local Pref, the customer must modify the AS_PATH length using an inbound policy on their primary router
   D. Instead of Local Pref, the customer must modify the AS_PATH length using an outbound policy on their primary router

35. You are working as a network engineer for an affordable events and wedding photography company. To achieve higher throughput and reduce the overall costs from their office in Washington D.C. to S3 and sometimes AWS Glacier, you are adding a pair of 1G Direct Connect links to your US East AWS presence. Currently, you do not have a dedicated public AS number. Which of the following options can be considered as a valid architecture, in this case, to put both links in service as soon as possible?

A. Submit a request through ARIN online and receive a 4-byte public AS number. This ASN can be used on your side of the Direct Connect. You can run eBGP to AWS.

B. Since the AS number will not be exposed to the rest of the world, you can choose any public AS number. This ASN can be used on your side of the Direct Connect. You can run eBGP to AWS.

C. You can safely choose a private AS number. This ASN can be used on your side of the Direct Connect. You can still run eBGP to AWS.

D. Submit a request to AWS technical support and receive a 4-byte public AS number. This ASN can be used on your side of the Direct Connect by the same AWS account. You can run eBGP to AWS.

36. You are configuring your first 1Gbps AWS Direct Connect to achieve more affordable rates compared to your existing VPN connections. Which of the following options are NOT required by AWS to establish the connection between your devices and AWS? (Choose TWO)

A. Single mode fiber
B. 1000BASE-LX (1310 nm) transceiver
C. Port speed manual configuration
D. 802.1Q support on intermediate devices that you might have between the two routers
E. BGP timers set to the RFC standards
F. Asynchronous BFD

37. As a Solutions Architect, you are assisting a music retailer chain based in California. After a brief outage in their primary AWS Direct Connect location, which affected their 500Mbps connection, you are adding another AWS 500Mbps Direct Connect link to the same region to improve the network resiliency. Which of the following options is NOT accurate about the process required to provision the link?

A. You must work with an AWS Partner Network (APN) company to provision the new connection and cannot use the AWS Direct Connect console
B. This connection, once provisioned, can only be utilized for one VIF, and you'll need to apply for a new connection for any additional VIF
C. You do not have to have any presence (e.g., routers) at the AWS Direct Connect location
D. The LOA-CFA letter must be downloaded from the AWS console by you and presented to the APN

38. You are architecting a greenfield AWS solution for a City Council of Hope with 15 different departments. You are planning on using different subnets, route tables, and DNS servers for each department. The DNS server addresses will be distributed using the DHCP Option sets. Which of the following combination of AWS constructs will allow you to implement this architecture?

A. Create 1 VPC, 15 subnets, and 15 DHCP Options sets.
B. Create 1 VPC, 15 subnets, and 1 DHCP Options set.

C. Create 15 VPC, 15 subnets, and 1 DHCP Options set.
D. Create 15 VPC, 15 subnets, and 15 DHCP Options sets.

39. You are paged into a troubleshooting case with an AWS cloud customer where they are complaining of broken public domain name propagation when it's set for the default VPC through DHCP options sets. The issue is that the AWS console does not show their EC2 instance names with the configured domain name. Instead, all the Public IPv4 DNS entries are still in the form of "ec2-x-x-x-x.compute-1.amazonaws.com" where x.x.x.x is the elastic IP address associated with the EC2 instance. Which of the following options could be the potential root cause?

A. The customer has not set the enableDnsHostnames option to TRUE
B. The customer has not set the enableDnsSupport option to TRUE
C. The customer cannot update the default domain name for the default VPC
D. The domain name configured under DHCP Options Set affects the operating system within the instance and not the "Public IPv4 DNS" column of the EC2 management console.

40. You are working as a network architect for a video gaming company. Since the artists need to create, store, edit, upload, and download very large and sometimes small video files over time, the IT team has increased the SAN capacity. You have S3 buckets in the us-west-1 region, yet due to high latency, it was solely used for monthly project backups. The company also has a 10G Direct Connect into one of the us-west-1 locations with 3 VIFs to access the prod, dev, and clients VPCs. You are looking to deploy Amazon Storage Gateway to provide your developers low latency access to the S3 buckets. Instead of further expanding the SAN use them for day-to-day operations. Which of the following TWO architectures provide correct connectivity options for the Storage Gateway?

A. Create a private VIF on the existing Direct Connect link
B. Create a public VIF on the existing Direct Connect link
C. Create an IPSec tunnel to an unattached VGW in the us-west-1 region
D. Use HTTPS over the public Internet

41. You have a fleet of 55 Web servers behind an AWS Network Load Balancer. The fleet is comprised of 35 EC2 instances in a VPC and 20 legacy Web servers in your corporate data center, all running Apache 2.4. The long-term plan is to move all the Web servers to the cloud, but for now, you need to make sure all the Web server visits by the clients are logging. In the log files, the security team would like to see the actual IP address of the source client. How should you architect this solution?

A. Replace the Network Load Balancer with an Application Load Balancer. This change will enable source IP address preservation in this setup
B. Enable proxy protocol on the Network Load Balancer and obtain the source IP addresses from the proxy protocol header

C. Replace the Network Load Balancer with an Application Load Balancer. Use X-Forwarded-For headers to capture client IP addresses

D. Source IP address preservation should happen by default in this architecture without any modifications

42. A large retailer with over 6 million dollars in credit and debit card transactions annually is subject to the PCI-DDS level 1 audit. They have recently migrated their MySQL database instances from their local datacenter in Portland to Amazon Aurora in the us-west-2 region, where they have multiple VPCs and a 10G Direct Connect. Their security team is looking to use the AWS Key Management Service (KMS) to create and store the keys used to encrypt their data at rest. Which of the following TWO options can enable this architecture?

A. Use NAT to connect to the AWS KMS service

B. Create a VPC endpoint based on PrivateLink and connect to the AWS KMS service

C. Create a public VIF on the DX link and connect to the AWS KMS service

D. The AWS KMS service can be reached from within the VPC through a private IP address

43. A senior cloud engineer working for an online music store is tasked with implementing a Digital Right Management (DRM) solution in AWS. They are looking to implement a scalable and resilient key management solution using AWS CloudHSM in the us-east-2 region. As a standard company practice, to pass the architecture board, the solution needs to be spread across at least 2 Availability Zones and fully synchronized all the time for better availability. To get started, you create a CloudHSM cluster with HSMs in two different AZs. Which of the following set of actions completes the architecture to meet the customer's requirements?

A. A- Use an Elastic Load Balancer to spread the load across the two HSMs. Create an IPSec tunnel for synchronization between the two nodes. Make API calls to add or remove HSM devices in case you need to scale.

B. Load balancing the traffic across the HSM units will take place automatically. Create an IPSec tunnel for synchronization between the two nodes. Make API calls to add or remove HSM devices in case you need to scale.

C. Load balancing the traffic across the HSM units will take place automatically. Constant synchronization between the cluster members will take place automatically. Make API calls to add or remove HSM devices in case you need to scale.

D. Load balancing the traffic across the HSM units will take place automatically. Constant synchronization between the cluster members will take place automatically. The cluster will auto-scale as the load changes.

44. To improve the overall security posture of their database encryption and its key management in AWS, an international financial services company is looking to use CloudHSM. Currently, the database servers are located in a VPC called dba-102, while the eight HSMs are provisioned as a cluster in a shared VPC named svc-100. Which

of the following architectures is NOT valid to provide connectivity to the CloudHSM cluster by the customer?

A. Use an ENI endpoint in svc-100 VPC
B. Use an ENI endpoint in dba-102 VPC
C. Peering between dba-102 and svc-100 VPCs
D. Deploy the HSMs in the same VPC as the database servers

45. To be prepared better to cover a nationwide election, a news agency is adding another Content Delivery Network (CDN) provider to their network, and they selected AWS CloudFront for the purpose. As part of the deal, they also moved their origin servers from their data centers to AWS behind an Elastic Load Balancer. The ultimate goal is to use the same origin servers during the election days for both CDNs to serve over a billion requests. This architecture is agreed upon by the key decision-makers. However, they need to make sure the data scientists can analyze the origin logs based on which requests have come from each contracted CDN. How should they update the architecture?

A. Configuring CloudFront and the third party CDN to add custom headers to the requests
B. Create two Application Load Balancers and assign them the same origin serves as the target groups.
C. Create two Network Load Balancers and assign them the same origin serves as the target groups.
D. Configuring CloudFront and the third party CDN to add custom headers to the requests based on the user-agent field

46. As a cloud solutions architect you are presenting a high level design to a start-up customer. They are looking to offer their security tool as SaaS on AWS and project to increase the number of sessions into their environment to begin at 100s and reach to millions in 12 months. Wehn the traffic is received they need to perform path-based load balancing to route the requests to the correct server farm based on the URLs. They will have 6 server farms. Which of the following options presents an acceptable high level architecture?

A. The customer only needs an ALB with path-based policies. Their customers would need to deploy NLBs in their VPCs.
B. The customer only needs an CLB with path-based policies You need to enable cookies.
C. The customer needs to create an ALB as the target of an NLB. The path-based policies are defined on the ALB
D. The customer needs to create an NLB as the target of an ALB. The path-based policies are defined on both the NLB and ALB

47. Due to financial constraints, the cloud engineer of a New York-based real estate company is tasked with reducing their public cloud fees, including their AWS monthly bills. The initial investigations reveal that the company incurs significant fees for one of its old architectures to provide connectivity to DynamoDB and S3 through a NAT Gateway.

If their entire AWS footprint is located in the us-east-1 region, how should the engineer rearchitect the solution to reduce the costs?

A. Move the S3 and DynamoDB resources to the same Availability Zone in the us-east-1 region
B. Create two NAT Gateways dedicated to S3 and DynamoDB. Keep the number of sessions to fewer than 5000 per session per NAT Gateway
C. Create an interface VPC endpoint and keep the traffic within AWS
D. Create a gateway VPC endpoint and keep the traffic within AWS

48. After using VPN tunnels for several years to reach your AWS VPCs, you just provisioned your first AWS 10G Direct Connect in one of the US West locations. According to your failover strategy, as long as the Direct Connect link is up, your traffic should take the more reliable path, and if it fails, the traffic should failover to the VPN service to the virtual Gateway. Although you were told by your Cloud consultant that this would be the default behavior, you notice the VPN remains the preferred path, although the DX is up and functional. Which of the following options describes a potential root cause?

A. The prefixes advertised via the Direct Connect link might have a longer AS_PATH length
B. The prefixes received from AWS via the VPN might have higher Local Pref values
C. The prefixes advertised via the VPN link might be longer
D. For the architecture to function properly, for the first time, you need to shut the VPN tunnels for the DX to take over. Going forward, the DX will remain the preferred path

49. A national bank based in California has an AWS footprint of 120 VPCs, each assigned to a particular branch or internal department. The IT organization is creating a central services VPC to host all their web-based applications hosted on Linux servers. To process the access logs more easily, they need to make sure each VPC is represented by a single IP address in the WWW log files located in the directory of /etc/httpd/logs/access_log on each web server. Which of the following architectures provides a valid solution?

A. Create a Gateway Load Balancer in each VPC except the central VPC.
B. Create a Gateway Load Balancer in each VPC except the central VPC. Ensure the IP addresses assigned to each Load Balancer are unique.
C. Create a private NAT gateway in the central VPC and map each VPC subnet to a single IP address. Place the web servers behind the NAT gateway.
D. Create a private NAT gateway in each VPC except the central VPC. Ensure the IP addresses assigned to each Load Balancer are unique.

50. An auto manufacturer is going through a major AWS architecture overhaul. In their new architecture in Europe, they have 32 VPCs attached to a single transit gateway. One of the VPCs is a highly protected environment equipped with a pair of stateful firewalls. Behind the firewalls, the company is hosting its most sensitive patented information in a group of Windows and Linux servers. During the first phase of the migration plan, to minimize the number of firewall rules, the cloud engineering department has gotten

approval from the CISO to NAT each VPC to a single IP address. Hence, instead of creating rules for the IP addresses of thousands of EC2 instances individually, those 31 IP addresses will be permitted on the firewall. Which of the following options describes the correct architecture for this migration plan?

A. Create a NAT subnet in the secure VPC. Create a private NAT gateway in the secure VPC and map each VPC subnet to a single IP address on the NAT gateway.
B. Create a NAT subnet in each VPC. Place a private NAT gateway in each VPC and map each VPC subnet to a single IP address on the NAT gateway.
C. Create a NAT subnet in each VPC and place a public NAT gateway in each.
D. Create a NAT subnet in each VPC and place a private NAT gateway in each.

51. The network engineering team of a small grocery chain with only one VPC is looking to implement a low-cost security appliance based on Linux in AWS. Their goal is to inspect the Internet traffic to and from their Internet Gateway. This traffic flows between the Internet and the public subnet, where they maintain their 35 production servers. Which of the following high-level design options should their architect approve?

A. Use the same VPC. Deploy the security appliance to a separate public subnet in the same VPC.
B. Use the same VPC. Deploy the security appliance to a separate private subnet in the same VPC. Deploy a NAT gateway between the security appliance and the IGW.
C. Create a separate VPC for the security appliance. Create a public subnet in the VPC and deploy the security appliance there. Create VPC peering between the two environments.
D. Create a separate VPC for the security appliance. Create a private subnet in the VPC and deploy the security appliance there behind a NAT gateway. Create VPC peering between the two environments.

52. You are working as a cloud architect for a software security company. Their latest product, an EC2-based packet filtering software with a single Elastic Network Interface, needs to be extensively tested by the Q/A team on AWS. To support this initiative, you create a sandbox VPC with two public subnets of A and B. The VPC has its own Internet Gateway. You place the security appliance in subnet A and all the target servers, including the honey pots in subnet B. This new VPC will not communicate with the rest of the company. Which of the following options indicates the routes that must exist as you architect the routing strategy for the Q/A VPC? Choose THREE.

A. Create a gateway route table and assign it to the IGW. Create a route to direct the traffic destined for the servers' subnet to the IP address range of the subnet hosting the appliance.
B. Create a gateway route table and assign it to the IGW. Create a route to direct the traffic destined for the servers' subnet to the ENI of the appliance.
C. Create a route table for the security appliance's subnet. Create a route to direct the traffic destined for the servers' subnet to the ENI of the appliance.
D. Create a route table for the security appliance's subnet. Create a route to direct the traffic destined for the Internet (0.0.0.0/0) to the IGW.

E. Create a route table for the servers' subnet. Create a route to direct the traffic destined for the Internet (0.0.0.0/0) to the IGW.

F. Create a route table for the servers' subnet. Create a route to direct the traffic destined for the Internet (0.0.0.0/0) to the ENI of the appliance.

53. You are reviewing the architecture created by one of your engineers to implement a security solution in AWS by deploying a group of 4 Next Generation firewalls that reside in a VPC called FWCLSTR01. The goal is to route any traffic between the Internet and a group of servers located in 5 subnets in a VPC called APPS01. The team has decided to use Gateway Load Balancers. Which of the following options indicates the right architecture for the endpoint block of the design?

A. Create 5 VPC endpoints, one in each server's subnet.
B. Create 1 VPC endpoint and place it in a dedicated subnet.
C. Create 5 VPC endpoints and place them in a dedicated subnet.
D. Create 1 VPC endpoint and place it in the same subnet as the GWLB.

54. Your team has deployed a Gateway Load Balancer solution to use a group of 2 firewalls to inspect any traffic flowing between the Internet and 25 servers in the APPS01 VPC. They have placed the GWLB endpoint in a dedicated subnet in the same VPC and created another VPC with dedicated subnets for the GWLB and firewalls. Which of the following TWO options indicate the correct inbound and outbound flow of traffic?

A. IGW>GWLBE>GWLB>Firewalls>GWLB>GWLBE>Servers
B. IGW>GWLBE>GWLB>Firewalls>Servers
C. Servers>GWLBE>GWLB>Firewalls>GWLB>GWLBE>IGW
D. Servers> Firewalls>GWLB>GWLBE>IGW

55. A customer is asking you about Gateway Load Balancers in AWS. They are keen to deploy a group of 4 firewalls to inspect any inbound and outbound Internet traffic. Currently, they only have one VPC and use simple VPC ingress routing to send the traffic to their only firewall. Which of the following statements is accurate about their future architecture? (Choose THREE)

A. The GENEVE protocol must be supported by the virtual firewalls.
B. The GENEVE protocol will be used ONLY between the GWLB and firewalls.
C. The Gateway Load Balancer endpoint can reside in the same subnet as the servers.
D. The GWLB and targets must reside in different subnets.
E. The security groups for the EC2 instances running the security tool must allow UDP 6081.

56. You are evaluating AWS Gateway Load Balancers to deploy a group of 4 security appliances in a dedicated VPC called FW01. The group will be used to inspect the traffic flow between all your servers in the other 5 VPCs owned by the company. Which of the following statements is accurate about the traffic between the GWLB and the firewalls? Choose TWO.

A. For TCP sessions, the GWLB will use the source and destination port numbers, in addition to the source and destination IP addresses and transport protocol, to choose the receiving firewall.
B. For UDP sessions, the GWLB will use only the destination port number, in addition to the source and destination IP addresses, to choose the receiving firewall.
C. For non-TCP/UDP sessions, the GWLB only uses the source and destination IP addresses to choose the receiving firewall.
D. The sessions will always remain sticky in both directions.

57. As a principal architect, you are being asked by an engineer how the Internet Gateway knows how to send the inbound traffic straight to (into) the Gateway Load Balancer endpoint. She is asking this because you are about to deploy a GWLB to distribute load across 2 firewalls in your AWS network. Which of the following statements presents a more accurate response?

A. The IGW uses the main route table of the VPC to route traffic to the endpoint.
B. The IGW uses a dedicated Gateway route table of its own to route traffic to the endpoint.
C. The endpoint is associated with the IGW, and the IGW is aware of its presence and IP address.
D. The IGW uses the route table of the subnet where the endpoint is located to route traffic to the endpoint.

58. You are running a single Availability Zone Proof of Concept (POC) for AWS Network Firewall in one of your VPCs with a dedicated Internet Gateway. The goal of this architecture is to inspect the traffic between a group of servers located in a subnet called SRV007 and the Internet. Which of the following high-level architectures shows the placement for the Firewall endpoint in this POC?

A. Place the endpoint in the SRV007 subnet.
B. Create a dedicated subnet in the same VPC and place the endpoint there.
C. The goal, in this particular scenario, cannot be achieved without creating a dedicated VPC for the endpoint.
D. Both A and B.

59. You have been using Flow Logs for quite some time to monitor traffic in and out of one of your EC2 instances called server1. Now to obtain more packet-level details, you are planning on deploying a traffic mirroring solution in your VPC. To accomplish this goal, you create a traffic mirroring session with the source Elastic Network Interface (ENI) of server1. Also, as the target of this mirrored traffic, you use the ENI of server2. The filter rules are set in both inbound and outbound directions for any TCP traffic. After waiting for some time and establishing a number of TCP connections to and from server1, the tcpdump command of "tcpdump -i eth0" on server2 does not catch any traffic from server1. Which of the following options below can be a potential route cause? Choose TWO.

A. The security groups on server1 do not permit inbound VXLAN traffic (UDP 4789).
B. The security groups on server2 do not permit inbound VXLAN traffic (UDP 4789).
C. Instead of TCPdump you should use tools such as Suricata (Linux-based IDS).
D. To see the traffic, you need to use tools such as Nubeva to decrypt SSL/TLS traffic.
E. The instance type of either the source or target might be T2.

60. You are evaluating AWS traffic mirroring to inspect UDP traffic in and out of a group of 15 EC2 instances. The traffic will eventually be mirrored to 4 appliances running your licensed packet analysis software. Which of the following statements is an accurate suggestion to ensure the scalability of the architecture? Choose TWO.

A. Add a secondary Elastic Network Interface (ENI) to each one of the sources of the traffic.
B. Place the packet analysis software servers behind a Network Load Balancer (NLB).
C. Place the packet analysis software servers behind a Gateway Load Balancer (GWLB).
D. If you have targets in more than one AZ, enable cross-zone load balancing.
E. In case of congestion in large-scale designs, the user will be responsible for assigning higher priority to production traffic to ensure it won't have to compete against mirrored traffic.

61. As a senior cloud security architect, you are using AWS traffic mirroring to monitor all the HTTP/HTTPS traffic in and out of server102, server103, and server104, all located in VPC1. The mirrored traffic is sent to a group of 2 appliances behind an Elastic Load Balancer. The SecOps team has brought to your attention that server02 has been taking an unusual load of ICMP traffic. Before taking any drastic actions, you need to mirror the ICMP traffic off server102 and send it to a third appliance that you set up for this purpose in a peering VPC in the same region, VPC2. The third appliance is NOT behind the ELB. You are planning on dissecting the packet and studying the payloads. Which of the following solutions architectures can be implemented to meet the requirements in this scenario?

A. You need to move the third appliance to the target group behind the Elastic Load Balancer. Then you need to create a filter rule to ACCEPT any ICMP traffic to server102. The target for this new rule will be the load balancer.
B. You need to move the third appliance to the target group behind the Elastic Load Balancer. Then you need to create a filter rule to REJECT any ICMP traffic to server102. The target for this new rule will be the load balancer.
C. You need to create a filter rule to REJECT any ICMP traffic to server102. The target for this new rule will be the Elastic Network Interface (ENI) of the new appliance.
D. You need to create a filter rule to ACCEPT any ICMP traffic to server102. The target for this new rule will be the Elastic Network Interface (ENI) of the new appliance.

62. The operations team of a college basketball club needs to closely monitor the traffic between a C4 instance and the Internet. The instance is used to run a few home-grown loyalty and membership applications, including several chat rooms for the fans and students. Although only one legacy application uses HTTP instead of HTTPS,

the application team assures you that the tool deals with no confidential data. The CISO is still keen to mirror the HTTP Internet traffic in and out of the instance to constantly analyze in case there is any trace of confidential information, including the fans' personal data. Which of the following options describes the best set of filter rules for the source instance?

A. Create a pair of inbound and outbound filter rules to ACCEPT HTTP traffic to and from the instance. With a higher rule number, create a pair of inbound and outbound filter rules to REJECT any traffic for the CIDR block of the VPC.

B. Create a pair of inbound and outbound filter rules to ACCEPT HTTP traffic and REJECT HTTPS traffic to and from the instance. With a higher rule number, create a pair of inbound and outbound filter rules to ACCEPT any traffic for the CIDR block of the VPC.

C. Create a pair of inbound and outbound filter rules to REJECT any traffic for the CIDR block of the VPC. Create a pair of inbound and outbound filter rules with a higher rule number to ACCEPT any HTTP and HTTPS traffic in and out of the instance.

D. Create a pair of inbound and outbound filter rules to REJECT any traffic for the CIDR block of the VPC. Create a pair of inbound and outbound filter rules with a higher rule number to ACCEPT any HTTP traffic in and out of the instance.

63. As a solutions architect, you are assisting a customer in migrating from a VPN on Virtual Gateway design to VPN on Transit Gateway. Their goal is to build 4 tunnels and increase their bandwidth by using aggregating multiple tunnels and using Equal Cost Load Balancing (ECMP). Which of the following options might pose a serious challenge that would need to be investigated before the migration? (Choose TWO)

A. The Autonomous System number selection on the customer gateway
B. The number of routes received from AWS
C. The number of routes sent to AWS
D. The possibility of asymmetric routing and how the customer gateway handles that
E. Whether the transit gateway supports 4 equal paths
F. Whether the customer gateway supports 4 equal paths

64. After a security breach that made it to the news as a cloud architect working for a theme park with branches across the United States, you are tasked with redesigning the cloud Internet access strategy for the company. The network in AWS has grown organically over time and has been designed by multiple architects. Your company currently has 23 VPCs, where 12 of them have their own Internet Gateways with public IP addresses, and the rest have Internet Gateways, NAT gateways, and private IP addresses. The breach happened to one of the VPCs with direct Internet access. Your new high-level idea is to remove all the Internet and NAT gateways and consolidate them in one egress VPC (called VPC_Egress), where you will also have your IDS/IPS deployed later on. All the VPCs will be connected to a transit gateway and would need access to the Internet. Which of the following statements is accurate about the routes present in the proposed architecture? (Choose THREE)

A.   0.0.0.0/0 pointing to the transit gateway in the spoke VPCs
B.   0.0.0.0/0 pointing to the Internet gateway on the transit gateway
C.   0.0.0.0/0 pointing to the NAT gateway on the transit gateway
D.   0.0.0.0/0 pointing to the attachment for VPC_Egress on the transit gateway
E.   0.0.0.0/0 pointing to the Internet Gateway on the NAT Gateway
F.   0.0.0.0/0 pointing to the NAT Gateway on the Internet Gateway

65.   An insurance company has just recovered from a major security breach where a worm
      was able to make its way from their extranet VPC to all the other VPCs ad eventually
      infect 17 VPCs via their only transit gateway. The issue was not identified for months
      until the security team accidentally noticed unauthorized exfiltration of data. As a
      remedy, their cloud team decided to build a shared VPC to house 2 sets of stateful 3rd
      party firewalls in two Availability Zones. The new policy will require any inter-VPC
      traffic to be routed through the new shared VPC. Which of the following is accurate
      about this architecture?

      A.   Use the AWS console to enable appliance mode on the transit gateway
      B.   Use the AWS CLI to enable appliance mode on the transit gateway
      C.   Use the AWS console to enable appliance mode on the subnets hosting the firewalls
      D.   Use the AWS CLI to enable appliance mode on the subnets hosting the firewalls

MOCK EXAM 2 - Detailed Answers

1. (D) While AS_PATH prepending is one of the most efficient ways to influence inbound traffic using BGP, since the customer is using the same AS number, they are using iBGP. The AS_PATH prepending technique is only available to eBGP peering scenarios. And in order to have eBGP over the GRE tunnels, they would need to use different AS numbers.

2. (A) This is an example of deploying SD-WAN appliances on AWS as opposed to on-prem. In cases similar to this, the overlay, as usual, would be made of GRE tunnels that are built over the Connect attachments, which in turn form over the VPC attachments of the Transit Gateway. Each GRE tunnel is capped at 5Gbps, and the customer would need to run 3 tunnels to achieve 15Gbps.

3. (B)(C) While the first part of the question is fairly easy, choosing the correct second option could confuse the candidates. First off, since the appliance is virtual and in AWS, we won't need any Direct Connect. Then we know that the appliance needs to communicate with the rest of the world. So, it makes sense for the Connect VPC to have an Internet Gateway and use it via the default route. Lastly, the Connect VPC needs to provide a way for the appliance to reach the Transit Gateway and build and maintain the GRE overlay. This is done by creating a route to the CIDR block addresses of the Transit Gateway. Keep in mind, one of these addresses is used by the appliance as the destination of the GRE tunnel. In other words, the outer IP address of the encapsulated packets between the appliance and the Transit Gateway. Finally, remember the BGP addresses are only seen inside the tunnel. The outside network does not need any routing logic to support them.

4. (A) Although it would be nice and actually pretty intriguing to extend MPLS into the cloud or have end-to-end IPv4 or IPv6 multicast via different BGP address families, currently, the only viable use case among the choices provided here is when the customer has both IPv4 and IPv6 unicast routes. In such cases, on the peer side, you would need to configure both ipv4 and ipv6 address families under BGP.

5. (D) Although D involves some work that can be scripted if done via the AWS APIs, it's the most practical and, of course, secure solution. The default option is to deny all

that would stop the solution from working, and opening up the entire subnet to Global Accelerator won't be a great idea.

6.   (D) The only acceptable form of endpoint for Custom Global Load Balancer at this stage is a VPC subnet type. You could increase the number of servers to increase the mappings on different servers, but adding more ports to the same servers would not be an option.

7.   (B) All the options are inaccurate except B. While the custom type is ideal for cases like the one described here (pining a group of users to the same endpoint – such as the students in one virtual class), it does not support any health check mechanisms as the Standard type does. With the standard type, you can have TCP-based health checks for the backend servers to detect outages and act upon them within one minute.

8.   (C) This question demonstrates one of the bizarre nuances of the Global Accelerators. There is nothing wrong with the design proposed here; internal ALBs (as well as EC2 instances) can be designated as endpoints and use internal subnets. In such architectures, you must have an IGW without the typical default route that plays no role but to mark the fact that the Internet traffic can flow through those private subnets. Interesting. Isn't it?

9.   (C) This is a classic use case of AWS Outposts where you can leverage AWS hardware and setup but keep the racks local to your data centers. In other words, the AWS racks will be considered "on-prem" from your network's perspective. All the other options could easily breach the requirements.

10.   (A) Fail open is the safest option. If the service fails, the queries won't be blocked. The risks are obvious as the queries won't be firewalled during the outage, but the availability requirements will be honored.

11.   (B) In this scenario, you are creating a SaaS application for users. This option creates a dedicated load balancer for the scanner servers, which can be connected to the customer's VPCs as a service provider using AWS PrivateLinks. This is a typical design when you have a service you want to offer to the other departments of your corporation or the rest of the world. The level of trust required between the client and server VPC is at the minimum compared to more invasive solutions such as VPC peering.

12.   (D) AWS PrivateLinks are designed for such cases where the consumers of a central service need secure and scalable access to it without leaving the AWS network. Regarding option C; please note that the AWS Gateway VPC endpoints are used to connect to AWS native services such as S3 and DynamoDB and still keep the session internal to AWS without traversing the public internet. This case is about a non-AWS service (i.e., user-created service).

13. (A) As discussed previously, the SaaS provider and end consumers do not have to be located in the same region. In fact, they can easily ride the existing VPC peering sessions in two specific scenarios. First, users in a consumer VPC in a remote region can access their company's endpoints in a different region; the endpoint that is connected to the Elastic Load Balancer of a SaaS provider. Second, as shown here in this question, a SaaS provider, without having to build costly software stacks in every region, can just drop an Elastic Load Balancer into each remote and new region. The new load balancer can have the original software stack as its target if you have a VPC peering between the remote and the original VPC.

14. (C) Although the keywords around lack of security concerns might sound tempting to use VPC peering, that cannot be an option as the two VPCs have conflicting IP addresses. As a general rule of thumb, any attempt to re-IP an existing production environment is considered very taxing and should be avoided if possible. In this scenario, you can create a VPC endpoint in the smaller business's VPC and connect to the destination VPC. By doing so, you resolve the issue of conflicting IP ranges and as a bonus point keep traffic away from the public Internet. Although the latter was not explicitly asked.

15. (A)(C) The PrivateLink consumable resources (usually EC2 instances) and the end-users do not have to be located in the same region. Option A demonstrates the costly possibility of building a local stack in the new region. However, Option C presents a smarter solution. Here as indicated above, we prove that it is possible to ride the VPC peering sessions and connect the Elastic Load Balancers to resources in other regions.

16. (B) CloudWatch (and S3 buckets) can receive log feeds from Flow Logs and process them using filters. Option B briefly explains the process. In this case, as you can imagine, the port scanner applications such as nmap are hitting a wide range of ports on a large number of systems. This pattern will result in a large number of REJECTED messages in Flow Logs which can easily be detected by the right CloudWatch filter. You can create an alarm in CloudWatch to receive notifications when the logs are received.

17. (B) Using AWS CloudTrail, you can track the history of API calls initiated by users in your AWS infrastructure. For instance, Console Login is considered an event and is logged with some useful details such as the exact time, user, and source IP address. Similarly, when a user deletes an Elastic Load Balancer, the operation initiates an API that is logged with all the details about the time of deletion, username, and the source IP address. The original API (such as deleting a load balancer) may result in other API calls by the AWS infrastructure (for instance, to delete the network interfaces related to the deleted main object). AWS CloudTrail can be very useful in forensics and post-mortem, where you are attempting to find out precisely what was going on within your AWS deployment when an outage, breach, or other major events have occurred. You will see a list of API calls with ample details to figure out who, when, and how changes were made to the infrastructure. This captures changes made through both the console and AWS

CLI. Finally, the threat detection mechanism offered by GuardDuty can analyze the logs generated by other services such as AWS CloudTrail Events and VPC Flow Logs.

18. (D) This scenario is a typical use case of end-to-end encryption by relying on backend servers for encryption and mutual authentication. In such cases, the session is established directly between the target (backend server) and the end-user without any man-in-the-middle (or offloading) operation by the ELB. This might be an ideal solution if you need end-to-end encryption and also need to support millions of clients/sessions across a large number of targets at the same time. The downside of this architecture is the burden of managing certificates and other related settings on potentially a large number of backend servers – which in modern days could be automated using third-party tools or, in some cases, AWS Systems Manager.

19. (D) You would need an inbound endpoint in your VPCs to receive queries from on-prem and forward them to the CIDR+2 address.

20. (D) Both VPN and Direct Connect are acceptable choices. You just need to choose the right type of endpoint to receive queries from on-prem and forward them to the Route 53 resolver.

21. (A)(D) To have end-to-end name resolution in a hybrid environment, you would need a combination of inbound and outbound endpoints as indicated in A and D. Pay very close attention to the direction of the queries and where we use inbound versus outbound.

22. (B)(D) You can either use a public certificate from ACM or import one in the East region. It's a hard requirement by AWS. The imported certificate cannot exceed 2048 bits.

23. (B) AWS Network and Application Load Balancers both support target groups where you can define instances and IP addresses as your load balancer's targets. In addition to that, with the ALBs, you can also have a Lambda function as the target. In this case, our choice of the load balancer is limited to NLB and ALB. You can use the second requirement (need for sticky sessions to send the traffic to the same server) as a tie-breaker to choose option B. The scenario does not require connection draining (i.e., deregistration delay). Please note that AWS added sticky sessions to the NLB type of load balancers in 2019, but even that won't change the correct option here.

24. (A)(B) S3 can be accessed via the public Internet and through proxy servers that you need to set up in your VPC. Some CISOs might not like the former option, but that's not a requirement here. Option D would work with a hundred issues if you had an unlimited budget. In this case, we don't.

25. (C) This scenario is a typical use case for path-based routing one of the key features of Application Load Balancer. Similar to most traditional physical or virtual load balancers, the AWS ALB can also have path-based rules to inspect URLs and serve them through

pre-‹　ıdy in many cases. For example,
to su　have separate target groups for
the sε　l on the URLs such as /en or /fr
the lo　them to the right target group.
Simila　ɔn, you can have separate target
groups　l and /v2 or /old and /new.

26. (A) Wii　lancing is always enabled. This
feature　all 100 targets almost evenly.
Both loa　ɔpraying their traffic across the
two Avaı　and Gateway) load balancers,
cross-zon　you can enable the feature at
any time

(handwritten annotations: "① focus on SD-WAN ② Custom Global Accelerator")

27. (A) Netwɔ　ıcts to distribute millions of
TCP-basec　ɾe also need to keep in mind
both Appli　IP addresses in their target
groups to h　ɔn to the EC2 instances you
might alreac　ıest risks are associated with
moving the ₅　r bare-metal servers) to EC2
and replacing　though in real life, you may
come up witı　a seamless transition plan
where you en　moving all your servers to
EC2 in one sh　..per ιcsting, you will have one window to put your ELB(s) in
service with on-prem clients. Subsequently, the rest of the maintenance windows will
be allocated to moving the servers in batches of 10 from the external/on-prem target
group to the VPC target group by registering and deregistering them. Finally, you need
to remember this solution will depend on either a Direct Connect Link or VPN tunnel
between AWS and on-prem.

28. (C) A target group associated with a Network Load Balancer can have targets from
the same VPC (EC2 instances), on-prem (virtual or physical servers), or peered VPCs.
You can use the IP address to register all three to the same target group. Although not
mentioned here the customer needs to consider their data transfer fees very carefully.

29. (C) One of the key benefits of Application Load Balancers that still hasn't been offered
by any other type of Elastic Load Balancers is the ability to have Lambda functions as
their targets. For example, Classic Load Balancers can send traffic to EC2 instances.
Network Load Balancers upped the game when they supported both instances and IP
addresses to cover on-prem servers. However, Application Load Balancers offer all three
options. You can have targets identified by their instance-IDs or IP addresses. You can
also have Lambda functions (such as the Python code in this scenario) as the target of a
load balancer as long as they are in the same account and same region.

30. (B) In this scenario, we need to craft a rule with two conditions. The first condition is met when the source IP address is that of the QA department, AND the second condition is met when the user agent field in the HTTP requests is set to Mozilla (for instance, Mozilla/5.0). If both conditions are satisfied, the THEN statement kicks in and routes the traffic to the designated target group for the non-production version of the application. There will be a default rule (catch-all) for the non-matching traffic to route them as usual to the production target group. Furthermore, keep in mind the ALB rules can inspect many different HTTP fields to discriminate traffic based on a wide range of HTTP Request header options.

31. (B)The session has been reset by AWS because the border router violated the maximum number of routes a customer can advertise to the VGW. Although you could technically filter out the new routes, this would likely lead to connectivity issues as you would be missing some paths. Also, turning the data center into the default gateway for the AWS subnets is considered too invasive and would potentially interfere with other settings, such as another default route to an IGW. This is a hard limit set by AWS, and assuming the prefixes are contagious, the aggregate-address command (on most platforms, including Cisco, Arista, Ericsson, and Juniper) would be the best option to reduce the number of routes being advertised to the VGW.

32. (A)(C)(E) To maintain symmetry, it is essential to ensure the inbound traffic also takes the same path via R1 into the network. With multiple Direct Connect links, BGP prefers the path with higher LOCAL_PREFERENCE, shorter AS_PATH, or higher MED. In this scenario, option A gives a higher metric to the routes learned from R2 on the AWS side (less favorable). Alternatively, option C does a similia job by making the routes learned from R2 less attractive when they arrive at AWS's routers. Finally, option E has the same effect by using pre-defined BGP communities. The community tag of 7224:7300 is used to signal the AWS routers to assign higher LOCAL_PREFERENCE to the routes learned via R1 and, in turn, make them more favorable. Please note the community tags of 7224:7100 and 7224:7200 are used in different scenarios to signal low and medium preference.

33. (D)Advertising routes with longer AS_PATH out of the 1G circuit will make it less preferred from the neighbor's perfective, in this case, AWS. Two points to keep in mind (1) The question explains phase 1 of a plan which makes sense. In this type of scenario, you need to engineer both directions of traffic, inbound and outbound, to avoid asymmetric routing and unpredictable failover/performance scenarios. (2) Although it goes against technical best practices, there still is nothing to stop you from using circuits with different bandwidths for one site, especially during a migration or transition phase. The downside is obvious, what if the 10G circuit fails and it has more than 1G load on it? The users will experience severe packet loss from which you cannot easily recover until the primary circuit is down.

In real-life scenarios, if you have such circuit configurations, it's recommended to use tools such as Netflow to closely monitor the current amount of traffic.

34. (B) The iBGP session between the two border routers plays a very critical role in propagation for some key attributes in this and similar architectures. For instance, just like this scenario, when you manipulate the Local Preference value of the routes received from your neighboring AS, all the other iBGP peers within your AS will learn about it and take the new Local Preference value into account when computing the path selection algorithm. Similarly, without a healthy iBGP session, your changes will remain on the local router and won't get propagated across your AS, which in turn might lead to undesired path selections. In this case, a potential manifestation of the issue could be as follows: you increase the Local Preference value from 100 to 500 to choose a preferred outbound path. It's set on one device and never gets propagated to the other border router. The device that has never heard of the better Local Preference via its peer will not stop at that decision point and will continue running through the BGP decision process. If you're not lucky, the next step (for instance, the AS_PATH) could favor the less preferred device, and the traffic is put on the wire out to the neighboring AS.

35. (C) AWS allows you to use private AS numbers. Option A is also possible but would take time and cost money.

36. (E)(F) BFD and BGP timer settings are not required to set up a Direct Connect link between your facilities and AWS. However, you must have single mode fiber with 1000BASE-LX (for 1G) with manually set port speeds. Also, to carry the VLAN tags from multiple VPCs, your device needs to support 802.1Q.

37. (D) Since the bandwidth required in this scenario is sub-1G, you cannot work directly with AWS as of 2020. The AWS console solely supports 1 and 10G connections, and anything else (sub-1G), in this case, needs to go through an AWS Partner (APN). Similar to dedicated Direct Connect links, you do not have to have any equipment at the Direct Connect location, and you may use any 3rd party WAN provider to connect your premises to the location. In such a setup, the Letter of Authorization and Connecting Facility Assignment (LOA-CFA) is not processed through the AWS console and will not be required, and the process of provisioning the Direct Connect link is handled by the partner.

38. (B) DHCP options set configurations are done at the VPC level. This means in this scenario that to use DHCP options sets and still have 12 different NTP server addresses and 12 different domain names, you will have to have 12 VPCs. This makes options A and B our only candidates. However, the interesting point here is that with NTP servers (if they're all accurate and perhaps of the same stratum with the same source), it really cannot be the most significant design challenge. Needless to say, this customer can later consider NTP consolidation to use only 2 NTP addresses.

39. (D) With AWS DHCP option sets, you can configure the domain name for your EC2 instances. For example, a server called srv01 with a domain name of farm1.local will respond to srv01.farm1.local. The issue reported by the customer here is that the console does not show the change. This is by design. However, the operating system does receive the change as part of the DHCP update and will update its respective files or settings.

40. (B)(D) You can use AWS Gateway Storage as an on-prem solution to provide low latency access to your data stored in AWS. In this case, through caching the most recently used data, the solution would give users high speed, low latency access to their S3 buckets. From on-prem, since AWS Storage Gateway uses public endpoints, you can use either a public VIF or direct HTTPS over the public Internet to connect to Amazon S3, where, if required, you can work with local proxy servers.

41. (B) Although Network Load Balancers are known to preserve the client IP addresses yet, by default, it only happens when the targets are registered by their instance-IDs. In this case, in addition to the Web servers on EC2 instances, you also have 20 on-prem legacy servers that must have been registered using their IP addresses. In this situation, enabling the proxy protocol will help you carry and preserve the source IP address (the client's) in the proxy headers. Please keep in mind after migrating all the servers to AWS and registering them using their instance-IDs, you should be able to natively preserve the source IP address of your clients, which is the method described by option D and can be considered as a future solution.

42. (A)(B) Amazon Aurora is a rational database service compatible with MySQL and Postgre-SQL. It also supports encryption of its database instances and uses AWS KMS, a managed service, to create, store, and manage the encryption keys. This mechanism helps customers, including this retailer, pass major audits such as PCI Level 1, HIPAA, and SOC 1, 2 and 3. Before 2020, the service could only be reached via IGW/NAT solutions, but recently AWS has added support for VPC endpoints to connect to the service and keep your traffic end to end on the AWS network.

43. (B) For a long time, Hardware Security Modules (HSM) were extensively used in computer networks to perform critical security-related operations such as digital key management to meet strict regulatory obligations. The same logic is replicated to the cloud, and now you can still use single-tenant dedicated hardware for the same purpose by using the CloudHSM service powered by the Luna SA 7000 hardware. CloudHSM allows you to perform the same security key management operations based on the strict government standards such as the FIPS 140-2. CloudHSM, once set up, acts as a secure key storage able to conduct a wide range of cryptographic operations. CloudHSM is a managed service where AWS remains in charge of the backup process, firmware, or failure management without user intervention. In keeping with its single-tenant protected nature, CloudHSM must be provisioned inside a VPC.

44. (A) Although you have several choices to provide connectivity between the two VPCs, if you are using the logical endpoint, they would need to reside inside the source VPC (in this case, dba-102). Please note the ENI endpoint automatically distributes the incoming load across the HSM devices.

45. (A) This question is one of the typical benefits of adding or updating custom headers to requests received by a CDN, in this case, CloudFront. With most CDNs, you can add such headers or update them if they already exist in the requests using the management console or API. This feature can also be used in other scenarios, such as networks where you have a large CloudFront footprint with multiple distributions and want to uniquely identify requests coming from each one. Furthermore, you can use the same feature in cases where you need to prevent users from bypassing the CDN and accessing the origin server or their load balancers directly.

46. (C) With the most recent updates to the ELBs you can have an ALB as the target of an NLB. This was extensively discussed in the book and offers the best of both worlds. With the NLB you can reach millions of session and have a static IP and with the ALB you can perform path and host-based routing. They traffic is received by the NLB and kicked over to the ALB(s)

47. (D) In contrast to the interface VPC endpoints, to access AWS services such as S3 and DynamoDB that used to be only accessible via the Internet, you can use a gateway VPC endpoint. By using the gateway VPC endpoints, you can keep the traffic on the AWS network and avoid hourly and data transfer charges in both directions. Without this solution, the customer will be charged for the NAT gateway and all the data transfer fees. In real life, beware of the NAT Gateway charging models and the fact that their hourly charges start being incurred as soon as they are created and are not necessarily used. Please note this question is about DynamoDB. If it were about S3, given the 2021 updates the architects would have the two options of gateway and interface endpoints.

48. (C)AWS always prefers Direct Connect over VPN for similar routes and tweaking BGP attributes will not affect the default behavior. However, the behavior will be impacted if you start advertising more specific routes through VPN connections.

49. (D) this scenario demonstrates the high-level architecture of one of the use cases of private NAT gateways introduced in 2021. In scenarios like this, the private NAT gateway sits in the spoke VPC and translates the private IP addresses of the private subnets to a single private IP address belonging to the same VPC. In this case, unless the bank has overlapping IP ranges assigned to their VPCs, which would be a bigger problem, the IP addresses allocated to private NAT gateways should be unique. Please note; currently, the NAT gateways do not support manual address mapping. Furthermore, keep in mind, AWS supports only 5 NAT gateways in each Availability Zone. In large architectures, you might run into issues with this limitation.

50.   (D) This customer needs a private NAT solution. To design such a network, you would need to create a NAT subnet in each spoke VPC and route the traffic from the other subnets of each VPC to the private NAT gateway of the VPC. The NAT gateways would, in turn, use the route table of their subnet to route their traffic to the transit gateway. Please note, the NAT gateways will have a network interface with a private IP address assigned from the IP range of the subnet, in this case, the NAT subnet.

51.   (A) This scenario depicts the simplest form of architecting packet inspection using the VPC ingress routing technique for single-NIC security appliances. In this scenario, all you need is a separate subnet to host the security appliance. The subnet needs to be public as it's sitting directly behind an IGW. The building blocks in this architecture would be the public subnet hosting the 35 servers, the public subnet containing the security appliance, and the IGW, all inline. As you will see in the upcoming scenarios, you can instruct the IGW to route the traffic destined for the production servers subnet to the Elastic Network Interface of the security appliance.

52.   (B)(D)(F) This architecture can be validated by tracing the flow of packets in two sections; between the IGW and security appliance and between the security appliance and the servers' subnet. The traffic comes in from the Internet. The IGW, using the ingress routing feature, has a dedicated "gateway" route table with a route pointing to the Elastic Network Interface of the appliance. That route sends the traffic straight to the ENI of the appliance. The appliance's subnet also has its own route table to forward all Internet-bound traffic (0.0.0.0/0) back to the IGW. This completes the first section between the appliance and IGW. South-bound from the appliance down to the servers, the security appliance's subnet uses the general route (x.y.z.t/p->local – not shown here) to communicate with the servers. The servers' subnet has a dedicated route table with a route to forward all the Internet(north)-bound traffic to the ENI of the security appliance. And this completes the second section of the routing strategy. Please note, the gateway route table is a term used to refer to the route tables assigned to IGWs and VGWs as part of the ingress routing architectures.

53.   (B) A typical GWLB architecture has the three main components of endpoints, Gateway Load Balancers, and target groups. This scenario is about the building block of the endpoints. To "catch" the traffic and route it to the GWLB, you need a single endpoint. This endpoint, similar to a NAT gateway, needs to be placed in a separate subnet. All you need to do to route traffic to the endpoint is to create a route in each server's subnet for 0.0.0.0/0 with the next-hop of gwlbe-xyz; which is the endpoint. This way, the servers will take this route and cross the boundary of subnets to the endpoint. From the endpoint, the traffic will get routed securely to the other VPC, the GWLB, and the firewalls behind it. The return traffic will take a similar path back to the servers. Keep in mind, the traffic between the GWLB and its targets (in this case, the firewalls) is encapsulated using the GENEVE protocol.

54. (A)(C) On ingress, the endpoint is fed by the VPC ingress routing route on the IGW. The traffic is captured and sent over to the GWLB and its backend targets. Once inspected, and if permitted, the traffic will go back through the GWLB to the endpoint and from there to the servers. Keep in mind, although the GWLB and targets can reside in the same or different subnets, the endpoint and servers must be placed in different subnets. This allows you to configure the 0.0.0.0/0 route with the next-hop of the endpoint for each one of the servers' subnets.

55. (A)(B)(E) Communications between the GWLB and its targets (in this case, the firewalls) is done over GENEVE. The firewalls, similar to the GWLB, need to support the protocol, and EC2 instances need to permit its port, UDP 6081. All the other statements are inaccurate.

56. (A)(D) The GWLB uses what is called a 5-tuple hash to decide where to send the initial conversation of each session. From that point on, the session remains sticky in both directions. The 5-tuple used to generate the hash includes: the transport protocol, the source, and destination IP addresses, and port numbers. Please note, if your session is non-TCP/UDP, a 3-tuple including the protocol and source and destination IP addresses will be used.

57. (B) In scenarios like this one, we use a technique called VPC ingress routing, where we create a dedicated route table and associate it to the IGW. The route table will contain a route to direct the inbound traffic destined for the backend servers to the endpoint as its next hop. The VPC ingress routing technique came out first, and subsequently, after a while, AWS released the concept of GWLBs to better scale the deployment of security appliances.

58. (B) Strictly speaking, the endpoint and the to-be-protected servers cannot be placed in the same subnet. In fact, if they are, you won't be able to route the traffic to the endpoint, and they cannot be protected. Also, while in more complex and scalable solutions, you can have a centralized design with a dedicated VPC, in this case, it is not required.

59. (B)(E) In order to land a mirroring session on an EC2 instance, you need to make sure the target permits the inbound traffic of UDP 4789 (VXLAN), as all the traffic will be encapsulated in VXLAN packets. Also, both the source and target need to be Nitro-instances or some of the Xen-based instances, including M4, R4, and C4. Very specifically, the mirroring won't work on R3, I2, and T2 instances. This can be a challenge to users with economic instances such as t2.micro that are eligible for free-tier charging models. Moreover, although Suricata as an IDS provides great visibility and Nubeva provides decryption for SSL/TLS-based sessions, they cannot be the root cause of the issue here where TCPdump is capable of providing raw packet data (perhaps encrypted) with their VXLAN headers. Finally, if you are planning on running traffic mirroring alongside your traditional Flow Logs, keep in mind that the mirrored traffic

will not be captured by Flow Logs and will not show up in its logs. This could easily confuse the operations teams if they try to map the sessions to the amount of traffic!

60. (B)(D) In large-scale mirroring designs where you have more than one server, it's always a good idea to place the targets behind a high-performance NLB. Furthermore, to ensure healthy resources in any Availability Zone are engaged, you need to enable cross-zone load balancing. Please note, what is suggested by option D is automatically done by AWS, and the user has no built-in and practical way to set a lower precedence value for the mirrored traffic versus production.

61. (D) The new filter rule can perfectly mirror the traffic to the third appliance as a new target. This rule needs to have the rule action of "ACCEPT" to admit the traffic to the mirroring process. As you will see later, we use the REJECT action to define exceptions. For instance, the REJECT action can be used to define the types of traffic out of a broader spectrum that we do not intend to capture.

62. (C) Similar to the logic of traditional Access Lists (ACLs), here we follow the same process. We reject the narrow traffic, which in this case is everything that belongs to our AWS footprint (the CIDR), and then accept the HTTP traffic between the instance and the Internet. You might ask, why don't we only have one filter rule to ACCEPT and mirror the HTTP traffic and drop everything else? This idea won't work because you would also catch the wrong fish. In this scenario, all the HTTP traffic inside the VPC.

63. (D)(F) In order to run ECMP and bundle 4 links, the customer would need to run BGP and not static routes. Assuming full BGP and BGP multi-path support, their device also would need to support performing multi-path across 4 links. Furthermore, especially if it is a firewall, it also needs to be configured to work with asymmetric traffic patterns, which might surface as an issue when using multiple for the same purpose. Please note the number of routes is not changing when they migrate from VGWs to TGWs.

64. (A)(D)(E) It is definitely a good security hardening idea for the company to remove the random local Internet Gateways in favor of a central NAT location. For this solution to work, each VPC needs to send its Internet-bound traffic to the transit gateway. This is achieved by the default route pointing to the transit gateway. Also, the transit gateway would need to pass the traffic on to the egress VPC. Subsequently, within the egress VPC, the traffic will be forwarded to the Internet Gateway after the translation on the NAT gateway. In order to achieve this, we would need a default route on the NAT route table pointing to the Internet Gateway. The return traffic, although it isn't asked by this question, will leverage the more specific routes for the VPCs pointing to the transit gateway on the NAT gateway. And then similar routes pointing to the VPCs on the transit gateway. Designer version. The latter will be learned through propagation by the transit gateway, so the transit gateway knows how to reach each one of the private subnets in the spoke VPCs.

65. (B)While this is a typical architecture adding the stateful firewalls to the picture makes the scenario a bit more complicated. The issue that the cloud team needs to resolve applies to scenarios similar to this: a user in VPC1 tries to establish a session to VPC2, and the session goes through the shared VPC. The outbound session hits the firewall in AZ1, the firewall takes note of it, and eventually, the session makes its way to VPC2. The return traffic leaves VPC2 and goes to the shared VPC, but this time hits the firewall located in AZ2 that has no prior knowledge (i.e., state) of the session. The firewall drops it, and the session fails. Transit gateway has a feature called appliance mode that can be configured via the CLI only (as of 2020) using the create-transit-gateway-vpc-attachment and modify-transit-gateway-vpc-attachment commands to resolve this issue.

CHAPTER 23

ANS-C01 MOCK EXAM 3

1. The cloud engineering team of a fast-food chain is evaluating AWS placement groups as a potential option for their distributed and replicated database. Which of the following statements is accurate about this service? (Choose TWO)

    A. There is no charge for creating an AWS placement group.
    B. Some AWS placement group strategies are billable.
    C. Regardless of the strategy type, all the EC2 instances in one placement group are always placed in the same AZ.
    D. Regardless of the strategy type, all the EC2 instances in one placement group are always placed on the same underlying hardware.
    E. If the AWS Partition strategy is selected, a hardware failure in AWS physical servers would still impact all the instances.

2. An ERP software company, after providing on-prem solutions for years, is turning its best-seller application into a SaaS offering in AWS using initially 30 EC2 instances running Windows Server. The clients of the ERP application will all be Windows Server EC2 instances located in customers' VPCs. According to their Go-To-Market .(GTM) strategy, the first marketing wave is expected to acquire 500 new customers with an existing AWS footprint with the key promise that their traffic to and from their ERP servers will never leave the AWS network. Which of the following architectures best satisfies the requirements?

    A. Place all the ERP server instances behind at least one Elastic Load Balancer and provide the customers with the public IP address of the service.
    B. Place all the ERP server instances behind at least one Elastic Load Balancer and provide the customers with the private IP address of the service.
    C. Place all the ERP server instances behind at least one Elastic Load Balancer and instruct the customers to create a PrivateLink endpoint to the service.
    D. None of the above.

3. A fast-growing startup company is planning to use AWS to market their Machine Learning application to other cloud-based customers as a SaaS offering. They currently only have one VPC with 20 servers in us-west-2 behind an Elastic Load Balancer, while all of their 30 AWS customers are located in the same region. The sales team is forecasting rapid growth in the region to over 230 customers in the next 6 months or perhaps sooner. Which of the following architectures provides the customers with access to their servers without unnecessarily exposing their entire VPC to them and, at the same time, can guarantee that the traffic will stay within AWS?

    A. Set up a pair of VPN servers on two EC2 instances in the central VPC and have the customers build IPSec tunnels back to both instances for redundancy. They can use features supported by the VPN vendor to limit the customers' access.
    B. Set up a pair of VPN servers on two EC2 instances in the central VPC and have the customers build IPSec tunnels back to both instances for redundancy. They can use Security Groups in the central VPC to limit the customers' access.
    C. Use AWS VPC peering between the central VPC and the customers' VPCs. Limit the scope of routing to a very specific subnet and routes that need to be exposed.
    D. Use the PrivateLink technology between the customers' VPC and the Elastic Load Balancer of the central VPC.

4. To route inbound HTTP traffic to different pods hosting your web services in an EKS environment, you are looking into deploying an AWS Elastic Load Balancer. Which option best describes the pieces required to implement the architecture? Choose the option with the minimum number of absolutely required steps.

    A. Use the EC2 part of the AWS console to deploy an Application Load Balancer in two subnets in two different AZs. Create a path-based policy to route the traffic to the right pod.
    B. Use the EC2 part of the AWS console to deploy an Application Load Balancer. Create a path-based policy to route the traffic to the right pod.
    C. Install an AWS Load Balancer controller. Use the kubectl tool to apply a manifest file containing an ingress resource. Include the HTTP routing policy in the YAML file.
    D. Use the kubectl tool to apply a manifest file containing an ingress resource. Include the HTTP routing policy in the YAML file.

5. As a cloud architect working for a start-up, you are moving a containerized application from a testing EKS environment to production. Choose the architecture that best describes the load balancing setup in the new environment?

    A. The AWS Load Balancer Controller must be used to provision the ALBs and NLBs and later cannot be removed from the cluster.
    B. The AWS Load Balancer Controller must be used to provision only ALBs but later can be removed from the cluster.
    C. The AWS Load Balancer Controller or Helm can be used to provision the ELBs. Later both can be removed from the cluster.
    D. The AWS Load Balancer Controller must be used to provision any type of ELBs. But its presence is not necessary to manage them after the deployment is complete.

6.   You are architecting an EKS-based solution to receive inbound HTTPS traffic from the Internet and, depending the URL, route it to different pods that will be provisioned for your website in different languages (/en, /fr, /de and /es). Choose the core action that best describes how the AWS Elastic Load Balancer is provisioned.

A.   Use kubectl to apply a YAML file that describes an ingress object. The file must also include a rule that describes how the routing decisions are made.

B.   Use kubectl to apply a JSON file that describes four ingress objects. The file must also include a rule that describes how the routing decisions are made for each ingress.

C.   Use kubectl to apply a YAML file that describes a service with the type of Loadbalancer. The file must also include a rule that describes how the routing decisions are made.

D.   Use kubectl to apply a JSON file that describes a service with the type of Loadbalancer. The file must also include four rules that describe how the routing decisions are made.

7.   You are planning to deploy a Network Load Balancer in front of a large EKS cluster. This solution is expected to be the main architecture for the next 3 years. The Load Balancer will route millions of sessions to over 5000 pods deployed in your cluster. Which statement depicts the most reliable and stable approach to deploy the NLB?

A.   Install the AWS Load Balancer Controller. Apply a manifest containing a service with the type of load balancer.

B.   Install the AWS Load Balancer Controller. Apply a manifest containing an ingress resource.

C.   Install the AWS Cloud Provider Load Balancer Controller. Apply a manifest containing a service with the type of load balancer.

D.   Install the AWS Cloud Provider Load Balancer Controller. Apply a manifest containing an ingress resource.

8.   For a long time, your company has been a customer of a SaaS security provider processing some confidential data for your development department. Both businesses have VPCs in the us-west-1 region and you use PrivateLink to connect an endpoint in your VPC to their Elastic Load Balancer in the SaaS VPC. Your company has recently acquired one of its competitors in Europe with a presence in eu-central-1. You are using inter-region VPC peering to connect the two companies. Your new task is to ensure that the European branch has access to the same SaaS security service. The SaaS provider informs you that they have no presence outside their original region; us-west-1. Which of the following options demonstrates a valid architecture meeting the customer's requirements?

A.   Create a new VPC with at least two subnets in us-west-1 and place the European services that need to talk to the SaaS provider in the new VPC. Create an endpoint pointing to the SaaS ELB.

B.   Create an endpoint in the European VPC in eu-central-1 and point it to the SaaS ELB using its public IP address.

C.   Create an endpoint in the European VPC in eu-central-1 and point it to the existing endpoint in your VPC in us-west-1 over the inter-region peering.

D. As long as the security groups associated with the endpoint service in your VPC in us-west-1 allow traffic from the European VPC, instances in eu-central-1 should be able to communicate with the endpoint over the inter-region peering.

9. After a merger, you are now designing a load balancing solution for the new company. Each company has one VPC in AWS dedicated to their Web servers. The development team, after replicating the contents, confirms that the pages on the Web servers are identical and can be treated as members of the same pool. You connect the two VPCs using the VPC peering feature and need to spread traffic across the instances in both VPCs. Which of the following options can help you achieve the goal? (Choose TWO)

    A. Create an Application Load Balancer with one target group and register all the servers of both VPCs in the same group.
    B. Create a Network Load Balancer with one target group and register all the servers of both VPCs in the same group. Ensure cross-zone load balancing is enabled.
    C. Create two Network Load Balancers, one in each VPC. Assign two Elastic IP addresses to each Load Balancer and create two DNS entries, www1 and www2. Provide both URLs to the users.
    D. Create two Application Load Balancers, one in each VPC. Use DNS to spread the load across the two load balancers.

10. Shortly after a successful maintenance window to put your first Elastic Load Balancer in service, your NOC team is receiving numerous reports that the load balancer is no longer reachable. Your initial investigations reveal that the IP address of the Network Load Balancer has changed. You communicate the new IP to the users and update the whitelisting ACLs on their firewall. Which of the following TWO options explain the issue and a potential permanent solution? (Choose TWO)

    A. Use AWS CloudTrail to find out who called the APIs and when, to change the IP address. Link this to a CloudWatch alarm
    B. Use AWS Config to be notified as soon as a key configuration change against your templates is made
    C. The change of IP address is normal behavior for all Elastic Load Balancers
    D. The change of IP address happens only to Network Load Balancers
    E. Assign an Elastic IP address to the Load Balancer

11. You are designing a load balancing solution in AWS for a SaaS company. Their Office of CISO needs to ensure Apache access logs on all their Web servers contain the actual IP addresses of the visitors. Which of the following statements are accurate about your options to design this network?

    A. With Network Load Balancers with TCP listeners, Client IP addresses are preserved only if the targets are registered with their Instance-ID
    B. With Classic Load Balancers Client IP addresses can never be preserved
    C. For Application Load Balancers with HTTPS listeners, to capture client IP addresses you must use X-Forwarded-For headers

D. All Elastic Load Balancers except Classic preserve client IP addresses natively without any configuration changes

12. You are using an AWS Network Load Balancer for a UDP-based application. All of your application servers are registered using IP addresses. Which of the following statements is TRUE about the source IP preservation when they are received by your application?

A. The source IP address cannot be preserved if UDP is used
B. The source IP address cannot be preserved regardless of the protocol if the targets are registered by their IP addresses
C. You need to use proxy protocol version 2 to send additional connection information to the application, including the source IP address of the clients
D. With no further changes the source IP address of the clients will be preserved in this architecture

13. Your company is running a large fleet of Nginx and Apache RHEL Web servers behind an AWS Application Load Balancer to use their path-based routing feature. Inspecting the Nginx access logs reveals that instead of the source IP addresses of your clients, the IP addresses of the Load Balancer have been captured. Which of the following options together form the right solution? (Choose THREE)

A. Update the Web application to support X-Forwarded-For header
B. Update the listener configuration of the Application Load Balancer to add X-Forwarded-For header to the requests.
C. On the Nginx servers, update the log format section of the /etc/nginx/nginx.conf file and add $http_x_forwarded_for on each one of the servers. Restart the nginx service using the systemctl command.
D. On the RHEL servers update the log format section of the /etc/apache2/apache2. conf file and add %{X-Forwarded-For}I for each one of the servers. Restart the httpdservice using the systemctl command.
E. Migrate the Nginx servers to Apache on RHEL and restore the same content on the new servers

14. You are using an Internet-facing Network Load Balancer in AWS in front of 24 TLS-based Web servers to serve millions of sessions per second. Which of the following options describes the best approach to preserve the IP address of the clients for future inspection in the access logs of the Web servers?

A. Since Network Load Balancers are used with no modifications, the source IP addresses captured by the Web servers are the IP addresses of the clients.
B. Update the listener configuration of the Network Load Balancer to add the X-Forwarded-For header to the requests.
C. Migrate the Network Load Balancer to Application Load Balancer with a TLS listener
D. Enable proxy protocol using AWS CLI.

15.   You are troubleshooting a Web server saturation case in one of your company's VPCs. The VPC has an AWS Network Load Balancer that is in a healthy state. Behind the load balancer in 2 different Availability Zones, you have 10 servers in each subnet. The SRE team has reported that one of the servers (WWW103) is attracting far more user sessions than any other instances, and when it starts, the situation exhausts its resources very quickly. After a few hours, the load moves from WWW103 over to another server WWW112, and again after a few hours, it moves to WWW107. The SRE team confirms that recently the company has onboarded a large new customer. Which of the following two statements together could potentially explain the issue? (Choose TWO)

   A.   The new customer is using 1:1 source NAT on their side.
   B.   The new customer is using PAT on their side.
   C.   The new customer is being taken advantage of by external attackers to ultimately DDoS your VPC.
   D.   Your Network Load Balancer has its sticky sessions setting enabled.
   E.   Your Network Load Balancer has its cross-zone load balancing setting disabled
   F.   You are using DNS to select the target and the configured policy unevenly favors one target.

16.   You are designing a load balancing solution for a group of 30 Web servers running TLS 1.2 and serving a popular public HTTPS website. To achieve maximum performance and minimize latency, you pick the Network Load Balancer option for this single-tier architecture. The Web development team informs you that the servers need to maintain state information to provide a predictable and continuous experience to clients. Which of the following statements is correct about this architecture?

   A.   Elastic Network Load Balancers cannot support IP source preservation if the targets are registered using their IP addresses.
   B.   Elastic Network Load Balancers can support sticky sessions but not with TLS listeners and TLS target groups.
   C.   Elastic Network Load Balancers can support sticky sessions but not with TLS listeners and TLS target groups with targets running TLS 1.2.
   D.   Elastic Network Load Balancers cannot support IP source preservation if the targets are registered using their Instance-ID.

17.   You are designing a 2-tier Web application in AWS where in each region, an Elastic Load Balancer will spread the traffic across a group of 55 Web servers. Then the outcome will hit another Elastic Load Balancer before it reaches a group of application servers. The development team informs you that, since their software does not natively provide cookies, they need the load balancers to issue session cookies and control their lifetime. This has to be done on both tiers. Which of the following would NOT present a major challenge to your design?

   A.   If you choose Application Load Balancers for both tiers, the same cookie name of AWSALB will be selected.

B. If you choose an Application Load Balancer for the first tier and a Classic Load Balancer for the second, path-based routing won't be available on Classic Load Balancers

C. If you choose Network Load Balancer for either tier with TLS listeners, session stickiness will not be supported.

D. If you choose Classic Load Balancers for both tiers, the same cookie name of AWSELB will be selected.

18. Which of the following approaches would enable the cloud engineer of a small SaaS provider to provide session affinity (session stickiness) to its set of servers sitting behind a Classic Load Balancer with minimum cost and impact on the existing architecture? The application does not natively support cookies.

A. Modify the application code to support cookies natively. This would guarantee session stickiness when users visit the frontend servers.

B. Update the Load Balancer's configuration to enable duration-based session stickiness. This will guarantee session stickiness when users visit the frontend servers.

C. Update the Load Balancer's configuration to enable application-controlled session stickiness. This would help the Load Balancer generated cookies to follow the expiration time set by the application cookie.

D. The Classic Load Balancer can be migrated to Application Load Balancer using the AWS console wizard. Update the Load Balancer's configuration to enable application-controlled session stickiness.

19. To better meet the increasing demand, an online betting company is expanding its cloud footprint. Part of the new architecture includes 3 different groups of EC2 instances for each geographical area where the company has a major customer base. The new URLs would be aussiecert.com/apac, aussiecert.com/emea, and aussiecert.com/na. This will give them a few key advantages, including independent cookie settings. Which steps should you take to implement this idea?

A. Choose Application Load Balancing. Create 3 different target groups and split them into different Availability Zones. Create a rule for host-based routing and forward traffic as needed.

B. Choose Application Load Balancing. Create 3 different target groups and split them into different Availability Zones. Create a rule for path-based routing and forward traffic as needed.

C. Choose Network Load Balancing. Create 3 different target groups and split them into different Availability Zones. Enable cross-zone load balancing.

D. Choose Network Load Balancing. With Network Load Balancing, the goals can be achieved with only one target group at Layer 4 without having to inspect the request URL.

20. You are working as a Cloud Optimization architect for a well-established Online History Channel. Currently, they have an identical presence in 8 AWS regions. One of the first pain points to address is to retire a large fleet of 10 proxy servers deployed to every region. They are prone to security breaches if not patched regularly and are

expensive in terms of AWS compute charges as well as third-party licensing. The proxy servers are used to route traffic based on the URLs entered by users: cyrus.aussiecert. com, cambyses.aussiecert.com, bardiya.aussiecert.com, and darius.aussiecert.com; each needs to be routed to a specific target group. Which of the following migration strategies would meet the requirements of this company?

A. Choose Application Load Balancing. Create 4 different target groups and split each into 2 different Availability Zones. Create a rule for host-based routing and forward traffic as needed.

B. Choose Application Load Balancing. Create 4 different target groups and split each into 2 different Availability Zones. Create a rule for path-based routing and forward traffic as needed.

C. Choose Application Load Balancing. Create 4 different target groups and split each into 2 different Availability Zones. Create a rule for method-based routing and forward traffic as needed.

D. Choose Application Load Balancing. Create 4 different target groups and split each into 2 different Availability Zones. Create an AND combination of a path-based and a host-based routing rule and forward traffic as needed.

21. You are architecting the Application Load Balancing strategy for the Web site of an APAC-based airline in AWS. The platforms team has slated 3 different groups of Web servers to provide a customized experience to different groups of customers. The table below demonstrates how traffic needs to be routed in the future architecture. How can you implement this policy using AWS load balancing tools?

URL	Destination Target Group
ap.aussiecert.com	Southern Cross Target Group
ap.aussiecert.com/vacation	Southern Cross Target Group
*.aussiecert.com/promotions	North Star Target Group
All else	Lcarus Target Group

A. IF (Host is ap.aussiecert.com) THEN (forward to Southern Cross)
   IF (Host is ap.aussiecert.com AND Path is /vacation) THEN (forward to Southern Cross)
   IF (Host is *.aussiecert.com AND Path is /promotion) THEN (forward to North Star)
   IF (Requests otherwise not Routed) THEN (forward to Lcarus)

B. IF (Host is *.aussiecert.com) THEN (forward to Southern Cross)
   IF (Host is *.aussiecert.com AND Path is /promotion) THEN (forward to North Star)
   IF (Requests otherwise not Routed) THEN (forward to Lcarus)

C. IF (Host is ap.aussiecert.com) THEN (forward to Southern Cross)

IF (Host is ap.aussiecert.com AND Path is /vacation) THEN (forward to Southern Cross)

IF (Host is ??.aussiecert.com AND Path is /promotion) THEN (forward to North Star)

IF (Requests otherwise not Routed) THEN (forward to Lcarus)

D. IF (Host is ap.aussiecert.com) THEN (forward to Southern Cross)

IF (Host is ap.aussiecert.com AND Path is /vacation) THEN (forward to Southern Cross)

IF (Host is *.aussiecert.com AND Path is /promotion) THEN (forward to North Star)

Requests otherwise not Routed will be sent to the remaining Target Group

22. As a chief architect you are reviewing the latest list of the security groups to be implemented on the ALBs of your network. Your engineers have recently learned that NLBs do not support those and are planning those only for the fleet of ALBs. Which of the following statements is accurate about such policies. (Choose TWO)

A. For the ALBs receiving sessions directly from the clients the source address of the security group needs to be 0.0.0.0/0
B. For the ALBs receiving sessions directly from the clients the source address of the security group needs to be 255.255.255.255/32
C. Fro the ALBs defined as the target of an NLB the source address needs to be set to the static IP address of the NLB
D. Fro the ALBs defined as the target of an NLB the source address needs to be set to the IP ranges of the clients

23. You are optimizing a 40G Link Aggregation solution that one of your customers has put in place in one of their Direct Connect Locations in EU Central (Frankfurt). Their main issue is that they had 3 outages last year in which 2 links went down briefly. They have overprovisioned the Direct Connect capacity to tolerate outages, but losing more than 50% of the link at a time could result in severe packet drops. They would like to make sure that if an outage takes place again, their traffic does not stay on the remaining two links. How would you architect this solution?

A. Spread the links across 2 different Direct Connect locations and create 2 LAG connections.
B. Take the links out of the LAG configuration and architect the solution with 4 standalone 10G links.
C. Set the LAG attribute to determine the minimum number of active links to 2
D. Set the LAG attribute to determine the minimum number of active links to 2. Configure a Lambda function to make the LAG port non-operational if the number of active links is equal to or lower than 2.

24. As a chief architect, you are reviewing a Standard Operating Procedure (SOP) prepared by your network engineering team. Currently, you have a single 10G Direct Connect link and a single VPN backup tunnel and advertise the same set of prefixes out of both connections. The preparation part of the SOP is calling for a temporary AS_PATH prepending of 2 ASN instances for the prefixes advertised to AWS via the Direct Connect. The logic is to make the Direct Connect less preferred while your bad SFP is being replaced. The AS_PATH settings will be reset once the fieldwork is complete. Which of the following options highlights the issue with this approach?

A. The AS_PATH is checked before the Local Pref and the SOP overlooks the fact
B. The AS_PATH length has to be increased by at least 3 instances
C. Regardless of the AS_PATH length, the VPN in this setup will not be preferred over the Direct Connect
D. Replacement of the faulty SFP (or any other physical related equipment) in a Direct Connect location would need an LOA/CFA letter which should be obtained from the AWS console 72 hours before the maintenance window.

25. You are investigating an AWS access failover issue. The customer has a 1G Direct Connect and a VPN tunnel running BGP. The reported issue is that during the last DX outage, it took the traffic well over a minute to transition from DX to VPN. This time was enough to trigger some authentication and database replication issues. Which of the following options provides the quickest fix for this architecture to achieve a sub-second convergence time?

A. Enable BFD on your side of the DX connection. Contact AWS support to enable BFD on their side of the link too.
B. Enable synthetic transactions between your on-prem devices and your AWS footprint. Repeat the transaction every 300 seconds, and as soon as it fails 3 consecutive times, update the BGP policy to shift the traffic over to the VPN link
C. Enable BFD only on your side of the DX connection
D. Enable synthetic transactions between your on-prem devices and your AWS footprint. Repeat the transaction every 100ms. As soon as a single failure is detected, have the BGP policy shift the traffic over to the VPN link

26. You are studying the current AWS architecture of one of your customers. They have one large VPC in ap-east-1 and several S3 buckets in the same region. Last year, they also replaced their IPSec VPN connection with a dedicated 10G AWS link in the same region. As part of the implementation, they configured one private VIF to access the VPC and one public VIF to access AWS public services, including their S3 buckets. Due to the nature of their business, they cannot take their service down for testing any time soon, but they would still like to know how their access to AWS would converge if they were to lose the Direct Connect circuit. Which of the following statements describes the event more accurately?

A. Without BFD, within 180 seconds their access would be restored to both S3 and VPC.

B. With BFD, within 1 second their access could be restored to both S3 and VPC.

C. They would completely lose access to their VPC, but access to S3 will be restored over the public Internet.

D. Access to both VPC and S3 will be restored over the public Internet

27. You are architecting a Split-View (Split-Horizon) name resolution solution for a small company with a single VPC in AWS. Your goal is to use the same domain name for public (users coming from the Internet) and private (users coming from within the VPC) name resolution. Your solution should work in such a way that the source of requests is always taken into account, so queries from the Internet will be responded to with the public IP address of the resources, and queries from within the VPC will be responded to with the private IP address of the resource. How should you implement this architecture using Route 53?

A. Create one public hosted zone and create similar A records for both public and private services in it

B. Create one private hosted zone and create A records for both public and private services in it

C. Create one public hosted zone and place the public records in it and create a private hosted zone with the same name and associate it with the VPC. Place the private records in it

D. Create one public-hosted zone and place the public records in it. Create a private hosted zone with an arbitrary name and associate it with the VPC. Create CNMAE records pointing to the public records in it

28. You are troubleshooting a Split-Horizon DNS case with a customer new to AWS. The case notes indicate that although external name resolution from the Internet is working as expected, the customer's EC2 instances are not able to resolve the same names from within one of their VPCs for most resources. Furthermore, the zone files attached to the case reveal that the A records in the private hosted zone are a subset of those in the public hosted zone. Which of the following TWO options could resolve the issue? (Choose TWO)

A. Associate the private hosted zone with the VPC

B. Associate the private and public hosted zone with the VPC

C. Ensure the records required for Split-horizon are available in both zones

D. Ensure both enableDnsSupport and enableDnsHostnames

29. To meet the High Performance Computing (HPC) requirements of a medical research company, you are architecting their first VPC in the us-east-1 region. The new VPC will have 4 subnets and a total number of 120 EC2 instances. There will also be a 10G Direct Connect link connecting the existing data center to the AWS deployment. Currently, the company is using a number of DNS servers on Windows in their data center for local and external name resolution and a single Route 53 Private Hosted

Zone for name resolution within the VPC. Select the two possible architectures that can enable on-prem users and servers to resolve the records stored in the Private Hosted Zone in AWS?

A. Create a conditional forwarding rule on the on-prem Windows DNS infrastructure and add the CIDR+2 IP address of the AWS subnets as the destinations. The resolver will respond over the Direct Connect.
B. Deploy at least one AWS Directory Service in the VPC. Configure the on-prem servers to conditionally forward the queries related to the Private Hosted Zones to the Directory Service instances. They will automatically forward them to Route 53.
C. Configure a Route 53 Resolver Inbound Endpoint within the VPC to receive the queries over the Direct Connect. Configure the on-prem servers to conditionally forward the queries related to the Private Hosted Zones to the Inbound Endpoint
D. Configure a Route 53 Resolver Outbound Endpoint within the VPC to receive the queries over the Direct Connect. Configure the on-prem servers to conditionally forward the queries related to the Private Hosted Zones to the Outbound Endpoint

30. You are architecting a scalable solution on AWS for an online travel and hospitality company. Your goal is to deploy a NAT gateway to provide connectivity between 100 sensitive EC2 instances in a single public subnet and 2 external hosts on the Internet. The EC2 instance will be contacting the two external servers to book flights internationally at a maximum rate of 10 new connections per second. Although you are certain that the total number of simultaneous connections to each one of those destinations won't exceed 25K, you still have concerns about the "climbing rate," which could be around 1000 new sessions per second per destination after high-season marketing campaigns. How would you address this concern?

A. Split the existing subnet into 2 public subnets with 50 EC2 instances and assign each subnet a dedicated NAT gateway
B. Assign an elastic (public) IP address to each instance and remove the NAT gateway from the design
C. Increase the number of NAT gateways for the existing subnet to 2. Direct 50 instances to each NAT gateway
D. Replace the existing EC2 instances with the Nitro type and reduce the number of instances from 100 to 50

31. As a part-time Cloud solutions architect working for a community college, you implemented a single VPC with 25 EC2 instances in a single public subnet with a NAT Gateway and an Internet Gateway. The instances are used for after-hours Linux training programs. It is brought to your attention that, at times many EC2 instances are not able to update their packages from the Internet or simply are not able to browse the Internet. Someone also anonymously tips you off that one of the students has been witnessed using a tiny script supplied by his dad to DoS, the NAT Gateway of the Linux virtual lab from one of the instances. You need to detect the situation as soon as it happens again. Which of the following two CloudWatch metrics would come in handy in this case? (Choose TWO)

    A. ErrorPortAllocation
    B. IdleTimeoutCount
    C. PacketsDropCount
    D. ActiveConnectionCount

32.   You are hired as a cloud architect by a popular paid entertainment channel to evaluate a newly implemented but apparently flawed content delivery design. After implementing a comprehensive request analysis policy at the edge using a Lambda function to redirect unauthenticated users to the main login page of their service, it appears to the accounting team that some users have been able to bypass CloudFront as a CDN and access the EC2 origin servers directly. Which of the following design options can resolve the issue to prevent users from bypassing the CDN?

    A. Implement an NACL policy and limit access to the origin servers to the requests coming from CloudFront
    B. Move the Lambda function closer to the origin servers and deny access if the user fails authentication
    C. Instead of the Lambda function, add the login page to the client application as the first step.
    D. Configure CloudFront to add a custom header to the incoming requests. On the backend, only accept requests with the custom header

33.   You are paged into an AWS troubleshooting case. The issue is that a CloudFront customer is complaining about CloudFront still returning the objects that had been retrieved from the origin server before they implemented a change to enforce HTTPS between the EC2 origin servers and CloudFront during the day. As part of the same maintenance window, they had also updated the CloudFront cache behavior settings to require HTTPS connections. You run a few tests, and it appears the communication is encrypted for the new objects. This issue is in clear violation of their regulatory obligations, and they must have end-to-end encryption for every object provided to the end-users as soon as possible. Which of the following choices demonstrates the issue and a potential solution?

    A. The behavior is by design. You just need to wait until the object expires.
    B. The behavior is by design. You can manually invalidate the objects in CloudFront edge locations.
    C. Wrong CloudFront configuration. They need to update the Origin Protocol Policy to HTTPS only
    D. Wrong CloudFront configuration. They need to update the Origin Protocol Policy to Match Viewer and enforce HTTPS between the clients and CloudFront

34.   An international education company that has just begun to use AWS CloudFront in the US and EU to run online exams has received multiple reports from the test takers about the Web site's availability. Further investigations by their SRE team reveal that the issues were all related to a planned maintenance window on the 4 origin servers that had been poorly communicated to the end-users. Now, you, as a cloud architect, are tasked with

ensuring the users are redirected to a simple HTML page clearly showing the downtime details and apologizing to the users for the inconvenience. How should you architect this solution?

A. Create a simple HTML page and place it on all 4 origin servers. Redirect the users to the maintenance page when there is an outage.

B. Create a simple HTML page and place it on one of the origin servers. Redirect the users to the maintenance page on the server hosting the page when there is an outage.

C. Use Lambda@Edge to run a piece of Python code to generate the response and serve the HTML page as static content without hitting the origin servers when there is an outage.

D. Create a simple HTML page and place it on all 4 origin servers. Use Lambda@Edge to run a piece of Node.js code and fetch the HTML page from an origin server that is responding during the window.

35. You are evaluating CloudFront as a global CDN to deliver video-on-demand content using Microsoft Smooth Streaming to millions of users. The delivery system will be adapting the quality of the content to the changes in the available bandwidth and CPU condition on the receivers' side. Which of the following statements CANNOT be considered as a definite benefit of the service?

A. Eliminates the risks associated with Distributed Denial of Service (DDoS) attacks

B. The ability to couple with Lambda@Edge to read cookies and deliver customized content to the viewers based on the value of the cookies

C. The ability to couple with Lambda@Edge to manipulate the HTTP error status codes that are being sent to the viewers

D. To provide both encrypted and unencrypted options between CloudFront and origin servers

36. To automate the future deployment of your AWS stack, you are planning to use AWS CloudFormation. The goal is to create a VPC with a /20 CIDR block with 2 EC2 instances acting as your Web servers hosting static pages to be accessible by the outside users. Which of the following options include the most complete set of resource types without any extra types? (the steps are in no specific order)

A. AWS::EC2::VPC, AWS::EC2::Instance, AWS::EC2::InternetGateway, AWS::EC2::Route

B. AWS::EC2::VPC, AWS::EC2::Subnet, AWS::EC2::Instance, AWS::EC2::SecurityGroups, AWS::EC2::Route, AWS::EC2::InternetGateway, AWS::EC2::VPCGatewayAttachment, AWS::EC2::NetworkAcl

C. AWS::EC2::VPC, AWS::EC2::Instance, AWS::EC2::SecurityGroups, AWS::EC2::Route, AWS::EC2::InternetGateway, AWS::EC2::VPCGatewayAttachment, AWS::EC2::RouteTable

D. AWS::EC2::VPC, AWS::EC2::Subnet, AWS::EC2::Instance, AWS::EC2::SecurityGroups, AWS::EC2::RouteTable , AWS::EC2::Route, AWS::EC2::InternetGateway, AWS::EC2::NetworkAcl

37. As part of an automated deployment in AWS, you have received the following CloudFormation template. Which of the following statements is accurate about the code?

T2:
Type: AWS::EC2::Route
DependsOn: T3
Properties:
RouteTableId: !Ref T1
DestinationCidrBlock: 0.0.0.0/0
GatewayId: !Ref IGW01

A. T2 is used to create a routing table
B. The creation of T2 is completed before IGW01
C. If needed T1 is deleted before T2
D. T2 will not be processed until T3 is created

38. As a Cloud Solution Architect working for a Value Added Reseller (VAR), you are assisting a customer in choosing the right monitoring solution for their future microservices environment. Their ultimate goal is to have visibility into resource comsumption at the container level; however, they are still not sure whether ECS or EKS would be the best choice. Currently they are evaluating CloudWatch Container Insights. Which of the following statements are FALSE and CANNOT be added to the next customer presentation? (Choose TWO)

A. CloudWatch Container Insights offers full support for ECS and partial support for EKS
B. CloudWatch Container Insights is an agentless service
A. CloudWatch Container Insights can provide insights into disk as well as memory and CPU
A. CloudWatch Container Insights collects data in JSON format

39. You are architecting an AWS solution for a software development company. Currently, they have a physical data center connected with a dedicated 100G Direct Connect link to their AWS presence in the ap-east-1 region in Mumbai. The goal is to enable the EC2 instances in VPC-dev023 to download updates every night at 10PM. You have two options to receive the updates. They can either be downloaded from Amazon RDS in another VPC in the same region and same Availability Zone called VPC-dev101 or directly from the physical data center through the Direct Connect. Which of the following architectures can meet the customer's requirements with minimum cost?

A. Establish VPC peering between VPC-dev023 and VPC-dev101. Download the files from the servers in VPC-dev101
B. Download the files directly from the servers in the datacenter
C. Create an Interface VPC endpoint to download the files from VPC-dev101

D. Place the contents in an S3 bucket in the same region and use a NAT Gateway to download the updates

40. After implementing a geolocation routing policy in Route 53 for an international Gas and Oil company with AWS resources in 5 regions, you constantly receive complaints from users in Denmark. After reviewing the tickets, it turns out the general theme of the issues is around: (1) Users load pages designed for the Norwegian customers (2) Users cannot successfully resolve the resource names. As the first step, you successfully confirm that the source IP address of the impacted users is indeed registered in Denmark. You also confirm that the DNS resolver used by those corporate customers is based in Norway and is in a healthy condition. Which of the following options show TWO potential root causes of the issue? (Choose TWO)

   A. The default (catch-all) record is missing from the zone
   B. A firewall along the path is dropping UDP packets larger than 512 bytes
   C. The users' local DNS resolver does not support EDNS0 (edns-client-subnet)
   D. The users' local clients do not support EDNS0 (edns-client-subnet)

41. The AWS footprint of a global online off-road equipment store has fallen victim to a deliberate security breach. Detailed forensics done by a third-party security company revealed that numerous changes were made to their AWS resources, including the Security Groups to open up backdoors to databases related to shocks and snorkel kits, although the attackers only had root access to the environment for minutes. The platforms' team assures the leadership that they have extensively hardened their environment, but everyone is still worried about the AWS resources and components. How would you go about tracking such changes to the AWS resources in case of another similar breach in the future?

   A. AWS Config
   B. AWS CloudTrail
   C. AWS Macie
   D. AWS GuardDuty

42. You are paged into a Direct Connect troubleshooting incident where the customer is having issues with manipulating AS_PATH to influence traffic from AWS S3 buckets into their network via the two 10G Direct Connect links that have just been put in service. The customer is running eBGP between their AS (AS#64513) and AWS and iBGP between their border routers. Their goal is to have an active/passive setup. Before opening a case with their router manufacturer, which of the following options might be true about their architecture?

   A. The customer must replace the current AS number with a public AS number that they own.
   B. The customer must replace the current AS number with an AS number in the range of 65000-65535.

C. The customer can keep the existing AS number but with the caveat that they cannot use AS_PATH to engineer their traffic. They can instead use AWS BGP communities to set Local Pref on the AWS side into their network.

D. The customer can keep the existing AS number but with the caveat that they cannot use AS_PATH to engineer their traffic. They can instead announce more specific prefixes out of the preferred link.

43. A small business has a star architecture for its 6 VPCs, all connected to the same transit gateway. As a cloud architect, you are helping them implement a private NAT strategy for 5 of their VPCs. Those VPCs will eventually be accessing resources located in the servers' VPC. To get started, they added a NAT subnet to each of the 5 VPCs and placed a private NAT gateway in each. Which of the following options describes the most suitable routing design for this customer? (Choose FOUR).

A. Ensure each VPC is attached to the TGW and associated with the main route table. Ensure propagation takes place between each VPC and the TGW.

B. Ensure each VPC is attached to the TGW and associated with a dedicated route table. Ensure propagation takes place between each VPC and the TGW.

C. Add a route pointing to the TGW to each route table of each VPC.

D. Add a route pointing to the private NAT gateway of each VPC to the other route tables of each subnet of each VPC.

E. Add a route pointing to the TGW to the route table of each NAT subnet of each VPC.

F. Add a route pointing to the TGW to the route tables of the server's VPC.

44. As a solutions architect, you are helping a customer with their migration to the cloud project. As part of the migration, they need to deploy private NAT gateways in each one of their 24 VPCs. The cloud engineering team is informed that the office of the CISO for certain EC2 instances would like to have a 1:1 NAT. The rest of the subnets in each VPC can be translated by Port Address Translation (PAT). Which of the following options is accurate about this migration?

A. The AWS private NAT gateway construct does not support 1:1 mapping. The customer would need to use a Linux box with IPTablesto implement such a design.

B. The AWS private NAT gateway construct does not support 1:1 mapping. The customer would need to use a public NAT gateway to implement such a design.

C. The customer can safely use the private NAT gateway construct to define the 1:1 mapping statement, but the PAT configuration cannot be done on the same gateway.

D. The customer can safely use the private NAT gateway construct to define the 1:1 mapping statement and the PAT configuration as needed.

45. As a chief cloud architect, you are contracted to review the roll-out plans prepared by the cloud engineering team of a startup. In their architecture, they created a dedicated VPC called ONPREM_ATTCH and connected that back to their data center using a single 1Gbps Direct Connect link to be backed up by a VPN connection. The idea is to use this VPC and its NAT gateway to reach the other VPCs as an intermediary platform. Also, there might be resources in ONPREM_ATTCH that would be accessed by the users in

the physical data center. All the 12 VPCs owned by the customer are connected to the main route table of a single transit gateway. How would you evaluate this architecture?

A. This is a flawed architecture, and the physical data center will not be able to consume any resources in any VPC.
B. This is a flawed architecture, and the physical data center will not be able to consume any resources in any VPC, except the ones located in ONPREM_ATTCH.
C. This is a valid architecture, and the physical data center will be able to consume any resources in any VPC.
D. As it stands now, this is a valid architecture, and the physical data center will be able to consume any resources in any VPC, but if the customer fails over to the VPN, the physical data center won't have access to any resources except the ones in ONPREM_ATTCH.

46. A small insurance company with only one VPC is trying to architect an inline firewall solution to protect 25 servers that they have deployed up in a subnet called Servers with public IP addresses. They reached an agreement with their firewall vendor to bring their on-premises license to the cloud. The firewall will have two inside and outside interfaces, run on an EC2 instance and protect the servers from the inbound traffic from the Internet. The VPC is connected to the Internet via an Internet Gateway. Which of the following options shows the correct high-level architecture to support this idea?

A. Create two separate subnets for the inside and outside interfaces. Configure a gateway route table for the IGW. Add a route to direct all traffic destined for the servers to outside ENI of the firewall. Add a route to the servers' route table to direct all traffic destined for the Internet to the inside ENI of the firewall.
B. Create two separate subnets for the inside and outside interfaces. Add a route to the route table of the outside interface to direct all traffic destined for the servers to the outside ENI of the firewall. Add a route to the servers route table to direct all traffic destined for the Internet to the inside ENI of the firewall.
C. Create a dedicated firewall subnet and place the inside and outside interfaces in it. Configure a gateway route table for the IGW. Direct all traffic destined for the servers to the outside ENI of the firewall. Add a route to the servers' route table to direct all traffic destined for the Internet to the inside ENI of the firewall.
D. Create a dedicated firewall subnet and place the inside and outside interfaces in it. Configure a gateway route table for the IGW. Direct all traffic destined for the servers to the outside ENI of the firewall. Add a route to the servers' route table to direct all traffic destined for the Internet to the IGW.

47. A high school with a single VPC is looking to insert a dual-interface Next Generation firewall in their existing AWS design to protect their servers' subnet. Currently, they do not have any public addresses on the servers, and their reachability to the outside world is established through a NAT gateway, then the Internet Gateway attached to the VPC. The virtual firewall will be running on an EC2 instance. Which of the following partial architectures should the chief architect approve to maintain connectivity and improve their security posture before the full design is prepared?

A. Create a dedicated subnet for the outside interface of the firewall. Place the inside interface of the firewall in the same subnet as the NAT gateway. Add a route to the route table of the NAT subnet and direct 0.0.0.0/0 to the inside interface of the firewall.

B. Place both interfaces of the firewall in the same subnet as the NAT gateway. Add a route to the route table of the NAT subnet and direct 0.0.0.0/0 to the inside interface of the firewall.

C. Place both interfaces of the firewall in the same subnet as the NAT gateway. Add a route to the route table of the NAT subnet and direct 0.0.0.0/0 to the outside interface of the firewall.

D. Create a dedicated subnet for the outside interface of the firewall. Place the inside interface of the firewall in the same subnet as the NAT gateway. Add a route to the route table of the servers' subnet and direct 0.0.0.0/0 to the inside interface of the firewall.

48. A principal architect is being consulted by the cloud engineering team of a legal firm. They only have one VPC in AWS and need to deploy a Next Generation firewall to protect their 16 subnets from the Internet reachable via an Internet Gateway. Currently, all the servers have public IP addresses and run host-based firewalls. The company is looking to use VPC ingress routing on the IGW to eventually remove all the host-based firewalls, centralize security rules at the firewall and maintain connectivity and security. If they are assured in terms of security, their IT leadership has no issues with keeping the public IP addresses on the servers. Which of the following high-level architectures can help the team achieve its goals?

A. Install the virtual firewall on an EC2 instance with 17 elastic network interfaces; 16 on the inside and 1 on the outside. Place each inside interface in one of the server's subnets. Remove the host-based firewalls.

B. Install the virtual firewall on an EC2 instance with 17 elastic network interfaces; 16 on the inside and 1 on the outside. Place each inside interface in one of the server's subnets. Remove the host-based firewalls. Remove the public IP addresses.

C. Install the virtual firewall on an EC2 instance with 2 elastic network interfaces; 1 on the inside and 1 on the outside. Place a NAT gateway between the servers' subnet and the firewall. Create 1:1 NAT map entries for each subnet. Remove the host-based firewalls. Remove the public IP addresses.

D. Install the virtual firewall on an EC2 instance with 2 elastic network interfaces; 1 on the inside and 1 on the outside. Place a NAT gateway between the servers' subnet and the firewall. Remove the host-based firewalls. Remove the public IP addresses.

49. As a solutions architect, you are helping an AWS customer to expand their security stack in the cloud. Currently, in their only VPC, they have a single firewall that processes the traffic between the Internet and a group of 32 servers. The solution uses the concept of VPC ingress routing with a dedicated route table for the IGW to send the traffic to the Elastic Network Interface of the firewall. After experiencing some performance issues, the cloud engineering team is looking to increase the number of firewalls by adding

3 more units. Which of the following two high-level architectures indicate valid and independent options for this customer? (Choose TWO).

A. In the same VPC, place all the servers in one subnet and the GWLB, its endpoint, and the group of firewalls in another.
B. In the same VPC, place all the servers, the GWLB, its endpoints, and the group of firewalls in one subnet.
C. In the same VPC, place all the servers and the GWLB endpoint in two different subnets. Create another VPC and place the GWLB and the group of firewalls.
D. In a dedicated VPC, place all the servers in as many subnets as needed. Create another VPC and place the GWLB, its endpoint, and the group of firewalls.

50. You are completing a Gateway Load Balancer architecture for an online education company. The company inherited this half-done design after its previous architect abruptly left the firm. The goal is to deploy a group of 4 firewalls in-path of every packet that travels between their AWS environment and the Internet. In his architecture, before his departure, the previous architect provisioned 5 VPCs for the main departments with their own Internet Gateways. The design also had a dedicated VPC for the firewalls. Finally, the documents indicate he had plans to place one GWLB endpoint in each of the 5 VPCs. Choose the right set of routes for this architecture (Choose THREE).

A. 0.0.0.0/0 to gwlbe-xyz for the servers subnet in each VPC
B. 0.0.0.0/0 to igw-xyz for the servers subnet in each VPC
C. 0.0.0.0/0 to igw-xyz for the endpoint subnets in each VPC
D. 0.0.0.0/0 to gwlbe-xyz for the endpoint subnets in each VPC
E. x.y.z.t/p (servers subnet) to gwlbe-xyz for the Internet Gateways of each VPC
F. 0.0.0.0/0 to gwlbe-xyz for the GWLB subnet in its dedicated VPC

51. As a chief architect, you are helping a team of cloud engineers with their security enhancement project. They currently have 10 VPCs, one for each team. They are all connected to the same transit gateway in the same region. Each VPC has a dedicated Internet Gateway, an idea despised by the new CISO. Their goal is to improve their security posture by centralizing the security stack in a separate VPC with a NAT gateway. They are also making a significant investment to purchase 4 Next Generation firewalls. Which of the following statements show a valid component of the central security VPC design? Choose FOUR.

A. Remove the IGWs from all the 10 VPCs. Create a new VPC for the GWLB, its endpoint, the IGW, and NAT gateway.
B. Remove the IGWs from all the 10 VPCs and place a GWLB endpoint in each one of the 10 VPCs. Create a new VPC for the GWLB, the IGW, and NAT gateway.
C. Attach the new VPC to the TGW and propagate the routes of each one of the 10 VPCs to its route table.
D. Add a route on the TGW associated with the VPCs to direct 0.0.0.0/0 to the security VPC.
E. Add a route to the route table of each one of the VPCs and direct 0.0.0.0/0 to the GWLB endpoint (gwlbe-xyz).

F. The subnet of the GWLB and its endpoint will have a route table containing two routes o direct 0.0.0.0/0 to the NAT gateway and the servers' supernet to the TGW.

52. You are architecting a security solution in AWS for a public company. Due to regulatory restrictions, the customer cannot place two groups of servers in the same subnet. In their original design, in the same VPC, those servers were simply placed in different subnets, and access control between them was implemented using network security lists. After three years, now the solution is difficult to manage and is not scalable at all. Your team's suggestion is to deploy a pair of stateful firewalls using Gateway Load Balancers between the two subnets. How would you rate this high-level architecture?

A. They would need to create two GWLB endpoints in two separate subnets. Each server's subnet would need a more specific route for the other servers' subnet via the endpoint.
B. They would need to create one GWLB endpoint in a separate subnet. Each server's subnet would need a more specific route for the other servers' subnet via the endpoint.
C. They would need to create a GWLB endpoint in each one of the server's subnets. Each server's subnet would need a more specific route for the other servers' subnet via the endpoint.
D. This architecture as it stands now is not supported.

53. After a major cloud redesign where you deployed a stack of 4 Next Generation firewalls behind a Gateway Load Balancer to inspect the Internet-bound traffic, the SecOps team is complaining about losing visibility into the IP addresses of their EC2-based servers when they communicate with the Internet. Your initial assessment indicates that the Next Generation firewalls only log the IP address of the NAT gateway and have no trace of the addresses of the EC2-based servers. In the current architecture, you have an Internet Gateway with ingress routing to direct any traffic destined for the servers to the Gateway endpoint. Also, from the servers, a default route sends all the traffic to the NAT gateway and then, from there, to the GWLB endpoint. Which of the following architectural changes can help the SecOps team regain visibility into the servers' IP addresses in the firewalls' logs without compromising any security enhancements?

A. Currently, the NAT gateway is between the GWLB endpoint and the servers. Move and place the NAT gateway between the IGW and GWLB endpoint.
B. Remove the NAT gateway from the design.
C. Replace the AWS NAT gateway with a Linux-based NAT gateway with Iptables.
D. Create a dedicated VPC for the security stack, including the GWLB endpoint, GWLB, firewalls, and NAT gateway.

54. You have architected a dual-Availability Zone security solution for a regional bank. In this design, you used 2 AZs in the us-east-1 region. Each of your 15 department VPCs has subnets in both AZs. You also have a dedicated security VPC with two subnets, one in each AZ. The security VPC has two sets of Gateway Load Balancers, endpoints, and stateful firewalls in AZ1 and AZ2. All the VPCs are connected to a Transit Gateway. The goal of your architecture is to inspect any east-west traffic between the servers in

the VPCs. You are asked by a junior engineer, "What would happen if we disabled the appliance mode on the TGW?"

Which of the following options accurately answers this question?

A. Since the firewalls are stateful, the setting can safely be turned off.
B. With the appliance mode turned off, we would not be able to failover immediately if we were to lose one AZ.
C. With the appliance mode turned off, one of the GWLBs would never be used. As a result, we would end up with an active-passive architecture.
D. With the appliance mode turned off, we would have connectivity issues if two servers in the different AZs of different VPCs were to talk to each other.

55. In order to inspect any east-west traffic between your group of 25 VPCs spanned across Availability Zone 1 and 2, you deployed a dedicated VPC. The security VPC has two subnets located in AZ1 and AZ2, each with dedicated a Gateway Load Balancer, its endpoint, and a stack of stateful firewalls. All the VPCs are connected via a single transit gateway. Which one of the following conversations will have issues if the implementation engineer forgets to enable appliance mode for the security VPC attachment?

A. Between server 1 in AZ1 VPC1 and server 2 in AZ1 VPC1
B. Between server 1 in AZ1 VPC1 and server 2 in AZ2 VPC1
C. Between server 1 in AZ2 VPC1 and server 2 in AZ2 VPC2
D. Between server 1 in AZ2 VPC1 and server 2 in AZ1 VPC2

56. In a large Gateway Load Balancer deployment, you have a dedicated VPC for the security appliances, and 65 spoke VPCs. In the security VPC, the GWLB has registered targets (appliances) in both AZ1 and AZ2 of the us-west-1 region. You have enabled cross-zone load balancing. Which of the following statements is correct about the behavior of the GWLB in this architecture when all the appliances in both AZs have failed?

A. The GWLB will drop all the traffic until at least one appliance recovers in one of the AZs.
B. The GWLB will drop all the traffic until at least two appliances recover in two different AZs.
C. The GWLB will keep sending new sessions to the last healthy target.
D. The GWLB selects a random target and sends the traffic to it.

57. You are configuring routing for a small AWS Network Firewall implementation. The customer only has one VPC with a dedicated Internet Gateway, and by creating a new subnet (10.1.254.0/24) for the firewall endpoint (vpce-123), you need to inspect the traffic between 2 servers subnets (10.1.1.0/24 and 10.1.2.0/24) and the Internet. Which of the following statements is accurate about the proper routing strategy? Choose THREE.

A. Add to the gateway route table of the IGW: route 0.0.0.0/0 to vpce-123

B. Add to the gateway route table of the IGW: route 10.1.1.0/24 to vpce-123 and 10.1.2.0/24 to vpce-123
C. Add to the route table of the endpoint's subnet: route 0.0.0.0/0 to igw-xyz
D. Add to the route table of the endpoint's subnet: route 10.1.1.0/24 to vpce-123 and 10.1.2.0/24 to vpce-123
E. Add to the route table of the servers subnets: route 0.0.0.0/0 to vpce-123

58. As an external consultant, you are evaluating a distributed AWS Network firewall deployment at an online vacation booking company. Currently, they have 12 VPCs in one region, and in a dedicated subnet in each VPC, they have placed an AWS Firewall endpoint. The ultimate goal of the architecture is to inspect any north-south traffic; between the servers in each VPC and the Internet Gateway. Which of the following statements is NOT accurate about this high-level design?

A. Any typo or other misconfigurations will remain contained within the same VPC and will not affect the other VPCs.
B. The customer does not have to deploy transit gateways for connectivity between these VPCs and the IGW.
C. The firewalls will have a common set of rules across all the VPCs which can easily be managed centrally.
D. The engineering team would need to add one route for each one of the server's subnets to the gateway route table of the corresponding IGW of each VPC.

59. You are architecting an AWS Network Firewall solution for a hardware manufacturer. Currently, they have 12 VPCs, all connected to the same transit gateway in the us-west-2 region. They also have two 100G Direct Connect links with MACsec attached to the same region via a Direct Connect gateway. The AWS footprint has dedicated connectivity to the public Internet. Your goal is to inspect the traffic between their VPCs and on-premises network. Due to the upcoming release date of their flagship chip, the company is unwilling to take any risks by adding any new subnets to the production VPCs, nor are they willing to update the route tables of any of the production VPCs. Which of the following options provides a valid high-level design?

A. Place a firewall endpoint in one of the existing subnets of each VPC.
B. Create a dedicated VPC, attach it to the transit gateway and add a single route to each VPC to direct the traffic to the new VPC.
C. Create a dedicated VPC with two subnets, one for the TGW attachment and the other one for the firewall endpoint.
D. Create a dedicated VPC with one subnet for the TGW attachment and the firewall endpoint.

60. A Colorado-based resort with a seasonal business has an AWS footprint of 8 VPCs, namely VPC1 through VPC8. They're all connected to the same transit gateway. The TGW also connects the on-premises network to their cloud presence via a single 100G Direct Connect circuit. Until last year, every VPC had its own IGW, and the IT team would rely on a number of host-based firewalls installed on most of their servers. After a

security breach, they rearchitected their AWS network and removed all the IGWs. They also added two new VPCs to their design, namely VPC9 and VPC10, connected to the same TGW. VPC9 is used to host an AWS Network Firewall endpoint in a subnet, and VPC10 hosts an IGW and a NAT gateway acting as the egress point of the network. The ultimate goal of the architecture is to inspect not just the traffic between the 8 production VPCs and the Internet but also the traffic between the VPCs themselves and the traffic between their AWS footprint and their on-premises networks. They create two route tables on the TGW called RT1 and RT2 to implement the design. RT1 is attached to VPC9, and RT2 is attached to VPC1 through 8 and VPC10. Which of the following statements is correct about their routing strategy on the TGW? (Choose FOUR).

A. RT1 will have a default route with the next-hop of VPC9.
B. RT1 will have a default route with the next-hop of VPC9.
C. RT2 will have a default route with the next-hop of VPC10.
D. RT2 will have a default route with the next-hop of VPC9.
E. RT1 will have a route for the subnet of VPC5 with the next hop of VPC5.
F. RT2 will have a route for the subnet of VPC5 with the next hop of VPC5.
G. The route table of the endpoint's subnet will have a default route with the next-hop address of the TGW.
H. The route table of the endpoint's subnet will have a default route with the next-hop address of the IGW.

61. You were hired as a cloud security consultant after a major malware outbreak that severely impacted a local government customer. The investigations revealed the malware had made its way to the network after one of the EC2 instances browsed an infected Internet public domain. The company has already started negotiations with major security vendors to develop a strategy and potentially block a list of such domains related to their line of business, but in the meantime, to prevent malicious websites from sending malware when they're browsed, the IT team needs to make sure no potentially harmful websites can be accessed from within the VPC. Which of the following architectures using Route 53 Resolver DNS Firewall can be a good starting point before the customer receives advice from their security vendors?

A. Create a rule with a single block action to block any non-business-related domain.
B. Create a rule with a single allow action to permit only business-related domains.
C. Create a rule with a single block action to block the AWS managed domain list of AWSManagedDomainsMalwareDomainList.
D. Create a rule with a single block action to block the AWS managed domain list of AWSManagedDomainsBotnetCommandandControl.

62. The SecOps team of a software business company has recently noticed a surge in the number of connections made from some of their EC2 instances to random domain names in the *.info range. Which of the following solutions using Route 53 Resolver DNS Firewall can help this customer receive a notification as soon as one of those connection attempts is made?

A. Add a rule for *.info with the action of BLOCK.
B. Add a rule *.info with the action of ALLOW.
C. Add a rule *.info with the action of ALLOW and Alert.
D. Add a rule *.info with the action of Alert.

63. As part of a network hardening campaign and ahead of their Initial Public Offering (IPO), the cloud engineering team of a startup is looking to put in place security measures to prevent any data exfiltration out of their 8 VPCs. Since their engineering teams need to regularly receive and process code from external parties, their biggest fear is a scenario where one of their EC2 instances is compromised, and the attackers are able to exfiltrate their Intellectual Property (IP) out of their environment. This attack could come from any of their competition or random hackers eager to gain access and sell their codes. Which of the following architectures can provide an acceptable but scalable level of security in this scenario?

A. Use Route 53 Resolver DNS Firewall and add a REJECT rule for a list of their competitions' domains.
B. Use Route 53 Resolver DNS Firewall and add two REJECT rules for the AWS-prepared lists of malware and botnet domains.
C. Update the list of malware domains developed by AWS and add the domain names of their completions. Use Route 53 Resolver DNS Firewall and add a REJECT rule for the new list.
D. A and B.

64. The cloud architect of a community college is trying to block access to any .edu website from their EC2 instances. The only exception would be their own public website (a .edu domain) hosted on Oracle Cloud. She is planning on using Route 53 Resolver DNS Firewall for this purpose. Which architecture can help her achieve the goal in this scenario?

A. Create two rules. Rule 1 to ALLOW their own website. Rule 2 to REJECT *.edu.
B. Create three rules. Rule 1 to ALLOW their own website. Rule 2 to REJECT *.edu. Rule 3 to permit *.*.
C. Create two rules. Rule 1 to ALLOW their own website. Rule 2 to REJECT *.edu. Give Rule 1 higher priority than Rule 2.
D. Create two rules. Rule 1 to ALLOW their own website. Rule 2 to REJECT *.edu. Give Rule 2 higher priority than Rule 1.

65. In preparation for an upcoming maintenance window, the cloud architect of a SaaS company is planning to redirect any DNS required to their external servers from within their VPCs to a maintenance page that she has placed on a temporary web server in a different VPC. How can she redirect the DNS queries for only 2 minutes to the new destination using Route 53 Resolver DNS Firewall?

A. Create a rule in every VPC with the action of BLOCK for the external website and configure the override option with a TTL of 120 seconds.

B. Create a rule in one VPC with the action of BLOCK for the external website and configure the override option with a TTL of 120 seconds.

C. Create a rule in one VPC with the action of ALLOW for the external website and configure the override option.

D. Since the website is hosted by an external party, this task cannot be done using Route 53 Resolver DNS Firewall.

MOCK EXAM 3 - Detailed Answers

1. (C) This question demonstrates a classic use case of AWS PrivateLinks where you create an endpoint service for endpoint interfaces in the client VPCs. The SaaS provider creates their pool of EC2 instances and places them behind a load balancer. The load balancer is then reached by other AWS users (the consumers) from their VPCs using AWS PrivateLinks by creating VPC endpoints pointing to the SaaS VPC and its load balancer. To make the service more palatable, the SaaS provider can confirm their DNS FQDN with AWS and provide it to the consumers for creating the endpoints. This traffic will remain within AWS, flowing from one VPC (provider) to another (consumer).

2. (D) The two key benefits of AWS PrivateLinks for this customer are security and scalability. The between the consumer VPC and provide VPC stays within the AWS network and the underlying environment to accommodate growth and will scale up automatically without any interaction with users to create more capacity. Both key points are used here, your choice of PrivateLinks will stop the traffic from going out to the Internet, and it can also accommodate more load even if the growth rate and its pattern are unknown.

3. (C) This solution requires an ALB, and in EKS, it can only be implemented as an ingress object that is provisioned by the AWS Load Balancer Controller. Keep in mind, if you are planning on deploying and managing AWS Elastic Load Balancers in such an environment, having the AWS controller in the cluster is not an option; it's a must.

4. (A) The AWS Load Balancer Controller must be used to provision ELBs and must remain active. Helm is a tool for Kubernetes environments that can offer functionalities similar to Linux package management. It can be used to install the AWS controller and has nothing to do with the ELBs themselves.

5. (A) In this case, you need an ALB. The ALB is automatically provisioned when you create an Ingress in EKS. This is done by applying the manifest file describing the Ingress and its rule.

6. (A) In order to provision an NLB in EKS, you need to use the kubectl tool to apply a JSON or YAML manifest describing a service with the type of LoadBalancer. The AWS Cloud Provider Load Balancer Controller was the older controller that was used to create Classic and Network Load Balancers. The support for the cloud provider controller is now limited to critical bug fixes.

7. (D) You can use PrivateLinks over inter-region VPC peering in two specific scenarios. This question shows one of them. In this case, as you see, as long as all the permissions are in place, you can use your existing endpoint services with a connection to a SaaS provider from any region to talk to that SaaS provider. In other words, you don't have to be in the same region as the SaaS provider. As long as you have one endpoint in a VPC in the same region as the SaaS's ELB, you can ride your existing VPC peering sessions to communicate with the SaaS provider. The other scenario which is also covered in this book is from the SaaS provider's perspective and shows you how to expand their infrastructure with minimum cost to offer services to customers in other regions.

8. (D) AWS Config can be coupled with other AWS services such as EventBridge. AWS EventBridge, in reality, is an event bus that can receive and feed events to other services such as SNS, Kinesis, and Lambda to trigger other events. In this case, although AWS Config does not natively send its notifications out via email, it can be tied to EventBridge and SNS. The SNS topic can be subscribed to, and provide notifications in the form of emails.

9. (A)(D) Your target groups can have members from the same VPC, peered VPC, and on-prem. Alternatively, you can always leverage other load-sharing tools at higher levels, such as DNS (or Route 53), to distribute the traffic across your load balancers.

10. (C)(E) AWS Elastic Load Balancers do change their IP address regularly in response to changes in their underlying infrastructure (such as scaling) which is beyond the users' control. Although, in most cases, users won't be impacted as they're using the FQDNs instead of IP addresses to reach the load balancer, there still are certain scenarios such as IP whitelisting where the actual IP address of the load balancer still matters. In those cases, you can assign an elastic IP address to the load balancer, which would guarantee its persistence over time.

11. (A) AWS Network Load Balancers will always preserve the clients' IP addresses if the targets are registered by their instance-IDs. However, if you register the targets using their IP addresses and you have TCP or TLS listeners (as you would have to do with on-prem servers), then you need to enable Proxy Protocol on the load balancer and carry the clients' IP address in the proxy headers to your Web servers.

12. (D) With Network Load Balancers, if you define the targets by IP address for UDP-based applications, the source IP address will still be preserved without any configuration changes. However, if your NLB has TCP or TLS listeners, then you must use proxy protocol.

13.   (B)(C)(D) For Application Load Balancers to pass along the original source IP address of the clients to the target Web servers, you need to enable the X-Forwarded-For header on them. Option B will take care of preserving client IP addresses. On the backend servers, on both Nginx and Apache, you need to make sure their logging format captures your X-Forwarded-For headers. This is done by updating the configuration files of the servers and restarting the Web service on both. In the case of Nginx, you restart the Nginx service, and in the case of Apache on RHEL 7, you restart the httpd service. After the restart, the services in addition to the default access logging details, will also log the client's IP address.

14.   (D) With Network Load Balancers and TLS listeners, you must use Proxy Protocol to preserve and carry the clients' IP address over to the Web servers. This change can be made through the CLI/API as well as the console.

15.   (B)(D) This question demonstrates one of the typical issues when you use NAT (especially PAT – Port Address Translation) and Sticky sessions together. One strong potential root cause of this case could be many clients on the customer side hiding behind one IP address (the one of the PAT). The Sticky sessions setting treats them all as one client and could pin/map them to one target.

16.   (B) At the target group level with Network Load Balancers, you can enable Sticky sessions. Although this feature has certain benefits, as of 2020, it is not supported with TLS listener and TLS target groups. Please note the earlier versions of Network Load Balancers were not able to support even basic sticky sessions, and your choices were limited to Classic and Application Load Balancers.

17.   (B) The AWS Elastic Load Balancers use cookies to support Sticky sessions. As indicated in (A) and (D), the ALBs use the cookie name of AWSALB while the CLBs use the cookie name of AWSELB. While you can always build multi-tier architectures using both, you cannot deploy either one in more than one layer of your architecture. If you do, since the cookie names are the same, the cookies would potentially be unintentionally re-written, created, or misused by the wrong load balancer that just happens to use or expect to see the same cookie name.

18.   (B) With most Load Balancers, including AWS Classic Load Balancer, you can have duration-based and application-controlled cookies to manage session stickiness. Duration-based cookies are created by the load balancer and their lifetime for the binding is also managed by the load balancer without any reliance on the application. They work just fine without any support from the backend server. However, if the application on the backend servers also supports cookies, then the Application-controlled mode can be used where the load balancer still generates a new cookie, but its lifetime follows that of the cookie generated by the application. In our scenario, the choices involving re-coding the application or changing the load balancer type are considered costly and impactful.

19. (B) To process the HTTP requests and forward traffic based on the URL paths, you should use Application Load Balancers. With ALBs, you can easily define rules to route traffic to target groups based on the path, such as example.com/test1 and example.com/test2 or based on the host address, such as test1.example.com and test2.example.com. This scenario is about the former; path-based routing.

20. (A) With AWS Application Load Balancers, you can have host-based and path-based rules to route traffic to different target groups. In this case, we are choosing the target group based on the host-names. Therefore host-based routing is the most suitable option. In real life, you can have more complicated rules.

21. (A) The first option provides the most precise statements compared with the other choices. First, we match and route the ap.aussieceert.com traffic to the right target group. This is followed by our decision to route the same hostname if a path called vacation is found. Then we route traffic similarly for all the other host possibilities. If the pathname is promotion, we assign the rest of the requests to our catch-all target group that is Lcarus.

22. (A)(D) The first mode is very straightforward. You need to permit the inboudn traffic coming from 0.0.0.0/0 (all). The second case, however; is tricky, the NLB is not a proxy and won't change the source IP address. Hence the source IP addresses will be preserved and needs to be permitted explicitly (e.g., VPC CIDR block or just the clients' IPs). Once again, we extensively discussed this topic in the ELBs chapters.Foro for thought; what is the traffic is coming from an endpoint such as the ones in SaaS architectures.

23. (C) Very similar to classic port channels and link aggregation solutions, with AWS LAG, you can configure the minimum number of links that need to be up for the LAG to be considered "alive" or production-worthy. If more links than the configured threshold fail, in some scenarios, you prefer the whole bundle to be marked as down/unavailable to take other actions, for instance, triggering a routing convergence.

24. (C) By design, AWS always prefers Direct Connect over VPN, and you cannot use the AS_PATH to reverse the decision. One way to affect this default setting (which is probably too invasive and not the best idea) is to have longer prefixes available through the VPN.

25. (C) BFD, in contrast to other settings such as MD5 BGP password, is optional and can be enabled on the customer side to improve failure detection. There is no need to do anything on the AWS side.

   In production networks, to improve your architecture resiliency, it is highly recommended to deploy redundant Direct Connect links in different DX locations and/or in LAG configurations.

26. (C) If you only have one Direct Connect link, it's strongly recommended to configure VPN tunnels for your VPCs as a backup channel. In this scenario, the customer has simply "replaced" their VPN with Direct Connect, which means in case of a Direct Connect failure, AWS would automatically route their S3 traffic through the public Internet while their VPC traffic (i.e., the private VIFs) would be dropped until the link is restored. This could be catastrophic to many customers and must be avoided.

27. (C) To use the same domain name for internal and external use cases, you can implement a split-horizon (split-view) DNS strategy using Route 53. The configuration is simple; a public and a private zone with their corresponding records. With this configuration, the external queries will be fulfilled using the records in the public zone, while the records in the private zone will be used when they are called from within the cloud environment.

28. (C)(D) To use AWS Private hosted zones you have to enable the two options of enableDnsSupport and enableDnsHostnames. Also, in a split-horizon architecture, you would need to have the same records in the public and private hosted zones to be able to respond to external and internal queries consistently.

29. (B) (C) This is a loaded question. AWS, over time, has changed their approach toward name resolution between on-prem and the cloud, and this question needs your knowledge of both. If you are working with architectures or taking exams developed before the 2018-2019 timeframe, most likely, you will need to work with proxy name servers placed in VPCs to receive and process name resolution requests. However, in newer versions, AWS introduced the concepts of inbound and outbound endpoints, which helped us eliminate the burden of managing any additional proxy servers. The only tricky option here is probably option A, which at first glance sounds reasonable; however, you need to remember the internal VPC DNS server (also known as CIDR+2 or 169.254.169.253) does not respond to requests from the outside (in this case, from on-prem). That is exactly why, before the age of endpoints, we had to set up name resolution proxy servers.

30. (A) While it is generally not a good idea to assign public IP addresses to sensitive EC2 instances, and you obviously cannot have more than one NAT gateway (or in general any gateway) per subnet, you can still split the fleet of EC2 instances and assign them dedicated NAT gateways, each able to handle 900 new connections per second. Option D, however; is an interesting one, you can always lower the number of instances to reduce the new connections per second rate on the NAT gateway, but you need to remember that the total number of new connections made by traditional EC2 instances or the next generation Nitro systems is driven by customer demand and not the capabilities of the instances. Hence, regardless of the instance type, the NAT gateway will have to accommodate roughly the same number of new connections per second. In production networks, you should closely monitor the NAT gateway in these scenarios. To do so, the ConnectionEstablishedCount CloudWatch metric indicates the number of established connections through the gateway. The ConnectionAttemptCount shows the number of tries to make that happen. Then the ErrorPortAllocation shows the number of times

your NAT gateway has failed to provide a source port during the translation process (limited to 55K per unique destination). CloudWatch, at this time, does not provide a metric to directly measure the average new connections made per second. This can be done using a simple script on the customer side.

31.   (A)(D) Currently AWS NAT gateway has two main limitations. The 55,000 connections per unique destination and the 900 new connections per second. In this case, the student is apparently saturating the NAT gateway by pushing the former limit.

32.   (D) You can use the AWS console or APIs to add custom headers to the viewer requests. Later, you have a few options to evaluate and pass only the requests with the customer header. For instance, you can update your application or add a layer 7 firewall to only accept requests containing the customer header.

33.   (B) Since your tests show the encryption is functioning properly between the origin server and CloudFront, this issue could only apply to the objects retrieved before the encryption was enabled using one of the two methods explained by options C and D. By design, CloudFront does not differentiate between the objects retrieved from origin servers using HTTP or HTTPS after they are received. They can both be provided to the end-users as long as they are valid. Consequently, the quickest course of action would be to invalidate those objects and let them be retrieved again once they are requested.

34.   (C) In this scenario, you simply cannot count on any of the origin servers to deliver the HTML page because they might be unreachable during the maintenance window. This alone eliminates the other three choices. However, AWS has an interesting service offering that can help in this situation. Lambda@Edge allows the customers to use the popular Lambda serverless compute service to customize delivery through CloudFront. The greatest advantage of Lambda@Edge is shown in its name. Similar to a Lambda function, it is serverless and allows you to execute Python or Node.js code. Furthermore, it is right at the edge (i.e., CloudFront), so the actions can be taken with the minimum latency and closer to the viewers. Using the Lambda@Edge service, CloudFront effectively intercepts conversations between the viewers and origin servers at 4 key spots in two directions and, if needed, take action on them. You can develop and execute Node.js and Python functions when a request is received from the viewer or right before it is forwarded to the origin servers. Similarly, when a response arrives from the origin servers or before it is sent to the viewers, it can be inspected and used to trigger certain actions. This offers a great deal of flexibility to track down messages and have them trigger a wide range of actions at the edge. For instance, you can inspect the User-Agent header and serve different pages or versions of your Web content on its values, or you can make calls to authentication systems and check the users' credentials before permitting them to reach the origin servers. Finally, as shown in this example, they can be used to serve simple static content to the end-users.

35. (A) CloudFront and Lambda@Edge can be used together to read cookies and take actions based on their content. They can also be used to update the status of error messages that are returned to the users. Also, you have the option to keep your traffic encrypted (HTTPS) or unencrypted (HTTP) between the users and CloudFront (through the cache behavior settings) and then the CloudFront POP and origin servers (through the Origin Protocol Policy settings). CloudFront, as a globally distributed service with quite a few built-in features, can certainly reduce the risks associated with DDoS attacks, but it still cannot completely eliminate all the aspects of it or, as the question requires, be a definite benefit of the service by itself.

36. (C) This option covers the most complete process without any extra steps. To launch a Web server (without any database or dynamic contents) from scratch, you need to create a VPC, define a subnet in a routing table, launch the EC2 instances with public IP addresses into the VPC and permit the Web ports (e.g., 80 or 443) through the Security Groups. You do not have to configure the NACLs. Finally, to make the service available to the Internet, you would need to create an Internet Gateway and attach it to the VPC. You will also need a default route (0.0.0.0/0) in the routing table pointing to the Internet Gateway.

37. (D) This is a great example of a dependent stack where CloudFormation needs to follow the steps in a certain order honoring all the dependencies. For instance, you can never insert a route in a non-existent routing table or point to an unattached Internet Gateway as its Next Hop. In the excerpt from the template, T2, as directed by AWS::EC2::Route, is used to build a route in a routing table called T1 that must have been created before using AWS::EC2::RouteTable (and is not shown here). In our template, both T1 and IGW01 are created (and deleted and updated if needed) before T2. This again forms the most logical flow of the process; the routing table and Internet Gateway both need to be created before T2, which simply is a route in the routing table. Finally, T3 is the IGW attachment which must be completed before CloudFormation can try to add the T2 route to the routing table.

38. (A)(B) The Insights provides visibilty into resources such as CPU, network, disk and memory for ECS and EKS and even K8s deployments on AWS. It needs an agent in EKS and K8s environments.

39. (B) The key to answering this question is the direction of the traffic. Since you are downloading (into AWS), there will be no data transfer charges added to the existing Direct Connect service. All the other solutions will have their own hourly and data transfer charges. In real life, always keep in mind with VPC peering, you incur charges for data transfer in both directions; send and receive if the transfer is inter-AZ and beyond. No data transfer charges are applied to VPC peering in a single AZ.

40. (B)(C) Nice scenario. The first symptom is about users in Denmark loading the Norwegian pages of the Web site while their client IP address is registered in Denmark

and geolocation routing in Route 53 is enabled. One strong possibility is that the edns-client-subnet extension of EDNS (Extension Mechanisms for DNS) is not supported by the local DNS resolver. This extension allows the resolver to expose parts of the client IP address to Route 53. This, in turn, improves the accuracy of the Geolocation service. However, if the EDNS0 extension is not supported, Route 53 will only see the IP address of the resolver itself, which is what is happening here. The resolver is in Norway and Route 53 sees the users as though they are based in Norway. The second symptom is easier to deal with. The additional bytes shared by the resolver with Route 53 result in larger UDP packets and firewalls may not like this behavior since it may come across as a violation of the DNS standards.

41.   (B) CloudTrail can store detailed information about changes to the AWS deployments. This information, since it's at the API level, can be traced and reconstructed later by cloud and security experts. The CloudTrail API calls store several key pieces of information such as CreateListener (Event name), Event time, User name, region, and source IP address that made the API call related to the change.

42.   (D) This question is about public VIFs. In that context, while AWS allows you to use private AS numbers similar to this scenario, you lose the ability to use AS_PATH prepending to perform traffic engineering. This will leave you with the option of advertising longer prefixes out of the preferred path as suggested by option D.

43.   (A)(D)(E)(F) The routing logic in this architecture is pretty straightforward. In each of the 5 VPCs, you need to make sure every packet destined for the servers' VPC goes through the corresponding private NAT gateway. To implement this, you need to add a route to the route tables of each of the 5 VPCs and direct the traffic bound for the servers' VPC to the private NAT gateway of the VPC (nat-xyz). Needless to say, each route table will maintain its "local" route used for internal communications within the same VPC. There are two more steps to take. First, you need to add a route to the route tables of your servers' VPC, pointing to the TGW to help your servers talk to the rest of the world. Second, you need to add a route for the servers' VPC to the NAT subnets of each VPC.

44.   (A) Currently, the AWS private NAT construct, or, in general, any NAT construct, does not support 1:1 mapping. Hence, you cannot define which IP address is translated to which IP address when passing through the NAT gateway. Instead, the current AWS NAT gateways' behavior is very similar to the traditional Port Address Translation (PAT).

45.   (B) In architectures similar to this case, you cannot route traffic to the NAT gateway via a Direct Connect link. The same limitation applies to VPC peering and IPSec VPN connections. In this scenario, they would be able to consume resources in the immediate VPC, but they could not leverage the NAT gateway. As a flashback, I suggest you go back to the VPC peering section of the lessons.

46. (A) This architecture is a typical scenario where we deploy a simple firewall with two interfaces, namely inside and outside. In such scenarios, for the first section, you create a dedicated route table (usually called a gateway route table) for the IGW. This route table will have a route to direct all the inbound traffic from the Internet to the outside interface of the firewall. The second section of this architecture is where you add a route to the route table of the servers' subnet to direct all the Internet-bound traffic to the inside interface of the firewall. This scenario does not need a NAT construct as all the servers have public IP addresses.

47. (A) This architecture is a classic scenario where the customer is not willing to assign public IP addresses to their backend servers and is using a NAT construct for Internet connectivity, but they still need to insert a firewall inline. To accommodate such scenarios, you can logically place the firewall between the IGW and NAT gateway. The outside interface of the firewall with a public address will face the IGW. The inside interface of the firewall with a private address will face the NAT gateway and share the same subnet with it. To route packets in this scenario, you need to add a route to the servers' route table for 0.0.0.0/0, pointing to the NAT gateway. Then you need to add a route to the NAT subnet for 0.0.0.0/0 pointing to the inside interface of the firewall. The subnet containing the outside interface of the firewall will have a route for 0.0.0.0/0 pointing to the IGW to complete the chain. The inbound traffic is handled by adding a route for the NAT gateway to the gateway route table of the IGW. Finally, please note the question is looking for a partial answer which is not uncommon when multiple teams are involved in a design process of a multi-phase effort. All the other choices contain wrong options. From a design perspective, this solution also helps the customer keep their AWS elastic NAT solution without worrying about scaling up the firewall to support the process-intensive NAT.

48. (D) The key to choosing the right architecture here is to pay attention to two facts. Firstly, the AWS NAT gateway does not support a 1:1 map; in fact, for the most part, it is a simple PAT (Port Address Translation) device. Secondly, AWS currently supports a maximum of 15 interfaces on one instance. Although this is the maximum for EC2, it does not necessarily mean you can run your firewall on that instance, or even that it financially makes sense. Hence, although you could have one interface per subnet in theory, this solution would not be scalable or even, in this case, doable. As indicated in D, the most reasonable option to achieve all the goals here would be deploying a NAT gateway and removing the public IP addresses from the servers. With that solution in place, you could grow the number of subnets to a much larger number until you start running into issues with the AWS NAT gateway's limitations, such as its total bandwidth (~45Gbps), the maximum number of existing sessions (55000), or the number of new sessions per minute (900). Once that point is reached, you could rearchitect your solution, for example, by deploying more firewalls. On a final note, you may exhaust your firewall resources before those of your NAT gateways. That is another reason why capacity planning and monitoring in such cases are critical. So is the new type of load

balancers, the Gateway Load Balancer (GWLB), and its specific architectures.

49.   (A)(C) The two options here present two major architecture options available to those customers with simple designs and north-south traffic flows as described here. They usually have a single VPC and would like to accommodate everything in there. Or they have a small number of VPCs and do not mind adding an extra VPC to centralize the GWLB function. The first architecture, as depicted by option A, is to create a dedicated subnet for the GWLB stack, which includes the GWLB itself, the group of firewalls, and the endpoint. The servers' subnet will have a route to direct everything north-bound to the GWLB endpoint. As described in C, the second architecture brings some centralization to the overall picture by allocating a dedicated VPC to the GWLB but leaving the endpoint in the servers' VPC. As you know, by this point, the endpoint and the servers are placed in different subnets. The latter gives the customer more flexibility to expand their design in the future by simply adding more VPCs with endpoint subnets instead of dropping another GWLB and a group of firewalls in each future VPC. As you can imagine, the extra flexibility comes at the cost of more overhead to manage two separate VPCs.

50.   (A)(C)(E) The logic behind this architecture is to have a dedicated VPC for the GWLB and its group of targets (the firewalls). The endpoints are placed in each one of the servers' VPCs. For such architecture to work, the servers would need to route their north-bound (Internet-bound) traffic to the GWLB endpoint of their VPCs (option E). The GWLB endpoints need to communicate with the IGW as well as the GWLB. You don't need to configure anything for the latter to take place; it's done by design. In fact, the return traffic from the GWLB to the endpoints also flows in the right direction by design. However, in order for the endpoints to talk to the IGW, you would need a route similar to option C. Finally, to properly direct the ingress traffic, you would need to use the VPC ingress routing feature and add a route for the servers subnets with the next-hop of the endpoint to the dedicated route table of each IGW. It goes without saying in large-scale scenarios, this solution can be automated or modified to a more centralized design.

51.   (A)(C)(D)(F) The key challenge in this architecture is to enable communication in two major areas. First, we need to set up routing inside the security VPC, and then we need to make sure the security VPC and all the other VPCs can seamlessly communicate with each other. The latter is pretty straightforward. All you need to do is make sure route the two route tables on the TGW have routes to both sides of the equation (the security VPC on one side and the servers VPC on the other). You also need to configure each server's VPC with a route to send its traffic out to the TGW. Next, we need to turn attention to the security VPC. In this VPC, you will have 3 route tables in a line. First, from the TGW, the packet hits the TGW attachment subnet and its route table. You would need a route to direct 0.0.0.0/0 to the GWLB endpoint. The endpoint is placed in the next subnet along with its GWLB. This subnet arguably forms the heart

of our design, where you would have two main routes, one directing the egress traffic to the NAT gateway and the other directing the ingress traffic to the TGW. The NAT gateway's subnet will have a default route to the IGW and a route for the servers pointing to the GWLB endpoint.

52.   (D) With the exception of gateway route tables defined on Internet Gateways and Virtual Private Gateways for VPC ingress routing, in AWS VPCs, you cannot have any route more specific than the VPC's main CIDR block to direct traffic from one corner of the VPC to another. In this case, an east-west traffic inspection within the same VPC, in theory, any intercepted traffic would have a more specific destination as it belongs to a subnet of the main CIDR block. You cannot have those more specific routes in AWS VPCs. This leads to very interesting design challenges that you will see at least one of in the following questions. In scenarios like this, depending on the customer's requirements and restrictions, your best bet might be to use separate VPCs (major architectural change) or simply automate host-based solutions such as network security groups of firewalls (usually significant overhead).

53.   (D) Here, you can easily rule out the two options of B and C. However, the choice between A and D needs to be made carefully. The issue as described in the scenario is that the NAT gateway is sitting between the servers and the GWLB endpoint. So, when the traffic leaves the servers, it hits the NAT gateway first and is PAT'ed to a single IP address. This is the IP address that the SecOps team captures in their firewalls' logs. An absolutely reckless architecture here would be to move the NAT gateway from where it is to a place between the GWLB endpoint and the IGW. Although this idea works in theory, as mentioned in previous questions, AWS will not allow you to create any routes more specific than the main CIDR of the VPC within a VPC. Why is this a requirement if we move the NAT gateway? If you place the NAT gateway between the IGW and the GWLB endpoint (which would make it similar to traditional data centers), you would need to configure a route for the NAT gateway's subnet to direct server-specific traffic to the endpoint. That route will be more specific than the VPC's main CIDR block and cannot be created. Hence, as this architecture demonstrates, you would need to keep the NAT gateway between the servers and the GWLB endpoint. This solution will address the AWS routing restriction but will expose you to other issues, including the one shown here. Your firewall logs will only record the outside interface of the NAT gateway. The AWS NAT gateway is effectively a PAT device, so although it would not scale, you still cannot create 1:1 NAT entries either. There are ways to get around this limitation, including creating a dedicated VPC for the security stack, as shown by option D.

54.   (D) This question is not limited to the concept of GWLBs. In fact, many engineers struggle with the whole concept of TGW Appliance Mode. The underlying reason why AWS needed this new mode is simple; the AWS TGW, by default, tends to keep

the traffic within one AZ (i.e., the originating AZ). What this behavior means in our context is that if a server in AZ1 tries to communicate with a server in AZ2, it would leave the server, hit the TGW, and intentionally be kept in AZ1. This effectively means the packets will subsequently hit the GWLB and its firewalls in AZ1. The stateful firewall in AZ1 will register and track this session. So far, we have no issues, and the packet is sent to its final destination server in AZ2. The issue starts coming to the surface when the destination server attempts to respond back. The response packets leave the destination server in AZ2, hit the TGW, and, according to the default behavior of the TGW, remain in AZ2 all the way to the GWLB and its firewalls located in AZ2. But, as you recall, the initial flow landed on the firewall in AZ1, and the unit in AZ2 has no clue about the response. Just imagine that bewildered face "response to what?" And the firewall in AZ2, not having a clue, will drop the packet. This conversation would go well if both servers were located in either AZ1 or AZ2. Because the TGW would keep the traffic in that AZ. But as you noticed, inter-AZ sessions will run into issues with stateful firewalls. This case and other similar scenarios constitute the small percentage of cases where you have to change the TGW's default behavior by enabling the appliance mode. After enabling the mode for the TGW attachment of the security VPC, the TGW will ensure both request and response traffic to the same appliance (or GWLB endpoint in this case).

55.   (D) By default and without appliance mode for the security VPC's attachment, the transit gateway will keep the conversation within the originating AZ. This works well until two servers in two different AZs try to talk to each other. The request will go to AZ1 and leave a trace on its firewall, but the response will be sent from AZ2 to an AZ2 firewall with no background of the session and will get dropped.

56.   (D) If cross-zone is enabled (or even if it's not) and there are no healthy targets, the GWLB will pick a random target based on the 5-tuples for TCP/UDP sessions and 3-tuples for non-TCP/UDP sessions. This behavior will continue until the session times out. Needless to say, the users will be having issues as the target appliances are not functioning properly.

57.   (B)(C)(E) The goal here is to make sure any traffic to and from the servers' subnet is sent to the endpoint. Hence, we add two routes for the two servers' subnets to the gateway route table of the IGW. They both direct the inbound traffic to the vpce-123 (the firewall endpoint). By the same token, we add a default route (0.0.0.0/0) with a next-hop of the endpoint to the route tables of the servers' subnets. Finally, the endpoint's subnet will have a default route for its Internet-bound (north-bound) traffic but uses the "local" route of 10.0.0.0/16 for its south-bound communications down to the servers. Probably the trickiest part of this scenario is where you rule out option D as the process will be done by the local route. As a bit of food for thought, you might also want to figure out why it cannot be done. Remember, this point was previously covered in the book.

58.   (C) While all the other options make sense, option C is not correct. In fact, each VPC

can have its own set of unique firewall policies without having to do any coordination with other VPCs. Also, option D is absolutely correct, as you would need to take the VPC ingress routing approach by creating specific routes for each of the serves subnets in the VPC. Please note, from a design perspective, a distributed firewall model, like the one presented here, can be implemented without any transit gateways. Given the billing model of transit gateways, to some customers, this is one way to potentially reduce costs, although one needs to carefully consider the endpoint hourly charges as the number of them increases in a distributed deployment model, like the one presented here.

59. (C) This scenario is the prime example of a simple centralized deployment. In this case, the customer does not need to touch their "spoke" (also known as satellite) VPCs at all. However, you would need to leverage a transit gateway to connect the VPCs and Direct Connect (and potentially the site-to-site VPN tunnels). As you have seen before, the endpoint will sit in its own dedicated subnet for the routing logic to work. Please note, option A and B clearly fail to meet the requirements of this customer. We will take a closer look at the centralized deployment model and its routing details in the following scenarios.

60. (A)(C)(F)(G) This scenario is an example of a fairly complex implementation of AWS Network Firewall. Having said that, the routing strategy is pretty straightforward if you track the flows and the logic of the architecture closely. In this case, RT1 is attached to VPC9 (security VPC) and will need a default route with the next hop of that VPC. This route table is associated with all the other VPCs, meaning they can consume its route, which effectively means all the other VPCs can only route traffic to the security VPC. According to the scenario, this is the desired behavior; no one talks to anyone else without going through VPC9. RT2, on the other hand, is attached to all the VPCs except VPC9 but is associated with VPC9. Hence, it has routes to each VPC with the next-hop addresses of their attachments, as you see in option F. Similarly, RT should have a route for the on-premises CIDR block pointing to the Direct Connect attachment. The most prominent route in RT2 is a default route pointing to VPC10 (egress VPC). This route is used by VPC9 (security VPC) to get to the exit gates of the network.

61. (C) For use cases similar to this architecture, AWS provides two lists of domain names called the AWSManagedDomainsMalwareDomainList and AWSManagedDomainsBotnetCommandandControl. While the former is focused on domain names involved in sending and spreading malware, the latter is about the networks that have already been infected ("owned") and could potentially turn into another source of infection. In this case, we need the former. The first two options are not practically possible.

62. (D) The Alert action is designed for cases like this where you are still testing the water. Probably it's too early to reject the queries, but you still would like to be notified when such queries are made. The Alert action will leave a notification in the Route 53 Resolver

logs.

63.   (D) This is a classic case of exfiltration-related concerns. In an exfiltration scenario, the actor uses a compromised device to smuggle usually confidential data out of the environment. In this scenario, the customer can reasonably reduce their risks by taking a number of actions in the Route 53 DNS Firewall. They need to create rules to reject queries of their competition, any web destination known for malware infections, and any web destination known for botnets. The first list is expected to be a very short list of domains that can be developed by the cloud team of our startup, but the other two are extensive lists that need to be constantly updated. To address the latter, AWS publishes two lists but, for a number of reasons, including AWS's Intellectual Property and security concerns, cannot be browsed or updated. This also automatically rules out option C.

64.   (A) All you need to do in this case is to permit their own website before dropping all the other queries for the .edu destinations. The order of action is key here, so you can use the console, for example, to move the permit action up the list.

65.   (A) In cases like this scenario, you can still use Route 53 Resolver DNS Firewall and redirect DNS queries by choosing the reject action. The only caveat here is that the Route 53 Resolver DNS Firewall settings are all done at the VPC level, so you need to make the configuration change to each and every VPC.

Made in the USA
Las Vegas, NV
08 October 2022

56764092R10181